City Housekeeping

Studies in Rhetorics and Feminisms
Series Editors: Jessica Enoch and Sharon Yam

The series promotes and amplifies the inter/transdisciplinarity of rhetorics and feminisms by connecting rhetorical inquiry and criticism with vital academic, sociopolitical, and economic concerns. Books in the series explore enduring questions of rhetoric's rich and complex histories (globally and locally), as well as rhetoric's relevance to current public exigencies of social justice, power, opportunity, inclusion, equity, and diversity. This attention to interdisciplinarity, gender, and power has transformed the rhetorical tradition as we have known it (white, Western, upper-class, public, powerful, mostly political, antagonistic, and delivered by men) into regendered, inclusionary rhetorics (democratic, deliberative, diverse, collaborative, private, and intersectional). Our cultural, political, and intellectual advancements continue to be enriched by explorations into the varied ways rhetorics and feminisms intersect and interanimate each other at the same time that they take us in fresh political, cultural, scientific, communicative, and pedagogical directions.

Cheryl Glenn and Shirley Wilson Logan served as series editors for *City Housekeeping: Women's Labor Rhetorics and Spaces for Solidarity, 1886–1911* by Liane Malinowski, guiding it through review, providing feedback, and shaping its development. They thank the current series editors, Jessica Enoch and Sharon Yam, for supporting its publication.

Books in the Series

Rhetorical Reception: One Hundred and Fifty Years of Arguing with Sex in Education by Carolyn Skinner (2025)

City Housekeeping: Women's Labor Rhetorics and Spaces for Solidarity, 1886–1911 by Liane Malinowski

Not Playing Around: Feminist and Queer Rhetorics in Videogames by Rebecca S. Richards (2024)

Inclusive Aims: Rhetoric's Role in Reproductive Justice edited by Heather Brook Adams and Nancy Myers (2024)

A Rhetoric of Becoming: USAmerican Women in Qatar by Nancy Small (2022)

Rhetorical Listening in Action: A Concept-Tactic Approach by Krista Ratcliffe and Kyle Jensen (2022)

CITY HOUSEKEEPING

Women's Labor Rhetorics and Spaces for
Solidarity, 1886–1911

Liane Malinowski

Parlor Press
Anderson, South Carolina
www.parlorpress.com

Parlor Press LLC, Anderson, South Carolina, USA
© 2025 by Parlor Press.
All rights reserved.
Printed in the United States of America on acid-free paper.

S A N: 2 5 4 - 8 8 7 9

Library of Congress Cataloging-in-Publication Data

Names: Malinowski, Liane, 1977- author
Title: City housekeeping : women's labor rhetorics and spaces for solidarity, 1886-1911 / Liane Malinowski.
Description: Anderson, South Carolina : Parlor Press, [2025] | Series: Studies in rhetorics and feminisms | Includes bibliographical references and index. | Summary: "City Housekeeping illuminates women's ways of reshaping rhetorical spaces to be more inclusive of women and gendered ways of communicating about labor"-- Provided by publisher.
Identifiers: LCCN 2025044828 (print) | LCCN 2025044829 (ebook) | ISBN 9781643175324 paperback | ISBN 9781643175331 adobe pdf | ISBN 9781643175348 epub
Subjects: LCSH: Women--Employment--Illinois--Chicago--History--19th century | Women in the labor movement--Illinois--Chicago--History | Feminism--Illinois--Chicago--History | Women--Employment--Illinois--Chicago--History--20th century
Classification: LCC HD6096.C4 M35 2025 (print) | LCC HD6096.C4 (ebook) | DDC 331.409773/11--dc23/eng/20260129
LC record available at https://lccn.loc.gov/2025044828
LC ebook record available at https://lccn.loc.gov/2025044829

2 3 4 5

Cover design by David Blakesley.
Cover image: Parade of women during the garment workers' strike in Chicago, Illinois, December 12, 1910. DN-0056264, *Chicago Daily News* collection, Chicago History Museum

Parlor Press, LLC is an independent publisher of scholarly and trade titles in print and multimedia formats. This book is available in paper and ebook formats from Parlor Press on the World Wide Web at https://parlorpress.com or through online and brick-and-mortar bookstores. For submission information or to find out about Parlor Press publications, write to Parlor Press, 3015 Brackenberry Drive, Anderson, South Carolina, 29621, or email editor@parlorpress.com.

Contents

Preface   *ix*

Acknowledgments   *xxi*

Introduction: Locating Feminist Rhetorical Histories of Labor   *1*

1 Settlement: Claiming Cosmopolitan Space   *31*

2 Tenement: Publishing Visual Rhetorics   *52*

3 Exhibition: Contesting Progress Narratives   *80*

4 Street: Allying Across Differences   *105*

Conclusion: Networking Labor Rhetorics   *128*

Works Cited   *149*

Index   *163*

About the Author   *169*

For Laura, Lucinda, and Jack.
In loving memory of my father, Tom Malinowski.

Preface

City Housekeeping: Women's Labor Rhetorics and Spaces for Solidarity, 1886–1911 focuses on women at the Hull House settlement in Chicago who used rhetoric to reimagine gendered labor relations during a period of rapid industrial upheaval. A feminist rhetorical historiography, the book traces the dynamic and emerging rhetorical interactions of diverse women experimenting with laboring differently and redefining labor's meanings and values. In taking up this topic, I was motivated by a disciplinary concern in rhetorical studies regarding how people use rhetoric to enable living and working together in the city, a space where diverse citizens have negotiated roles, resources, and visibility for millennia. Communication about political and economic life in the city is also a feminist concern because women have long been excluded from full participation in civic conversations. I began this project by gathering archival and published sources that spoke to how women used rhetoric to claim discursive space in industrializing Chicago. As I did so, I noticed women's responses to constraints on their full participation in civic life were often simultaneously responses to constraints on where, when, and how they could labor. Women across diverse identities and experiences shared an interest in rhetorically reimagining relationships to the exhausting and alienating labor within industrial capitalism.

I pursued inquiry into women's labor rhetorics in Chicago for personal reasons, too. I spent my childhood and young adulthood in Chicago and its surrounding suburbs learning about how women in my family and communities had negotiated the terms of their labor in the city's urban and suburban landscapes. Later, as a graduate student in composition and rhetoric living in western Massachusetts, I had the time and distance to begin imagining a Chicago-based study that might capture something about the lives of previous generations of women like those in my family who immigrated to Chicago in the early twentieth century and worked in the garment industry, which was for many working-class women an entry point into paid employment. While living in western Massachusetts, I spent countless hours in the libraries of Smith College, where I had access to an abundance of records about working-class and middle-class women who learned and practiced rhetoric throughout the Northeast. I began to wonder what institution I might consider a Chicago counterpart to Smith College, somewhere that had long been dedicated to supporting women's rhetorical engagement and practice and had also preserved records about a region's diverse women. Hull House was this kind of institution.

One of the first and the most well-known settlement houses of hundreds across the country in the late nineteenth and early twentieth centuries, Hull House was established by social reformers Jane Addams and Ellen Gates Starr to bring together college-educated, middle-class women and men with their working-class and poor neighbors. Hull House brought these groups together when the settlement's middle-class residents offered social welfare services such as childcare, medical care, and community education classes to their immigrant neighbors. By 1910, Hull House was serving nine thousand local neighbors weekly (*Hull House Yearbook* 6). Historical records that provided evidence of cross-class engagement at Hull House allowed me insight into the rhetorics of immigrant and working-class women who were in conversation with middle-class and elite women, and to notice patterns of interaction between the groups. Ultimately, I pursued a project focused on Hull House to capture emergent labor rhetorical practices among women with diverse class and ethnic identities and relations to whiteness, and to potentially glimpse moments of burgeoning solidarity.

As I followed women and their labor rhetorics beyond the settlement, I identified the tenement, the exhibition, and the street as additionally important and contested geographies of gendered labor, where the meanings of private and public, home and work, and feminine and masculine, were held in productive tension for the emerging collectives of women who sought to transform their labor. These spaces were far from ideal for the purpose of labor organizing. They were ephemerally and imperfectly made, and they shaped the power dynamics of their users in different ways. Yet, in each of these spaces, women were innovating labor rhetorical traditions and practices, pulling from both feminized rhetorics for communicating about labor in the home and from masculinized labor organizing traditions taking place in factories, saloons, and union halls.

Considering National and Global Influences on Local Rhetorical Spaces

In seeking to explore what was unique about women's labor rhetorics emerging in Chicago, I prioritized the influence of local spaces on the rhetoric happening during communicative events. In attending to space, I thought of Roxanne Mountford's argument that gendered locations provide "a physical representation of relationships and ideas," which she illustrates in her own work by focusing on the space of the religious pulpit for how it communicates relationships of gender and power among its users (42). I am interested in following Mountford's lead as I turn my attention to the gendered locations in the industrial city used by women rhetors in pursuit of solidarity.

As I began to unpack the meanings of gendered locations for labor rhetorics, I made sense of them by considering their global influences. Chicago, like other large northern cities in the US, experienced an influx of immigrants from southern Italy, Russia, Poland, and other Slavic countries beginning in the 1890s. These immigrants joined already-established groups from Ireland, Germany and Scandinavian countries. Chicago in the 1890s was also a hub of imperialist discourse, as the city's builders, boosters, and everyday citizens began mythologizing the city as both midwestern small town and global metropolis, especially during the 1893 World's Columbian Exposition. Taking a global point of view on local rhetorical spaces helped me to better account for how these spaces were not only gendered, but also physical representations of ideas about domestic and foreign identities.

Taking account of global influences on rhetorical spaces helped me to notice that at Hull House, labor became a topic around which to negotiate who could claim whiteness. Its founders and residents embraced a cosmopolitan outlook toward gendered labor, driven on one hand by embracing the diversity of immigrants from southern and eastern Europe on Chicago's west side and the labor experiences and traditions they brought with them, and on the other hand by valuing global knowledge as a marker of status, education, travel experience, and open-mindedness for affluent white American women. In a city emerging as a cosmopolitan hub, women leaders at Hull House explored the potentials of claiming authority in labor negotiations by drawing on their expertise as consumers in a world market. Consumers, after all, could purchase fairly traded household goods, remaking domestic spaces and opposing industrial manufacturers who exploited laborers in the process. Immigrant workers rarely had similar access to the cultural capital to claim expertise over diverse home goods, nor could they put aside their exhausting work as producers and wait for consumers to shift market trends. Hull House's interest in furthering labor equity by idealizing foreign and artisan-made goods ultimately commodified Irish, Italian, and Jewish identities while protecting whiteness from commodification. When immigrant women workers collaborated with Hull House residents, tensions emerged over the efficacy of a cosmopolitan and consumer-focused orientation to labor solidarity. Increasingly, over the first decade of the twentieth century, women garment workers organized their own collective action, centered themselves and their needs as producers and agents of change, and at times rebuffed the authority their white, wealthy collaborators claimed to decide who could inhabit the identities of white, American, woman, and worker.

Often absent in the local rhetorical spaces I investigated was explicit conversation about Black/white labor relations. This silence around race relations is a topic that might be best explained by noticing the national context of local rhetorical spaces. Specifically, this silence reflected white Northerners' tacit understanding that they were benefiting from the racist laws institutionalizing segregation in the South. Hull House's immigrant neighbors who organized in craft unions followed national trends and kept their unions segregated to keep hold over a limited number of jobs, and placed their racist attitudes above class interest that would have been ultimately mutually beneficial for white and Black workers[1]. Meanwhile, the social reformers living at Hull House shared a wider Progressive perspective that offered alliance to Black Americans in theory more so than in practice[2]. For example, Addams, like many of her Progressive colleagues,

---

1. Philip S. Foner's *Organized Labor and the Black Worker, 1619-1981*, provides a historical overview of how national labor organizations like the Knights of Labor and the American Federation of Labor attempted to bring together Black and white workers, but eventually ceded to the racist attitudes of white workers who refused interracial organizing. Allen H. Spear, in *Black Chicago: The Making of a Negro Ghetto, 1890-1920*, offers a detailed picture of white Chicagoans' racist exclusion of Black workers from neighborhoods and trades, especially as more Black Americans moved from the South in the lead up to and during the Great Migration.

2. I use the term Progressive in the book both as a standard historical marker and as a contested description of a time seemingly characterized by broad interest in making society better, safer, and more equitable. From the end of the nineteenth century to the end of World War I, Addams was a leading figure associated with the label "Progressive," and in speech and writing theorized improving society in response to the challenges of immigration, industrialization, and international relations. Addams attempted to live out her Progressive ideals through her work at Hull House and later through the Women's International League of Peace and Freedom. Historian Rivka Shpak Lissak has written extensively about Addams as a Progressive figure, and Hull House as a key place in furthering Progressive ideologies and myths, in the book *Pluralism and Progressives: Hull House and the New Immigrants, 1890-1919*. My book explores how the label "Progressive" describes Hull House residents' collective approach as labor theorists: they were committed to making progress toward more equitable relations between labor and capital, while skeptical that the outcomes of revolution would make life better for working-class people.

In addition, I use the term Progressive as a label that implied the exclusion of immigrants, working-class women, and African Americans from visions of what progress looked like. In this understanding, I am following the lead of historians

did not engage day to day with the national racial politics institutionalizing white supremacy and wide-scale disenfranchisement happening in the South. On an occasion in January 1901 when Addams publicly engaged with national politics to denounce lynching, she began from the premise of accepting that lynching's defenders believed lynching was just punishment for violent crime and assaults on white women. Addams proceeded to argue that lynching was nevertheless antithetical to the project of democracy. In May of 1901, Ida B. Wells rightly called the premise of Addams's denouncement "unwarrantable" and "baseless" and provided detailed statistics showing the wide range of excuses given for lynching, including many times no excuse at all (1134). Wells called on Addams and her readers to acknowledge the real reason for lynching was racism (1135). Even in taking up the topic of lynching, Addams managed to elide race and racism and frame the issue as one about self-government. In the body chapters of the book, I take note of these kinds of racial elisions by white labor rhetors, especially their marked silences surrounding including Black workers in spaces for labor solidarity. While attentive to the global influences on rhetorical spaces for labor, I also point to national context when it better explains the dynamics of Black/white labor relations. Considering labor rhetorics at the different scales of local, national, and global ultimately offers needed dimension onto the gendered rhetorical spaces and times that feminist rhetoricians place under investigation.

---

such as Nell Irvin Painter and Thomas C. Leonard who have argued Progressive Era immigration and economic policies deliberately excluded these groups. Immigrants and working-class women experienced marginal and ambivalent status regarding their inclusion in Progressive-era institutional change, but the era's racist exclusion of African Americans from participating as full citizens was particularly pointed. As William A. Link covers in *The Paradox of Southern Progressivism, 1880-1930*, white, middle-class social reformers in the South sought to give more people greater access to equal rights and protections while simultaneously limiting the power of rural and Black people to participate in creating change. In so doing, Progressive reformers not only excluded Black Southerners, but participated in or ignored more active efforts of white people who perpetuated racial violence and created measures to put into place systematic disenfranchisement. Northern social reformers like those at Hull House were indifferent or racist, and often took white Southerners' racist interpretations of society at face value. Elizabeth Lasch-Quinn's *Black Neighbors: Race and the Limits of Reform in the American Settlement House Movement, 1890–1945* offers extended explanation of the racial attitudes of Northern reformers associated with the settlement movement.

Moving Beyond the Primacy of Writing

To learn about women's labor rhetorics, I relied primarily on written records. In archives and general collections, I looked through written documents that included census and newspaper records, archived manuscripts, meeting minutes, collections of clippings, letters, yearbooks, memoirs, and printed oral histories that described strikes and negotiations, theorized about labor organizing, recounted conditions in garment shops, and reminisced about life in Hull House. Though my sources were written, they informed me about other, more ephemeral modes of labor rhetoric in sight and sound. What I learned from these sources was that writing itself posed unique promises and challenges for women wanting to express ideas about labor. Writing has been, and often still is, a resource intensive mode of expression. It requires literacy education and materials to produce and then circulate. In the early twentieth century, writing could be a barrier for some interested in claiming a middle-class identity and entry into professional fields, especially given the assumption that middle-class professional writing took place in English. In the labor organizing context, writing's ability to endure and circulate could make it at times a dangerous mode because it could reach unintended audiences like the managers and business owners against whom workers were organizing. Meanwhile, employers and the state leveraged power over workers by requiring compliance with written contracts, protest permits, and labor laws written in employers' favor. Because of the challenges posed by writing, many garment workers turned to visual and embodied public rhetorical practices such as protests, pickets, and parades to communicate their workplace labor was undervalued and exploited. Learning more about garment workers and their labor rhetorics helped me to reflect on the promises and perils of prioritizing writing as the mode under investigation and to appreciate the affordances of visual, aural, and bodily modes for historical subjects. In the book I explore a range of modes used by women labor rhetors and suggest speech and writing need not take priority in rhetorical histories. These histories can also include a focus on visual symbols, such as images and bodily gestures, as well as aural communication including and beyond speech.

As I sought out evidence of labor rhetorics delivered in modes beyond writing, I also began to expand my thinking about multimodal possibilities for crafting and thwarting progress narratives about gendered labor. Previously, I had thought of writing as ideal for narrating: one of writing's affordances is it allows composers to sequence and link events in time. I wondered how garment workers, with sometimes fraught relationships to writing, would complicate progress narratives about society becoming better, safer, and more equitable through multimodal labor rhetorics. In relation to this topic, I thought about the first member of my family to work in the garment trade, my great-great grandmother Tekla Maztak, who in 1900 immigrated from Poland at age twenty-three and soon after married. Family records that speak to her life around the time of her immigration are limited. A few photographs exist. When I see the photos in chronological order, I think I can glimpse Tekla participating in the progress narratives of assimilation through her Americanizing fashion choices and communicating her class mobility through a growing expertise in sewing. I had begun to think of an absence of written family records as likely a result of transnational moves and then subsequent moves across the city from tenement to tenement. I also imagined this absence of writing was perhaps evidence of Tekla's own agency in resisting a paper trail that could constrain her identity at a time she might have been interested in composing her own American progress narrative by eschewing a Polish past and embracing identities that were Anglicized, middle-class, and ever evolving.

Writing, though, eventually provided me with clues about Tekla's sense of herself as participating in and complicating American Progress narratives. Census records revealed that by 1910, Tekla was divorced and supporting herself and two young daughters as a machine operator in a tailor shop. She lived in a tenement on Chicago's northwest side among neighbors who also worked in the garment industry. At thirty-two, she was older than many of the garment workers who would participate in the city-wide garment strike that same year. By 1918, Tekla Maztak spoke to a *Chicago Tribune* writer and reported her name as Tillie Miller. In 1920, she told a census enumerator she was employed in the more specialized and higher paid role of dressmaker and lived in a different tenement. As I read these reported details, I imagined Tekla using the census enumerators' writing and bureaucratic processes to memorialize her assimilationist and economic progress narrative in her Americanized name, specialized work role, and physical movement across the city. Yet, this narrative of transformation and mobility diverged from common progress narratives about working-class women and upward mobility: by divorcing, Tekla had not used marriage as an exit from the work of garment making, a common strategy that hindered union organizers' efforts to encourage women to see themselves as workers long term. This personal connection helped me to be more imaginative in noticing how other garment workers narrated—even through other people's writing—what their own progress looked like.

In my own working life as a writing and rhetoric professor, it has been at times all too easy for me to want to believe my workplace labor of writing has offered me a path to class mobility and transformation. What I better appreciated from studying historical women garment workers like my great-great grandmother is that many experience writing as a fraught mode of expression because it is a site of inequitable access—it requires time, space, and materials to learn, produce and circulate—and is thus as much a barrier to claiming a middle-class identity and entry into a professional fields as it is a pathway. Learning about women garment workers' relationships to writing helped me to reimagine my own relationship to the mode as more complicated. For example, by talking with other writing professors about the difficulties of accessing the time, space, and resources needed for writing, I noticed that what seemed to be my individual workplace difficulties were in fact shared, as was the process of advocating for better conditions. In this way, I felt my own relationship to writing become more connected to the struggles and joys of other writers past and present.

I hope other researchers will join me in recovering historical multimodal rhetorics. Many teachers and scholars have already embraced multimodality as it suggests a more expansive notion of composing for students who use their knowledge of digital and social media to create texts. Yet, composing is not newly multimodal, and multimodality is not synonymous with digital formats. Though digital and social media make multimodal communication a timely issue, the concept of multimodality is important for understanding the range and accessibility of historical communication, too. It is also important so we might better understand the affordances and constraints of writing. This book, then, is a charge to interrogate an assumption that writing was a primary rhetorical mode for historical subjects. Using written sources for information about the uses of other modes of rhetoric is especially important when researching subjects for whom access to writing was limited. The project of historicizing multimodality going forward includes interrogating writing by asking who had access to the education, sponsorship, and technologies needed to do it. Ultimately, writing is a kind of labor, and noticing its accessibility and value across different moments of history is part of creating solidarity with research subjects.

Overview and Structure

In the broadest sense, this book features the stories of women who came to Chicago hoping to find new and better social and economic opportunities. In the city, they negotiated terms of labor at a moment when the modes of production—and the traditions and precedents that accompanied those modes—were rapidly changed by industrialization. Within debates about where and how women should labor arose possibilities for solidarity among stakeholders. In addition, tensions arose among settlement leaders and women workers as it became apparent that seeking solidarity by appealing to consumers to purchase foreign and artisan-made wares commodified the identities of producers with Irish, Italian, and Jewish ancestry and precluded them from claiming whiteness. Immigrant women garment workers began striking to enlist public solidarity and to disrupt the consumer-focused campaigns of their white, wealthy colleagues. Within these tensions, there emerged fleeting moments when women came together across differences and recognized organizing as mutually beneficial, setting the stage for more robust women's labor organizing opportunities to take hold in the twentieth century.

Bookended by Chicago's Haymarket Strike of 1886 and Garment Workers' Strike of 1910–1911, the chapters explore women's multimodal efforts to reimagine the spaces where they labored, organized, and built solidarity among each other, all-male unions, and the public. The introductory chapter offers additional definitions and framing for how I take up the book's central concerns of labor rhetorics and solidarity, and further introduces Hull House as an organization centrally located in Chicago's culture of labor and animated by a labor reform agenda. It also engages pressing conversations about writing feminist rhetorical histories on women, work and space by arguing labor is a useful category of analysis that points feminist rhetorical historiographers to look beyond the locations of home and workplace and across the spaces of everyday life.

Chapter one, "Settlement: Claiming Cosmopolitan Space," establishes Hull House as a place where women could speak about labor in Chicago in the wake of the Haymarket Strikes. By reconstructing the layout and design of Hull House, I extend the scholarly conversation about rhetorical space and women's authority to include women's place-making as a strategy for crafting ethos. I argue that the Hull House founders curated a cosmopolitan, or nationally diverse, aesthetic for the settlement that communicated their authority in a world market and opposition to employers who exploited industrial workers. I then recover rhetorics that circulated at early meetings meant to appeal to skeptical garment workers and conclude the space of Hull House largely reinforced differences across racial, ethnic, national, and linguistic lines and worked against speakers attempting to establish trust and solidarity.

Chapter two, "Tenement: Publishing Visual Rhetorics," turns to a close analysis of Hull House residents' collective bookmaking project during the 1893 World's Columbian Exposition. As tourists descended on the city, Hull House residents undertook a research project led by reformer Florence Kelley that resulted in the publication of the overlooked yet remarkable labor treatise *Hull-House Maps and Papers*. This book brought public attention to the tenement, a domestic space transformed into a workspace when garment companies outsourced manufacturing to employees' homes. Kelley's rhetoric, anticipating the rhetoric of contemporary consumer philanthropy campaigns, excluded workers in the project of building solidarity and comforted readers by providing visual evidence that the problems of the tenement were spatially contained and distant.

In chapter three, "Exhibition: Contesting Progress Narratives," I explore women's labor rhetorics that crafted and challenged notions of industrial progress. Beginning in 1901, exhibit makers at Hull House's Labor Museum cast immigrant women workers as representatives of an imagined past in which domestic labor was visible and valued. Then, in 1907, women affiliated with Hull House contributed to an industrial exhibit held downtown that even more explicitly positioned immigrant and racialized workers as primitive, while idealizing US-born white women as the modern vanguard in the American labor force. I reconstruct the visual and embodied rhetorics of these exhibitions, focusing on when tensions flared among exhibit makers, women workers, and the public. I argue women workers whose labor was on display contested exhibit makers' racist progress narratives through their performances and communicated directly with the public through striking.

Chapter four, "Street: Allying Across Differences," centers the embodied and mobile labor rhetorics of women garment workers during the citywide 1910–1911 Garment Strike, during which women formed alliances across gender, ethnic, racial, and linguistic differences, and unsettled the street as a marker of economic and social boundaries in the process. I read strikers' embodied appeals to solidarity as relying on and exceeding the meanings of Hull House residents' verbal negotiations on their behalf, and recover historical labor protest as an interactional, mobile, multimodal performance in the process.

In the book's conclusion, I explore how rhetorics of gendered labor have persisted and evolved over time and impact contemporary labor attitudes and ways of communicating about it. Through the process, I account for my own "politics of location," poet Adrienne Rich's term for locating oneself in wider networks of space, time, and history, to model how feminist rhetoricians might understand the embodied practices of writing and research as participating in networks of solidarity with women, workers, and other marginalized persons, past and present (210).

Together, these chapters offer a complex, multifaceted picture of the ways some women used rhetoric to reimagine gendered divisions of labor. By turning attention to the topic of historical women's labor rhetorics, I hope to contribute perspective to conversations about the persistent gender inequality embedded in America's labor relations. In the US, care is still largely seen as feminized, private labor excluded from economic and public debate. Meanwhile, labor laws and policies do not adequately accommodate pregnant persons or parents and reflect longstanding ambivalence to women working outside the home and for pay. The figure of the nineteenth-century garment worker in a tenement house resonates in the current moment as workers enter a gig economy and are encouraged to use their own homes as workplaces to save employers from renting workspace. Today we might recognize that rhetors have unequal access to technologies and the literacies required within new media ecosystems, which can lead to a failure of individuals and collectives to communicate with others across differences. The women's labor rhetorics I focus on give us glimpses into the history of modal inequality experienced by workers seeking to establish solidarity across differences of class, race, ethnicity, and language. *City Housekeeping*, I hope, will circulate historical rhetorics beyond their originating situations to provide insights for rhetoricians, writing instructors, feminists, and historians who are committed to learning from history to better understand today's labor crises and the role rhetoric plays in building solidarity.

Acknowledgments

I wrote this book in the hope of joining the community of feminist scholars working in the history of rhetoric and composition in ongoing conversation about women, gender, power, and possibilities. I am indebted to your contributions, perseverance, and insights, and I strive to live out the ethic of care modeled by this community in my roles as teacher and mentor. I owe my deepest gratitude to my teachers in the rhetoric and composition program at the University of Massachusetts Amherst who helped me find entry into scholarly conversations, begin archival research, and develop this project in its early stages. Special thanks to my mentor Haivan Hoang, who taught me how to design a research project with a solid foundation, helped me to critically imagine historical people and events, and supported me over time as I developed this book. David Fleming modeled for me how to think expansively about rhetoric and made it possible to imagine writing a book on the themes of rhetoric and Chicago in the first place. Thank you to Donna LeCourt, whose graduate seminars and scholarship have always made labor a pressing topic. I owe gratitude to Janine Solberg for teaching a seminar on "Historicizing Women's Literacies" that introduced me to archival research and to feminist rhetorics. Rebecca Dingo, Anne Herrington, Peter Elbow, and Rebecca Lorimer Leonard generously gave time to mentoring me and offered important feedback on this research. I appreciated the support of fellow graduate students and UAW members who created a community and sustained a culture of organizing.

I developed this book manuscript while working at the University of North Texas (UNT) and owe gratitude to the colleagues who supported me, especially Angela Calcaterra, Kyle Jensen, Aja Martinez, Kimberly Tweedale, Kimberly Moreland, Jill Talbot, and Robert Upchurch. Matthew Heard was a generous collaborator and friend who helped me work through countless ideas and drafts. Thank you, Matt, for believing in this project and for your much needed encouragement and support through the process of writing this book. Through UNT's American Studies Speakers Series, I connected with Cristina Ramírez who helped me write about methodology and provided feedback on my introductory chapter. To the undergraduate rhetoric and writing students at UNT: your enthusiasm and engagement are unmatched, and I remain inspired by the ways you showed up for each other and for the rhet/writing community.

xxii *Acknowledgments*

I completed this book project while beginning a new position in the Department of Writing Studies at the University of Minnesota. I am grateful for the support of my new colleagues Lee-Ann Breuch, Patrick Bruch, Dan Card, Jaclyn Fiscus-Cannaday, Richard Graff, Molly Kessler, Amy Lee, John Logie, and Tom Reynolds. Thank you for your collective warm welcome. Thank you also, UMN graduate students. I'm inspired to continue researching labor rhetorics by the ongoing labor organizing you are doing. Thank you for inviting me and others to join you in spaces for solidarity.

This book has been enriched by the scholars and teachers I have met through my participation in disciplinary networks, organizations, and publications. I am especially grateful to the Coalition of Feminist Scholars in the History of Rhetoric and Composition (CFSHRC) for connecting me with Lauren Obermark through their online mentoring program. Lauren helped me make progress on the manuscript and offered feedback on drafts of chapter two. Thanks also to my CFSHRC mentor Janine Morris for helping me in the final stages of writing the manuscript. The members of my writing group—Bethany Ober Mannon, Lillian Mina, Amy Reed, and Ryan Skinnell—played a big role in helping me write and finish this book. It was a joy to talk with this group each week over several years and work together to develop projects into books. Thanks to Stephanie Kerschbaum for organizing us into a group, facilitating our early discussions, and setting us up for successful long-term collaboration. Thank you to my undergraduate mentor Catherine Prendergast and to my graduate school friend Sarah Stanley for providing feedback on my book proposal. I'm glad working on the proposal provided a chance to reconnect. Kathleen Baldwin was generous with her time and energy in reading and commenting on drafts of two chapters. Thanks to Liesl Olson for her encouragement and feedback on my project during a National Endowment for the Humanities workshop at the Newberry Library in the summer of 2019. I was inspired to make more connections between past and present labor organizing rhetoric after learning about contemporary practices through the Labor Notes organization, especially through Luis Feliz Leon's labor organizing workshop in the winter of 2022. An early version of chapter one appeared as "Claiming Cosmopolitan Geographies: Space and Ethos at Hull House, Chicago," in *Rhetoric Review*, vol. 37, no. 4, 2018, pp. 406–20. I thank editor Elise Verzosa Hurley and the reviewers Lindal Buchanan and Wendy Hayden for their generous feedback. Portions of chapter three are derived from an article published as "Engendering Progress, Contesting Narratives: Women's Labor Rhetorics at the 1907 Chicago Industrial Exhibit," *Rhetoric Society Quarterly* vol. 50, no. 4, 2020, 283–96. I thank former *RSQ* editor Jacqueline Rhodes and anonymous reviewers for their feedback.

My sincerest thanks to David Blakesley for guiding this project through the process of publication with Parlor Press. I extend my deepest gratitude to Cheryl Glenn and Shirley Wilson Logan for invaluable feedback on my manuscript and for including the book in the Rhetorics and Feminisms Series. Thanks also to new series editors Jessica Enoch and Sharon Yam for your support. I'm grateful to Risa Applegarth for providing an insightful review that helped make the book better and to Fran Chapman for copyediting.

Finally and most important, I want to express my appreciation for my friends and family. To my dear friends Holly, Melissa, Megan, Stephanie, and Eva: thank you for always letting me know that I belong. I would like to thank my parents Tom and Diane and brother Alex for their love. I regret that my father Tom is no longer with us to share in family celebrations. Bill, Melinda, Warren, Sarah, Linda, and Don, thank you for your love and encouragement. My daughters Lucinda and Laura have been part of this research adventure for their entire lives. They inspire my continued engagement with feminism and make me hopeful about the future. My greatest thanks go to my husband, Jack Christian, who has helped me develop every part of this book, accompanied me on the research trips that made the book possible, and helped me find humor when the obstacles seemed too great. Thank you, Jack, for being a constant source of love and support and for helping me to appreciate the joy in domestic life and labor.

Introduction: Locating Feminist Rhetorical Histories of Labor

> May we not say that city housekeeping has failed partly because women, the traditional housekeepers, have not been consulted as to its multiform activities?
>
> —Jane Addams, *The Modern City and the Municipal Franchise for Women*

In March of 2021, women garment workers led a march through the streets of Yangon, Myanmar, to protest a military coup. As they marched, the protestors wore face masks and red scarves to protect themselves from COVID-19, to protect their identities, and as symbols of solidarity. Some wore hard hats and carried makeshift armored shields in anticipation of a violent response from the armed security forces stationed along their route. Many flashed a three-fingered salute, a sign of resistance originating from the *Hunger Games* films. As protestors walked through the city streets past concrete factory buildings and security barricades, their synchronous movement, symbolic gestures, and coordinated clothing worked in concert to communicate their unity in protest.

It is no coincidence women garment workers were leading an anti-coup protest. Across time and locations, women garment workers have developed rhetorical traditions to assert their equal rights to safety and economic equality, and demand governments, employers, and the public recognize their humanity. While the current locus of the garment trade is centralized in Southeast Asia, it was first located in industrial cities in Europe and North America in the nineteenth century. In all of these places, the garment trade has attracted young, rural women to cities by offering abundant and flexible work that does not require experience or specialized training. The industry has also exploited women. Manufacturers subject women workers to hazardous environments, underpay, and unpredictable hours, and military governments like the one that claimed power in Myanmar often restrict workers from organizing and reject efforts to pass protective labor legislation. The suppression of organizing under military rule is dire for all workers, but especially for women for whom organizing can secure gains across a spectrum of gendered social issues, such as access to fair housing, healthcare, education, and wage parity. Because exploitative conditions have spurred women garment workers to organize, they are often the group ready to mobilize and create visual and public displays in response to immediate exigencies, such as the coup in Myanmar. The rhetorical traditions developed by women workers have included strategies for coming together across differences—of rank, pay, and skill, but also of gender, race, ethnicity, nationality, language and more. Women garment workers' organized responses to violence and exploitation have often served as a bellwether for the development of a broader gendered class consciousness and interest in securing women's rights.

I focus my investigation of women's labor rhetorics on an earlier moment in industrialization, taking place primarily in the garment district of a northern US city in the late nineteenth and early twentieth centuries. As I turn my attention to historical women's labor rhetorics, I do so to illuminate the rhetorical resources women may draw upon when they speak, write, strike, and march today. As the scene in Myanmar reveals, women workers use labor rhetorics to prevent life-threatening violence in the immediate moment and to reimagine new conditions that make continued living possible in the future. For now, we might define labor rhetorics as the multimodal means by which rhetors negotiate the value and conditions of their work. Studying labor rhetorics, I hope, illuminates how rhetors draw from immediate surroundings and contexts as well as longstanding traditions in their responses. The street protest in Yangon is an example of a spontaneous collective response to the exigency of a coup, but it draws on historical precedents set within cultures of social movement organizing. The very act of marching is both a democratic and labor rhetorical tradition available to participants who have maintained collective memory around its meaning and effects. The march is an example of a rhetorical tactic that requires collective preservation in the labor field because it may remain an unused tactic in times when economic relations between labor and capital are relatively stable. In addition, it is used sparingly because it can be dangerous for workers to participate. As I will discuss, the labor march can be so threatening to governments and employers that workers often embody it under the guise of other traditions. The Yangon march, for example, was also a funeral procession; several garment workers had been killed by security forces the week prior. Marchers' spontaneous use of the three-finger salute, meanwhile, was meaningful because it had been previously adopted in Southeast Asia as a symbol of resistance during prior military takeovers of democratic governments. Now protestors were highlighting its gendered meaning; by referencing a film about a young female protagonist who leads a resistance movement through the gesture, the youthful women garment workers bolstered their own authority to lead. As I discuss discrete events like this march, I hope to show how labor rhetorics that respond to immediate exigencies also draw from longer-standing traditions and precedents.

In addition, labor rhetorics span local and global contexts, and their scope can teach us much about the ecologies in which symbolic acts make meaning. In Myanmar, as women collectively left the factory and marched in the streets to respond to a local political exigency, they also disrupted a global supply chain. The three-finger salute, too, was important for communicating across borders with a multinational public who bought fast fashion and could pressure manufacturers to protect workers from the abuses of military leaders through boycotting. The salute represents how industrial workers, whose livelihoods are made possible by transnational networks of distribution and consumption, use the geographic reach of their labor when they communicate. The three-finger salute was a symbol from an English-language American film with global reach, and by making use of a globally known reference when marching, women garment workers claimed authority in the street. In the process, they disrupted a key distribution channel and space of civic life rife with traditional and masculine notions of who has the power to assemble.

Overall, *City Housekeeping* explores how women have used rhetoric to conduct local negotiations about labor, and how those negotiations have been shaped by global contexts. Throughout, I emphasize how labor rhetorics resonate across spaces, times, and social movements. I do this as part of enhancing the broader feminist project of recovering women's rhetorical contributions to creating a more socially just world. I also take up this project to suggest women rhetors draw from unique experiences to offer insight into the gendered dimension of labor. Women who have reimagined labor through rhetoric create paths we might follow in the larger project of feminist solidarity building in a global economy. In the remainder of this chapter, I establish the context of my historiography and ground my study in feminist, rhetorical, and labor concepts. Finally, I describe my approach to gathering and analyzing archived and published sources.

Locating this Study

I located this study in Chicago in the late nineteenth and early twentieth centuries, a time when this city linked the industrializing American Midwest to the global market. It is also where women in my own family worked in the garment industry for generations. My great-great grandmother's migration from rural farm to industrial city was a transnational journey, from Poland to the US, in the early twentieth century. In Chicago, she and thousands of other immigrant women entered paid employment by making clothes in sweatshops and factories. There, they adapted to rapid shifts in the industry's technologies and to changing literacy requirements, and faced limited opportunities to seek labor protections as women and citizens. By locating this study in Chicago during the Progressive Era, I hoped to learn something about how women like my great-great grandmother used rhetoric to reimagine the meaning and value of labor.

To discuss labor and seek solidarity, women needed spaces to assemble. Certainly, as contemporary women garment workers continue to use it, the street is one important space where women have met collectively and communicated their mutual interests, and I recover historical instances of labor protest in the street. Yet, as a feminist researcher I wanted to expand the locations where I noticed labor rhetorics happening beyond public spaces associated with masculine traditions of civic life and protest. In a city Carl Sandburg famously described as the "Hog Butcher for the World,/Tool Maker, Stacker of Wheat,/Player with Railroads and the Nation's Freight Handler," there is little doubt Chicago women used numerous spaces to seek labor solidarity (191). They also, however, faced obstacles to accessing existing assembly spaces where they were welcome to discuss labor. Sandburg's poem captures labor's importance by figuring Chicago itself as a laborer who feeds, builds, and transports for the nation and world, yet industrial employers actively inhibited workers from sharing spaces and organizing their labor. Garment manufacturers, for instance, outsourced work to homes to save on rent and to keep workers from meeting and talking together in the same factory. In so doing, employers exacerbated already existing gender, ethnic, and racial divisions within trades and neighborhood enclaves. When garment workers managed to form unions around the turn of the twentieth century, members were overwhelmingly white, male, factory-based workers. Within the culture of organizing these men built around saloons and union halls, women were excluded.

Often, women had to make their own space before they could use it to reimagine labor. To locate women in the spaces that mattered to them, I took inspiration from Anne Ruggles Gere's call to historiographers to explore the "enormous number of individuals who meet in homes, community centers, churches, shelters for the homeless, around kitchen tables, and in rented rooms to write down their worlds" (76). Gere's study of historical women's clubs, for example, illustrates the importance of recovering women where they were located to remake culture and literacy in ways that studies of writing classrooms cannot capture. After collecting archived and published sources that spoke to emerging patterns of women's labor discourse in Chicago in the Progressive Era, I looked for recurrent mentions of the spaces women discussed or used when negotiating labor. The Hull House settlement house on Chicago's west side emerged as an important node in the larger network of spaces where Chicago women reimagined labor.

Hull House was the hub for crafting a women's labor agenda in a city that offered limited spaces for organizing. When reformer Florence Kelley arrived in Chicago in 1891, she first went to the Woman's Temple, the large and well-known headquarters of the Woman's Christian Temperance Union. There, an acquaintance learned Kelley wanted to work in labor reform and redirected her to Hull House, where she lived for nine years (Sklar 462). For Kelley and countless others, Hull House was unique in its status as a stable, visible, and reliable space for bringing diverse people together to have difficult conversations about labor. Founded by Addams and Starr in 1889, Hull House was one of the first American settlement houses of hundreds that eventually opened during the Progressive Era. Addams decided to open an American settlement house after visiting Toynbee Hall, the very first settlement house founded by elite university-educated men who lived and worked among East London's poorest citizens. Addams and Starr refigured the settlement house to serve college-educated women and their working-class and poor neighbors in Chicago. While working on labor reform was an exigence for the English Toynbee Hall founders, this project took on new dimensions in the Chicago settlement under the leadership of women grappling with momentous shifts in gender, labor, and race relations wrought by industrialization.

Hull House was also different from Toynbee Hall and other settlements in that it was centrally located within Chicago's unique culture of labor organizing. One of the most impactful events to happen on Chicago's west side was the Haymarket labor strike in 1886, which began when well-known socialist leader August Spies called for an eight-hour workday in response to police killing four striking workers at the McCormick Reaper Works. Attended by approximately 1,500 people, the gathering ended in chaos when an anonymous striker threw a bomb at a crowd of six police divisions. Newspapers reported at least fifty police were injured and one was killed. Police retaliated by firing on the crowd. The police response to the Haymarket bombing instilled fear in workers, the public, and the press about supporting labor organizing. Workers, after Haymarket, lost ground in advocating for the eight-hour workday as employers faced little resistance in returning to the ten-hour workday. Hull House opened at a moment when workers were reimagining what labor organizing could be in the wake of the Haymarket incident. Even for those who did not come to Hull House to work explicitly on labor reform as Kelley had, Haymarket's importance was obvious: "The Haymarket riot cast its sinister shadow on all of us working at Hull-House in the late nineties," reflected doctor and resident Alice Hamilton in her autobiography (59). After witnessing firsthand the ongoing labor conflicts on Chicago's west side, Hamilton went on to bring medicine and labor reform together as one of the originators of the field of occupational medicine. Residents like Hamilton ultimately participated in and were influenced by the neighborhood's labor politics because they were always among and responding to neighbors.

By focusing on a settlement house, this study contributes to a tradition of feminist rhetorical historiographies that center women's organizations such as women's clubs (Gere), temperance organizations (Mattingly), civic organizations (Sharer), Black educational societies (Logan), and moral reform institutions (Shaver). Such studies establish that in the era before suffrage, women's organizations were spaces for networking, collaborating, gathering resources, and creating counter publics, so women might better argue for political rights and shape culture. This study argues that the settlement house was an additional kind of organization that sponsored women's rhetorics; however, Hull House was a unique version of a settlement house *because* of its location at the center of Chicago's west side garment district. By emphasizing the importance of this singular organizational site, I network spaces together differently than many prior feminist rhetorical histories. Where prior studies synthesize findings across organizational sites, this book offers a contextualized and sustained portrait of one settlement—Hull House—and then demonstrates its influence by following women who were able to meet there, gather resources, and organize labor out to other locations in the city.

Ultimately, *City Housekeeping* responds to a central question: how did the diverse group of women who came together at Hull House reimagine gendered divisions of labor in a rapidly industrializing metropolis? One way I answer this question is to highlight that women negotiated the spaces, values, and conditions of their labor through using multiple and intersecting modes, or ways of communicating, to reach a variety of stakeholders separated by differences of language and identity backgrounds. Confronted with impossible domestic ideals and gender discrimination in both trades and professions, women leveraged available communicative resources that included their physical surroundings, materials for composing, and literacy and language training, to create and circulate messages. Women labor rhetors had varying levels of access to the resources required to produce and circulate messages through speeches, printed materials, performances, and protests. Wealthier women enjoyed greater ability to curate their surroundings to reflect their labor politics and easier access to the channels necessary for circulating their messages beyond immediate surroundings in print.

Despite unequal access to resources for composing, working-class women effectively used verbal, visual, and aural modes to shape their own messages about labor. To appreciate the variety of modes used to deliver labor rhetorics, I explore in each chapter moments when women came together and used multiple modes concurrently to communicate about labor. Their use of multiple modes during singular events both enhanced communication and led to cross-talk and missed opportunities to connect in solidarity.

A more in-depth answer to my question emerges from my analysis of the content of the messages women delivered in multiple, intersecting modes. In the heart of Chicago's garment district, Addams and Starr, along with the many colleagues who joined them in living in the settlement, and the thousands of workers and organizers who met at Hull House, used labor rhetorics to redraw divisions between domestic and factory labor, and between domestic and foreign labor. In so doing they complicated tidy, linear progress narratives about the merits of industrialization. While the women I discuss largely agreed on the need to reimagine gendered divisions of labor in the industrializing city, their different responses to this need were numerous. Labor rhetors debated whether women should be protected from industry's worst effects or should be able to fully join in employment alongside men. Some thought women should protect their authority over the home and a separate, domestic sphere of labor from encroaching industry, keeping the identities of woman and worker largely separate in the process. Others wanted to further integrate women with men across gendered divisions of labor and questioned whether integrating the workplace meant ceding gendered power over the home. Labor rhetors who were brought together at Hull House also differed in their approaches to dealing with differences of identity beyond gender, as negotiating the meaning of the categories woman and worker required more than regendering divisions of labor; it required reckoning with wider ethnic and racial tensions kindled by the confluence of mass migration and increased competition for work, housing, and visibility in the rapidly growing city. Throughout this book, I analyze interactional labor negotiations for what they reveal about the emergence of new ideas about gender, labor, ethnicity, race, national identity, and power in this era.

INTRODUCING KEY FIGURES

Those who met at Hull House were motivated to come together on Chicago's west side to create new possibilities for living and laboring. Among the many who met at Hull House to discuss labor, the settlement's founder Addams was an important figure. A prolific speaker and writer who influenced local, national, and international conversations about labor, democracy, social work, diplomacy, and suffrage, Addams served as the settlement's figurehead until her death in 1935.[1] Born in 1860, Addams spent her childhood in Cedarville, Illinois, where she developed an early sense of civic duty and interest in public service from her father—a miller, state senator, and friend of Abraham Lincoln. As a teenager, she attended the Rockford Female Seminary, where she met future collaborators and Hull House residents Starr and Julia Lathrop, and received a liberal arts education that included studying German, Greek, and French. Addams was also a leader in the school's expansive extra curriculum that included literary societies, scientific clubs, and a school newspaper. After college, she continued her studies by joining traveling parties in Europe and visited England, France, Germany, Greece, Italy, and Switzerland to learn more about art, language, and literature. For Addams, creating Hull House began as an attempt to expand roles for college-educated women and merge what she called the "family claim" over women's lives with the desire to become a "citizen of the world" ("The College" 4). The goal of expanding women's roles beyond the family not only motivated Addams's settlement project, but also her later contributions to the suffrage movement and to international diplomacy. In these contexts, as she campaigned for Theodore Roosevelt and held a leadership role in the Women's International League of Peace and Freedom during World War 1, Addams became a nationally and internationally known speaker and writer.

Addams is a key figure for this book because her rhetorical contributions connect the labor rhetorics that emerged at Hull House with rhetorical traditions across social movements. At a meeting of the nation's leading suffragists in 1906, for example, Addams's labor rhetorics intersected suffrage rhetorics when she argued women's diminished control over their labor should be a pressing concern in a feminist response to life at the turn of the

---

1. Addams has received prior attention within rhetoric and composition studies. For example, Gloria McMillan has published an article analyzing Addams's approach to conflict resolution during the Pullman Strike, and William Duffy considered Addams's book, *The Long Road of Women's Memory*, as a treatise on how women's memory is a site of rhetorical invention. In the edited collection *Women and Rhetoric Between the Wars*, Hephzibah Roskelly analyzed Addams's 1915 speech titled "The Revolt Against War," arguing that Addams created a rhetoric of pragmatism, encouraging rationality instead of emotion, and in so doing, became deeply unpopular with audiences hoping to hear more patriotic and impassioned arguments about war. Another book that features Addams's later career is Wendy Sharer's *Vote & Voice: Women's Organizations and Political Literacy, 1915–1930*. Sharer discusses Addams's rhetorical tactics in the context of her membership in the Women's International League of Peace and Freedom, a group that attempted to implement rhetorical reform within international politics in the 1920s.

twentieth century. To support this claim, Addams drew from her experiences living on Chicago's west side with working-class, immigrant women who crossed the Chicago River daily to work in factories. Many considered women's entrance into industrial employment a step toward gendered equality, but Addams argued that by working in industry, women were doubly disenfranchised: they lacked the power to vote *and* they lost control over their space and time when laboring. The idea of "city housekeeping" is one Addams invented when questioning whether the modern city suffered when men excluded women from municipal decision making. Addams wondered, "may we not say that city housekeeping has failed partly because women, the traditional housekeepers, have not been consulted as to its multiform activities" (4)? "City housekeeping" was the practice that Addams and her Hull House colleagues took up when the process of securing women's suffrage was frustratingly slow, ultimately not granted until seventy-two years after the Seneca Falls Convention. Addams engaged in the practice of city housekeeping, for example, when in 1895 she became Chicago's nineteenth ward garbage inspector, a role for which she received criticism from local politicians because it gave her a civic power previously only granted to men to demand the garbage collector fulfill his contract ("Jane Addams Wears a Star" 6). While repetitive and unglamorous, city housekeeping provided women like Addams an immediate path for claiming gendered power that did not require the right to vote. Addams joined many first-wave feminists who coupled labor reform with suffrage activism in this way. Throughout, I use Addams's rhetoric as a touchstone to demonstrate how labor rhetorics borrowed from, intersected with, or supplemented feminist and social movement rhetorics.

Describing Addams's labor rhetorics as intersecting larger social and political landscapes requires understanding them as motivated by and emergent from interactions with colleagues. At Hull House, Addams was joined by countless reformers, organizers, and workers across decades in watching women's labor conditions change and in debating the merits of the narrative that integrating industry across gender lines equated with progress. In each chapter I feature Addams in collaboration with a wide network of other women, together thinking through the social meanings of gender, labor, race, ethnicity, and nationality. In addition to Addams, I highlight the rhetorical contributions of Hull House cofounder Starr, a bookbinder who helped bolster the settlement's commitment to anti-industrial and protectionist labor politics. I also consider at length the rhetorical activities of reformer Kelley, who received a labor education as the daughter of a prominent member of the US Congress known for advocating labor protections for workers and as Frederick Engels's English language translator. From

Hull House, Kelley drafted some of the first labor legislation for women and children and served as project manager for the labor treatise *Hull-House Maps and Papers*. Kelley's sometime roommate at Hull House was Harriet Rice, a medical doctor and the first Black woman to live at the settlement, where she worked in the medical clinic, dispensary, and library. Also living in the settlement around the turn of the twentieth century was Alzina Parsons Stevens, a former president of the first women's labor union in Chicago; Isabel Eaton, a social scientist who later contributed to W.E.B. Du Bois's *The Philadelphia Negro: A Social Study*; Agnes Sinclair Holbrook, a statistician and mapmaker; and Grace Abbott, a child labor reformer, along with her sister Edith, an economist and labor historian. Mary Kenney (later Kenney O'Sullivan) was a bookbinder and, while not officially considered a resident—a designation that implied one had committed to a lengthy stay at Hull House and required a vote of acceptance by other residents—organized women's unions at Hull House and founded the Jane Club, a boarding house for women workers within the Hull House complex. Similarly, Chicago socialite and philanthropist Ellen Henrotin did not live at Hull House, but she worked with Addams on a number of high-profile labor negotiations and served as president of the Chicago branch of the Women's Trade Union League headquartered for a time at Hull House. These individuals were part of a social circle that consistently produced and circulated rhetoric regarding the status and value of women's labor in the city.

Rather than focus solely on these individuals, however, my recovery project situates Hull House's social circle in conversation with women workers who organized within and beyond the walls of the settlement. For example, I recover the rhetorical contributions of garment workers Hannah Shapiro and Bessie Abramowitz, who were leaders of a citywide garment strike in 1910. I also tell the stories of collectives, made up of women often unnamed in sources, who attended union meetings despite risking their employment and good character; who formed their bodies in coalition on the street to protest conditions in the garment factory; and who spoke to the press to enlist public support for improving their living and working conditions. In connecting the stories of individuals and collectives as part of rhetorical networks across space and time, I seek to illuminate labor as a crucial topic that brings more women into the fold of rhetorical histories.

Defining Labor Rhetorics

Before further introducing my methodology, allow me here to define key terms. To ground my subjects of women and labor in rhetorical theory, I define labor rhetorics as the multimodal acts of meaning-making that deliberate the terms of who, where, when, and under what circumstances humans reproduce the conditions that make living possible. I focus on individuals and collectives who negotiated the contested value of "labor power," Karl Marx's term for the labor that may be exchanged as a commodity over a set period of time, a term distinct from labor itself, owned by the individual (270–71). When individuals negotiate the value of their labor power with, for example, an employer seeking to make a profit, labor rhetorics take on spatial and temporal dimensions. Labor rhetorics enmeshed in the logics of space as ordered by industrialization include negotiations about safety, accessibility, cleanliness, and social and cultural norms. When individuals sell their labor power over a period of time, labor rhetorics crucially negotiate temporal frames, including the number of working weeks, days, and hours, and concerns over schedules, breaks, and vacation time. Labor rhetorics that articulate relationships of space and time occur across verbal, visual, and aural modes.

Labor and Work

In focusing on labor rhetorics, I join feminist rhetoricians who are bringing attention to "work-related rhetorics," a term Sarah Hallenbeck and Michelle Smith coin to make visible work as an undertheorized site of inquiry with potential to complicate "problematic culturally dominant narratives about women's historical absence from professional spaces and practices as well as their gradual but steady linear progression toward full participation in civic and professional life" (202). Alongside their call has arisen scholarship by the contributors to *Women at Work: Rhetorics of Gender and Labor*, edited by David Gold and Jessica Enoch, who spotlight a variety of women's work sites and thus offer breadth to the study of the challenges that women faced when entering workplaces and professions. In *Domestic Occupations: Spatial Rhetorics and Women's Work*, Enoch complicates facile home-to-work narratives by unpacking myriad and multimodal arguments about the spaces of home, school, and childcare center that linked women's authority in the domestic sphere to workplaces (6). This scholarship joins prior rhetorical investigations of women professionals in medicine (Skinner; Wells), teaching (Enoch *Refiguring*), anthropology (Applegarth), and journalism (Ramírez). To this emerging area of scholarship, I contribute the varied work histories of women who met at Hull House. Many of these women were garment workers; others dedicated their labor to making sense of how garment work and other industrial trades were rapidly changing social life and representing modern labor conditions as artists, writers, social workers, teachers, and government bureaucrats.

Labor and work, though, are not synonymous. In distinguishing between the two, Hannah Arendt points out that labor "never designates the finished product" in the way that work does, a phenomenon she traces to classical antiquity's historical contempt for labor done by enslaved people in the home and outside the polis (80). Arendt's observation makes clear that labor has been associated for millennia with the home, while work is what happened beyond it. Labor, then, has a locational history in the home/work dichotomy. Further, Arendt's observation implies temporal distinctions between labor and work. Labor is fleeting; work endures. Throughout *The Human Condition*, Arendt traces how this hierarchy implied between labor and work is not ancient history, but foundational in Western humanistic philosophy. Feminist rhetorical inquiry into work—absent a focus on labor—has the potential to leave this hierarchy unchallenged and in fact can reinforce it, as prioritizing work happening in designated workplaces can make labor happening in the home seem less valuable or important. A focus on labor, alternatively, invites inquiry into a fuller range of activities and practices that exceed the bounds of traditional notions of work and workplace. Inquiry into the lives of women who labored in the garment trade, for example, illustrates how their labor was not confined to a single kind of workplace. Though the tragedy of the 1911 Triangle Shirtwaist Factory fire in New York City looms large in the history of the historical garment trade and suggests the primacy of the factory in this history, in fact much of the work of garment making was outsourced to kitchen tables in workers' own homes, or to tenement houses converted into sweatshops. Flexibility regarding where garments could be made allowed many women to multitask and carry on domestic tasks alongside sewing. Distinctions between home and workplace collapse quickly when exploring where women made garments, along with home-to-work progress narratives about their labor.

Because work is often associated with a workplace and carries with it assumptions about the value and status of the work undertaken there, the term labor better encompasses the diversity of paid and unpaid activities that were happening across the spaces women inhabited in their lives. At Hull House, for example, paid work that residents undertook within their occupations was a part of their labor. To be considered a Hull House resident, one had to have an income that paid living expenses for a stay of at least six months, though many residents stayed for decades. The 1900 US Census offers a snapshot of the kind of occupations the residents held to pay for their room and board at the settlement. For the census category of "Occupation, Trade, or Profession," residents offered job titles that included writer, clerk, schoolteacher, art teacher, piano teacher, journalist, and typewriter. Starr was listed as a bookbinder, while Addams was listed as a manager (and head of household) (*Twelfth Census*). Hull House residents' occupations, though, do not concede where they labored, which was often from the settlement itself. The census, for example, does not explain that the art gallery, library, kindergarten, coffee house, and kitchen in which residents were working were also part of Hull House where they lived. In addition, a focus on women's occupations subordinates labor like the quotidian domestic chores necessary for continued living. Hull House residents experimented with dividing domestic labor among a large group rather than a normative family unit, which allowed women residents the time not only to work for pay but to invent and facilitate neighborhood-facing projects. The lenses of work and workplace fail to capture the labor required for community organizing, which Hull House residents did by supporting unions, opening a labor museum and labor bureau, and collecting statistics and writing reports about their neighbors' lives and labor. Labor is a more expansive term that captures a range of activities that made life meaningful and possible for the women who lived at Hull House.

Rhetoric and composition scholar Carmen Kynard has recently offered teachers and scholars a powerful example of how prioritizing professionally recognized work can overshadow labor valued by individuals and communities when she explains the difference between "the work" and "the job" (19). Situating her advice in Black culture and as passed down by her mentor Suzanne Carothers, Kynard troubles the hierarchy of work and labor by distinguishing between the labor an employer values ("the job") and the labor that disrupts white privilege in the academy and centers Black knowledge and language ("the work"). The "job" and the "work," Kynard argues, can only align for those who experience white privilege and share goals with racist academic institutions (19). In this configuration, Kynard's Black feminist labor rhetoric flips the traditional hierarchy of work and labor, subordinating work to the status of "job" and elevating community organizing labor that resists monetization and participating in the racism of institutions as "the work." Labor rhetorics such as Kynard's about where, why, and for whom one labors illuminate the narrowness of traditional definitions and understandings of work. By focusing on labor rhetorics, I aim to contribute to the feminist project of understanding women's explanations of how they value and prioritize labor in their lives.

Space and Time

To explore women's reimagining of labor on their own terms and beyond the workplace, I highlight how rhetoric is part of the ongoing process of making and remaking spaces for solidarity. By focusing on the rhetorical and material making of spaces for solidarity, this study contributes knowledge about spatial rhetorics—Enoch's term for the rhetorics that give spaces meaning—which are significant because they contribute to obstructing or authorizing women's communication and work within those spaces (6). Here, I multiply the kinds of spaces that might serve as the focus of investigation in rhetorical studies by identifying the settlement, tenement, exhibition, and street as central in ongoing debates about gendered labor. For example, the tenement emerged early in my research as a primary and contested space in the labor rhetorics I recovered. A tenement is a dwelling originally built for one family, but divided and used by several. While tenements in cities solved the problem of housing large numbers of people who needed to live in proximity to industry, they contributed to new problems of overcrowding, sanitation, zoning, and privacy. The tenement, furthermore, evoked questions about the nature of modern social life. What did it mean to live among strangers? Or, to turn a kitchen into a workshop? At the heart of discourse about the tenement was a debate over whether the tenement should be subject to government oversight and its inhabitants protected from industry, or whether the tenement was private, domestic space ruled by norms of the white, American family. Like the tenement, the other spaces I focus on are linked in their status as contested in their meanings and uses. Women rhetors used spatial rhetorics to debate the uses and boundaries of kinds of spaces and give them renewed gendered and racialized meanings.

In addition to focusing on the way labor rhetorics participate in imparting meaning on spaces, I also consider space as a constraint on communication. I explore space as a constraint by asking what happened when the settlement, tenement, exhibition, and street were used as the locations of communicative events. To highlight how space's existing meanings, histories, and traditions shape rhetoric on location, I fill the book with concrete, scene-setting details about instances when communication occurred. I questioned how I might recover historical instances of rhetoric as constrained (or enabled by) location when observation was not possible and there were no video or audio recordings of the labor rhetorics under investigation. I decided to reconstruct individual, ephemeral instances of rhetoric by triangulating as many textual sources as I could find that described rhetorical events and their contexts. For example, there was a robust textual record about how the labor exhibitions I focus on in chapter three were rhetorically and materially constructed, and also many texts in archives and newspapers that spoke to what happened during the exhibitions as temporal events with concrete beginnings and endings. I sought to recover the fixed details of exhibitions, such as their location, place names, and material items on display, along with the names and number of participants. Ultimately, I did so not to give definitive accounts of exhibitions, but to understand exhibitions that had existed in particular places and times for what they could reveal about exhibits more generally as kinds of spaces where labor rhetorics were interactional and dynamic. I also considered individual exhibitions as recurrences in a pattern, or variations on a theme, and set each against the backdrop of other, related exhibitions. By recovering physical locations and the rhetorics that happened there, I was better able to understand how space shaped possibilities for rhetoric.

Another key contribution this book makes is to highlight how labor rhetorics participate in negotiating time, especially on the large scale of societal and technological change that may go unnoticed in everyday discussions about the length of a work schedule. Women's labor rhetorics in the late nineteenth and early twentieth centuries created, and also resisted, narratives about historical time in which industrialization was equated with progress and modernity. Addams, for example, resisted the idea that women's factory work was a sign of gendered progress in her NAWSA speech. She argued instead that women's industrial labor of biscuit making was like their traditional labor of breadmaking. These kinds of making were connected, according to Addams, by an "unending procession of women who have furnished the breadstuffs from time immemorial" (9). Addams, in fact, argued that factory labor represented a setback for women's authority because "always before, during the ages of this unending procession, women themselves were able to dictate concerning the hours and the immediate conditions of their work" (9). By invoking a timeline extending beyond memory, Addams rendered women's recent loss of control over their labor conditions in the city all the more shocking.

Though critical of women's factory work as a sign of gendered progress, Addams's narrative was a stereotypically Progressive one in its temporal scope: it characterized all of women's history yet was still shortsighted in its elision of the differing experiences of women in a racist and classist society. The scope of Addams's "unending procession" concealed, for example, the more recent national past those in her audience had experienced in which many Black women had been enslaved and did not control their working conditions, a past that contradicted the idea of women sharing in authority over labor spaces and practices through time (9). Later in her speech, Addams located historical women in this too-broad progress narrative in an imagined "primitive village," merging a Marxist conception of "primitive" time as an era prior to capitalism and an anthropological and racist temporality in which foreign and nonwhite women were relegated to an indeterminate past and excluded from white American women's modern city (875). Throughout the book, I highlight women's labor rhetorics as inseparable from the context of US empire-building and imperialist progress narratives that at this time positioned white Americans as more advanced and progressive than citizens of other nations, and of Black and Indigenous people in the US. Women's labor rhetorics both perpetuated and contested these racist narratives of time.

Labor rhetorics are an important site of rhetorical recovery because they narrate relationships of power and progress across spatial and temporal dimensions. Labor rhetorics are often *about* space and time, as they negotiate the purpose, value and conditions of individuals' labor power. These local negotiations have global implications: workers on a local scene are interconnected to producers and consumers in chains of production that cross national boundaries. In addition, as rhetors imagine new kinds of labor relations for themselves, they build new worlds in narrative, and their rhetoric offers renewed understanding of what progress and solidarity can look like. Finally, in recognizing that labor negotiations are often dynamic and evolving interactions among stakeholders who have varying levels of authority, many women who reimagined their worlds through labor rhetorics did so by first remaking the material and symbolic surroundings where negotiations took place.

Multimodality

To explore how women's labor rhetorics both reimagined space and occurred within space, I make it a priority to go beyond a focus on rhetoric in the verbal mode and attend to how women intervened in their worlds using sight and sound. Multimodality, a term used in a variety of academic fields to highlight that there are multiple ways to communicate, suggests that meaning-making symbols are interconnected across formats and work in concert to create messages. I emphasize the multimodality of labor rhetorics because a rhetor's modes communicate about the labor required to produce a message. By focusing on communication beyond the verbal, I affirm the conclusions of communications scholar Mary E. Triece who describes how working-class women often enacted labor rhetorics through visual embodied actions, such as the strike, picket, and march, to interrupt and draw attention to the capitalist churn that left them exhausted and vulnerable when expected to fulfill the unreasonable demands of employers. Labor rhetorics, though, are not restricted to working-class subjects. Women with economic privilege had greater ability to plan and access the resources they needed to create and deliver rhetoric. The middle-class and affluent reformers I discuss, for example, communicated by designing model homes and exhibits that reimagined labor relations; they wrote about labor in books and articles, and they spoke about labor reform in public forums. During discrete rhetorical events such as union meetings, exhibit openings, or labor marches, women from diverse class backgrounds communicated across a variety of modes simultaneously, mixing combinations of verbal and visual symbols that included words, images, bodies, and landscapes to make meaning. By recovering the simultaneous labor rhetorics of working-class, middle-class, and affluent women rhetors together, I feature real examples of women's unequal access to rhetorical modes and demonstrate how the project of building solidarity could be aided or thwarted as modes interacted during events.

Solidarity

One of my aims in writing a feminist rhetorical history is to illuminate how the gender identity *woman* was constructed in an industrializing American city in relation to labor, and in so doing contribute to the larger goal of better understanding how gender categories have shifted to become both more inclusive and exclusive at particular times and places. To focus on this aim, I attend to women's uses of rhetoric to align the identity *woman* with the identity *worker*. I understand women's uses of labor rhetorics to align these identities as a project of pursuing solidarity. Women take a first step toward solidarity, according to Chandra Talpade Mohanty, when they recognize their "common interests as workers" while honoring their diverging experiences within a global capitalist economy that promotes division across gender, race, caste, and nation (168). This book illuminates the rhetorical dimensions of women both recognizing differences and working together to resist exploitation in labor contexts.

By solidarity, I mean a recognition of reciprocity, or that we rely on each other. This recognition does not necessarily need to manifest symbolically. In *Inessential Solidarity: Rhetoric and Foreigner Relations*, Diane Davis explores solidarity as an imperative preceding and motivating symbolic action to achieve social and communal purposes. Whereas Davis is interested in theorizing solidarity as a necessary openness that arises prior to persuasion, I am more interested here in analyzing what happened in actual instances of symbol using for solidarity. I discuss the claims, appeals, and negotiations rhetors used to express a recognition of reciprocity and to invite others to work toward shared goals and commonalities. These instances of communication include labor rhetorical traditions, like the strike, picket and parade, still commonly used in the labor movement today. I also discuss everyday labor rhetorical practices, ones that recur, but do not necessarily rise to the level of tradition. For example, in chapter one I discuss a salutation in an invitation to a union meeting for garment workers that is gender inclusive. This is an example of a writing practice that might parallel something like today's ubiquitous use of "in solidarity" in labor organizing as an email closing to signal communal membership and establish a trustworthy ethos for the writer. By exploring a range of labor rhetorical traditions and practices, I hope to show seeking solidarity as an ongoing process that relies on constant rhetorical invention and expression.

I focus on women who used rhetoric to seek solidarity because another of my aims is to add to a capacious and inclusive picture of women's contributions to rhetorical traditions and practices. To take stock of these contributions, I attend to women's labor rhetorics along a spectrum of effectiveness in actually creating solidarity. I provide a few glimpses of solidarity established and sustained, but also attend to women's labor rhetorics that created or maintained division, such as when women social reformers who were not employed imagined they could remain outside the fray of labor and capital. These complicated instances of labor rhetorics are the result of women bringing different motives, tactics, and willingness to recognize and potentially cede individual power in the service of creating collective power to communicative events. Analyzing these complicated or divisive efforts reveals just as much about gender and power relations among participants as analysis of overtly successful efforts. While at times, the women I focus on were visionary, at other times they were short-sighted, racist, or elitist. Through rhetoric, the subjects of this book expanded and constricted the meaning of womanhood, created new possibilities for women in the labor market, and mediated unequal social relations. They were constrained by discourses and circumstances and were unable to anticipate fully the consequences of their rhetoric and the difficulties of achieving solidarity.

Seeking solidarity is at times difficult because rhetors must deal with differences while working toward the goal of finding common ground. On its face, solidarity may seem to imply bonding with those who already hold similar identities, beliefs, values, or interests, yet it is a concept that actually suggests the need to recognize reciprocity is most pressing among those with differences. In describing solidarity within the feminist movement, bell hooks expanded on this idea by arguing that what gets in the way of solidarity is false or too easy notions of sisterhood (often historically voiced by privileged white women) that emphasize unity without confronting and addressing divisions. As hooks insists, "divisions will not be eliminated by wishful thinking or romantic reverie about common oppression despite the value of highlighting experiences all women share" (44). These divisions extend beyond gender and class. In the context of the early women's labor movement in Chicago, for example, divisions among women were shaped by race, ethnicity, language and literacy usage, citizenship status, and skill level or position within an industry, and implied distinct experiences with labor exploitation.

That seeking solidarity requires dealing with differences in the interest of coming together is what makes the term pertinent to rhetoric, an art and practice of persuasive discourse that, for some, exists in the first place because people inevitably have differences and need to find ways to induce social cooperation. By implying differences, solidarity shares much in common with Kenneth Burke's notion of consubstantiality, a term connoting a place of bridged differences through a rhetor's use of symbols to invite identification. As Burke explains, "to begin with 'identification' is, by the same token, though roundabout, to confront the implications of *division*" (22). We might think of Burke arguing that "if men were not apart from one another, there would be no need for the rhetorician to proclaim their unity" (22). I use the term solidarity over other terms that describe the pursuit of persuading people they have commonalities within differences (such as Burke's term identification) because solidarity is a labor term. It has a history of usage connoting finding common ground among differences constructed in divisions of labor and implying those who seek it acknowledge differences as produced within a system of economic exploitation.

Borrowed from French, the term "solidarity" began circulating in English by the mid-nineteenth century in discussions and publications about political alignment in the face of labor exploitation shared among workers ("solidarity"). In the 1890s, the French sociologist Émile Durkheim helped theorize the term's importance for labor discourse as he wrestled with how to characterize the social bonds of society during and after the industrial revolution when increasing divisions of labor made it difficult to assume that communities shared beliefs and values. Durkheim theorized that solidarity was a feature of a modern consciousness in which individuals came to understand themselves as interdependent on others' labor. On a more basic level, solidarity's root word *solid* suggests a physical and present quality and reminds us that solidarity is about people's lives as materially interconnected. The content of rhetoric in pursuit of solidarity often points back to shared material conditions required for continued living. Solidarity might suggest a desire for a fixedness or stability to these conditions, one that arises in contrast to a lived experience shaped by the constant motion of capital: as Marx famously asserted in the *Communist Manifesto,* "all that is solid melts into air" when describing capitalism as characterized by constantly changing modes of production and expanding markets (77). Many appeals to solidarity have imagined unity and stasis rather than change and motion. The writer and agitator Ralph Chaplin, for example, pushed back on the capitalist logic of perpetual change when he called for "Solidarity Forever," an anthem he completed for the International Workers of the World just before a hunger march began from Hull House in 1915 (167). The song's title expresses a wish for solidarity across a stable and unified temporal dimension—forever—and pushes back against a capitalist logic of perpetual change.

Solidarity is also a useful term for aiding in the feminist project of noticing how women used rhetoric to navigate complex power relations in labor contexts. In their project of tracing the theoretical and historical usage of the concept, activists Leah Hunt-Hendrix and Astra Taylor further define solidarity as "a form of power rooted in the acknowledgment that our lives are materially intertwined" (34). In seeking solidarity, power emerges in the shared project of coming together against exploitation. Solidarity as a form of power that emanates from reciprocity or intertwinement offers a key contrast to more static notions of power, or something individuals or groups possess and then bring with them to rhetorical situations. In analysis of labor rhetorics, I take stock of power relations among participants in rhetorical situations to understand whether their rhetoric furthers the goals of equality and justice or works to maintain power imbalances.

To draw out an understanding of power as emergent in interaction rather than as static, I am interested in thinking through possibilities for solidarity within the context of alliances. I do this especially in chapter four as I consider an alliance between workers and reformers created during a citywide garment workers' strike. In their work on education and identity development, Jamie Washington and Nancy J. Evans define an ally as "a person who is a member of the 'dominant' or 'majority' group who works to end oppression in his or her personal and professional life through support of, and as an advocate with and for, the oppressed population" (195). For example, an ally to the LGBTQIA+ community often refers to a person who is not a member of the community, but can show visible support and advocate for the community's members. Allies can work with oppressed groups to acknowledge differences and end exploitation, but in alliances, power is not necessarily emerging in the interaction between allies and oppressed groups; rather, allies may lend their power to an oppressed group for a time. When this happens, allies can sometimes reinforce power inequality between themselves and the group they are supporting. In 2014, Indigenous Action, a group that supports Indigenous sacred lands defense, published a critique of allies who maintain and even gain power from their position. Indigenous Action pointed out that ally can become its own powerful identity and hold a value easily commodified in a nonprofit environment where individuals' livelihoods are funded by organizations with agendas that may not align with the goals of oppressed groups (2). When holding onto the identity of ally becomes more important than the goals of ending exploitation and seeking equality and liberation, allies are not seeking solidarity with the group they are supporting. I take notice of the perils and possibilities for solidarity within alliances as part of the larger project of creating a picture of women's labor rhetorics along a spectrum of power dynamics and effectiveness in recognizing reciprocity among differences.

Finally, solidarity as a practice is not only something to analyze what others are doing, but to pursue as writers and researchers. While writing most of this book from a public research university in Texas, where public sector workers are banned from collective bargaining and many are fearful to even discuss possibilities of collective action, I recognized the kinds of labor rhetorical traditions and practices I write about were suppressed in my own workplace. Even in an academic context without a robust culture of labor organizing, pursuing solidarity can be an everyday practice when academics recognize writing and research as labor and collaborate with others to imagine the conditions that make this labor sustainable and accessible. Researchers and writers can also begin to seek solidarity by acknowledging their positionality, or the differences and commonalities between researcher and research subjects. In the conclusion, I develop the idea that writers of rhetorical histories might think of themselves as networked—connected in patterned ways, though not through direct or linear relationships—to research subjects by their shared relationships to labor. Researcher and subject are also networked through the shared possibility of using rhetoric in reimage progress narratives about gender and labor. Solidarity, then, is not for others to pursue, but for researchers and writers who recognize reciprocity with other workers in the academy and with the historical subjects they recover.

REVISITING 'SEPARATE SPHERES' DISCOURSE

Within the collective feminist project of articulating how rhetoric participates in socially constructing gender, many scholars have noted the power of domestic or "separate spheres" discourse to shape the spatial and rhetorical lives of women. I engage with domestic discourse as a framework in part to persuade feminist rhetorical scholars to revisit "separate spheres" ideology through the lens of labor. Labor matters to constructions of gender: when rhetors reimagined possibilities for women's labor, they simultaneously reimagined the category woman. For example, Mary Wollstonecraft was an early and famous critic of the gendered division of labor that relegated women's work to the private, domestic sphere in *A Vindication of the Rights of Woman*. In her 1792 pamphlet, Wollstonecraft questioned "how many women thus waste life away, the prey of discontent, who might have practiced as physicians, regulated a farm, managed a shop, and stood erect, supported by their own industry?" (156). The categories of woman and worker, Wollstonecraft suggested, need not be exclusive; they could align in their meaning for the benefit of individuals and society.

Several historians of domestic discourse, including Nancy Cott, Steven M. Beuchler, Barbara J. Harris, and Glenna Matthews, have attributed the rise of women's status in the home to increasingly unequal divisions of labor in the industrializing economy. Defining domestic discourse, Cott describes it as "the ideological presumptions, institutional practices, and strongly held habits of mind insisting that the home must be guided by a calm, devoted, and self-abnegating wife and mother" (xvii). In addition to associating women and femininity with the home, domestic discourse enjoined men and masculinity with public places and workplaces. As the US shifted from an agricultural to a manufacturing economy, the historiographic narrative goes, middle-class and affluent white women who had previously experienced relative access to public space, work, and money were excluded from the formal economy and the ownership of goods. As compensation, the cultural and institutional status of white women's domestic work was elevated. Domestic discourse, then, is a term that names the interrelated set of beliefs, values and material practices that structure ideals about white women's domestic labor in an industrializing society that newly excluded them from paid and public labor.

While many historians have explored industrial upheaval as foundational to nineteenth century idealized womanhood, feminist rhetorical historiographers have largely elided labor as a factor in their gender analyses of rhetorical spaces. For example, Nan Johnson, Lindal Buchanan, Jane Donawerth, and Roxanne Mountford have argued rhetorical convention discouraged women from taking up the public podium, academic platform, and religious pulpit, and instead prescribed the home as where women should speak. As Hallenbeck and Smith have pointed out, the rhetorical spaces of podium, platform and pulpit are also workplaces, yet remain underexplored as spaces of gendered labor (206). Relatedly, Karlyn Kohrs Campbell, Shirley Wilson Logan, Carol Mattingly, and others have inquired into what happened when nineteenth century women spoke in public. These scholars have found women speakers stoked such public anxiety that they often began by assuring audiences of their femininity, so that their gender, and for Black women, their race, did not disqualify their remarks. Gender and race, though, do not fully explain the resistance women rhetors experienced when speaking. Whenever nineteenth century women spoke on the podium, platform, or pulpit, they challenged traditional notions of womanhood *defined by* divisions of labor. Their presence in public and masculine spaces was additionally threatening because it suggested women could compete economically with men.

Domestic discourse was—and is—powerful because it constrained possibilities for how individuals could think, speak, and write about gender and labor. Virginia Woolf described ideal womanhood personified by the "phantom" of the "Angel in the House" as the greatest obstacle to writing truthfully about her experience as a woman. "It is far harder to kill a phantom than a reality," Woolf wrote about her struggle to work in the traditionally masculine profession of novelist (1254). As Woolf recognized, the practice of novel writing countered the idealized notion that women's labor should be relegated to private, domestic practices. Domestic ideals pervaded individual consciousness and collective cultural norms to such a degree that Woolf struggled to find the language she needed to describe actual womanhood. I join historiographers of gendered labor such as Cott, Mary P. Ryan, Christine Stansell, Sarah Deutsch, and Joanne J. Meyerowitz who focus on how real women contended with the ideals inscribed in domestic discourse. While Woolf battled with domestic ideals in a profession, working-class women struggled without the economic and social privileges someone like Woolf had when they challenged prescribed gender roles by working for pay. For example, in her study of unmarried wage earners in Chicago, Meyerowitz argues employers justified paying women inadequate wages because they assumed women were supported by family members and did not live independently (33). Throughout this book, I emphasize how domestic discourse not only structured women's experiences of labor, but also their responses to it.

I highlight domestic discourse as originating in industrialization's stark divisions of labor because it is all too easy for many to consider it a discourse solely about gender. Interrogating the origins of domestic discourse is important because it continues to shape gendered labor rhetorics today. One might detect the influence of domestic discourse in contemporary debate about the prospect of women "having it all," a phrase originating from the title of *Cosmopolitan* editor Helen Gurley Brown's 1982 book. This phrase, which broadly refers to whether women can have both a family and a career, is usually uttered with regard to white, middle-class professional women. A notable entry in this discourse is Sheryl Sandberg's argument for "leaning in," a phrase predicated on the idea that women have not yet gained equality in the corporate world and might actively choose to claim a place there and thus equalize the workplace (335). Both "having it all" and "leaning in" only make sense if one assumes contemporary women are afforded some or partial access to a whole life. Recently, the myth of having it all has been leveraged in arguments about whether pregnant persons should continue to have access to abortion services. In *Dobbs v. Jackson Women's Health Organization* (2022), for example, the state of Mississippi argued before the US Supreme Court that abortion protections are now unneeded because enacting the obviously gendered reproductive labor of childbirth and childcare is no longer an economic impediment to leading a full life at home and work (Miller). That abortion protections were legally encoded in the first place concedes a history in which few have reliably accessed this healthcare. As access to the material supports of healthcare, childcare, education, and transportation continue to be contested, the fantasy of having it all, even for the privileged, remains largely aspirational.

Cosmopolitanism

This book also revisits the framework of domestic discourse for what it reveals about the term "domestic" as produced in opposition to the foreign. Historians such as Kristin Hoganson, Amy Kaplan, and Mari Yoshihara have noted that when the term "domestic" connoted the nation, it implied an opposition with the foreign and created an opening for American women to participate in the project of articulating relationships between American and foreign identity and culture. Building on the insight of these historians, I offer a local history of women who expanded domestic roles and labor practices by adopting a cosmopolitan outlook. Some of the women I focus on actively claimed global citizenship, considered relationships between consumers and producers on a global scale, and intervened in labor discussions by centering the value and meaning of national differences. From Hull House, some women advocated for the purchase of foreign and artisan-made wares as a means of communicating an anti-industrial labor politics. Owning a cosmopolitan collection of clothing, art, books, and furniture could communicate an embrace of fair-trade politics and solidarity with foreign artisans and workers exploited by industry.

Cosmopolitan values were more generally circulating in Chicago and guiding citizens' ethics and behavior at the end of the nineteenth century. By cosmopolitanism, I am referring to the expansive notion that citizenship exceeds allegiances to towns, cities, and nations, and extends to a global community. As philosopher Kwame Anthony Appiah has argued, cosmopolitanism is a useful concept because it brings together two key ideas about the interconnectedness of humans. First, cosmopolitanism centers the ethical idea that strangers are universally obligated to be responsible for one another, regardless of geographic location. Second, the concept assumes that people who must coexist are different from one another, and their differences are a resource for exploring how to associate (xv). As a concept that positions difference as inevitable and as a resource, cosmopolitanism is one that can align theoretically with the project of building solidarity. A local version of cosmopolitanism began crystallizing in Chicago in the early 1890s during the lead-up to the 1893 World's Columbian Exposition, or World's Fair. The event, which brought up to twenty-seven million tourists to Chicago, was meant to counter Chicago's provincial reputation and establish it as a global city on par with New York, Paris and London (Gilbert 121). By featuring exhibitions representing countries from around the world, the World's Fair was both spectacle and educational space for understanding the interconnectedness of nations and cultures. It also promoted the economic benefits of global exchange.

The World's Fair helped to localize and politicize a gendered version of the cosmopolitanism outlook. The event especially influenced some women's responses to ethical questions about consumption in an increasingly global marketplace. That women would embrace a politics of consumption at this moment was not a foregone conclusion. Rhetoric scholar Kristy Maddux has argued Chicago's World's Fair was a hugely influential event where women speakers lamented the shift from domestic, handmade production to industrial production because it signaled a loss over gendered authority in the home. *City Housekeeping* furthers inquiry into this lament over the loss of domestic-based production to reveal some Chicago women responded, not by returning to producing goods in their own homes, but by consuming artisan goods others were making. I first came to understand that consuming foreign and artisan-made wares was a way to express a cosmopolitan outlook after reading historian Kristin Hoganson's book, *Consumers' Imperium: The Global Production of American Domesticity, 1865–1920*. Hoganson describes the phenomenon of white women who lived in provincial towns and interior American cities in the late nineteenth and early twentieth centuries demonstrating their appreciation for the wider world through purchasing goods made internationally. Hoganson argues that purchasing was a way some women could live out the cosmopolitan ethic and support diverse strangers across the globe. Once in the home, imported goods signaled a homeowner's cosmopolitan outlook. In *City Housekeeping*, I build on Hoganson's observations about women's purchasing to intervene in the global market and explore this practice as a local labor rhetoric.

Cosmopolitan consumption was ethically dubious and a political strategy unequally accessible to all. When white, well-to-do women purchased foreign-made goods, they not only communicated support for foreign producers, but also their economic power to intervene in the livelihoods of both domestic and foreign producers. In Chicago, this power play highlighted that local cosmopolitan ideals expressed through the World's Fair were always intermixed with an imperial project to assert the US's dominance in global trade. The World's Fair, after all, was not only a pedagogical space of encounter; it was also a marketplace to showcase how US manufacturers were collecting raw materials from around the world and turning them into industrial products. Imperialistic trade relationships were represented in the built environment of the Fair itself: the fairgrounds were populated with neoclassical revival style buildings and referred to as the White City, while a separate carnivalesque area called the Midway Plaisance featured exhibits from nations seen as primitive and racialized. These exhibits were often inaccurate, demeaning, and perpetuated a vision of nations beyond the US and Europe as existing outside technological and cultural progress narratives. At a time when international trade seemed to usher in cultural homogeneity rather than preserve differences, American women participated in this imperialistic relationship of global exchange as consumers who idealized products from so-called primitive nations and reified differences in the process. By attending to cosmopolitan consumption as a labor rhetoric, I reveal the practice's roots as a first wave feminist strategy. It is still a seemingly feminist strategy practiced today, for example, when privileged American women use selective purchasing as a primary mechanism to aid Southeast Asian women workers in sweatshops. Rather than realign power imbalances across the globe, consumer philanthropy instead reifies power relations between American consumers and foreign producers.

In late nineteenth century Chicago, women consumers who celebrated foreign labor cast local immigrants as foreign workers and valued their racial identities as part of the commodities they were making. By valuing local workers' foreign identities, some women consumers protected whiteness from commodification. At the time, local racial distinctions went beyond differences of white and Black and extended into negotiating the color of European immigrants. This period of mass European immigration was a time when historian Matthew Frye Jacobson argues it was possible for European immigrants to be "white *and* racially distinct from other whites" (6). Chicago Italians, Irish, and Russian Jews living on the city's west side were recognized as white and nonwhite simultaneously. As it became increasingly apparent that consumer organizing focused on purchasing foreign and artisan-made wares commodified Irish, Italian, and Jewish identities, some immigrant women workers began striking in part to disrupt the consumer-focused campaigns of their white, wealthy collaborators.

Finally, women who focused on cosmopolitan consumption as a labor rhetoric did so to elide domestic racial politics between Black and white workers. The Hull House residents I focus on were diverse in their class, ethnic, and national affiliations, but most shared in the privilege of whiteness. *City Housekeeping* explores how some white women who participated in the politics of cosmopolitan consumption excluded Black women from their projects of solidarity. Historians and legal scholars working at the intersections of race and labor such as Ian F. Haney López, Cheryl I. Harris, and Noel Ignatiev have shown that white people have often protected the value of whiteness above seeking labor solidarity with Black people. As historian Philip S. Foner documented in his history of women in the American labor movement, white women in the early movement protected racial divisions of labor by ignoring the multilayered oppressions Black women faced and excluded them from organizing efforts. Today, contemporary feminists such as writer Mikki Kendall point to patterns of white women excluding women of color in their feminist practices through the hashtag "#SolidarityIsForWhiteWomen" (1). This is a hashtag that could apply to situations across time to highlight long-standing patterns in the feminist labor movement. As my analysis attends to these racialized dimensions of labor rhetorics, I contribute to recovering the historical origins of a feminism in which white women often protected and defended whiteness above seeking solidarity. In so doing, I cast the work of recovering rhetoric as part of a larger feminist advocacy project to make visible histories of inequality that still impact contemporary efforts to create a world in which all have equal opportunities and rights.

NETWORKING LABOR RHETORICS

The past of women's labor rhetorics is connected to its present, and local labor rhetorics draw from rhetoric delivered in other locations. I draw connections between labor rhetorics across spatial and temporal networks and among stakeholders who share the conditions that provide their exigence. To recover a fuller picture of the circulation of labor rhetorics, I turned to the practice of garment making for the metaphor of the network. Networking, or engaging in a manufacturing process of weaving threads in a complex net or pattern, was useful for conceptualizing how singular rhetorical events were spatialized and linked to other rhetorical events. In a network, each thread is linked to others to make a larger net. There are patterns in a network, governed by limits of what is possible within the industrial processes of making, and women's labor rhetorics are interconnected by historical and industrial conditions that give rise to common exigencies and responses. The network is a particularly salient metaphor to apply to the study of the rhetoric of social movements because it is ultimately not possible to trace cause and effect in the complicated web of exigencies, participants, actions, and outcomes in social movements over time. In a call to study social movements, Nathan Crick invites researchers to think of a social movement as a network assembled in response to social changes, and participants as already connected to others as they act to make their interests rise to the level of movement. Crick writes that the work of the scholar of social movements is to "leave behind a map that indicates the significant aspects of that environment and traces out the different relationships between them so that future scholars can follow a different path. There is no ultimate explanation for any social movement, although there will always be more or less significant actors within a network" (23–24). Here, I hope to trace certain threads within networks that supported an emerging women's labor movement in Chicago. On the streets in the early twentieth century, for example, Chicago women newly protested the conditions of their labor in the garment industry in part because other labor movement participants located in other cities had by then developed shared traditions of labor protest that included stopping work, leaving the workplace, and taking to the streets to enlist public support against employers' exploitative practices. In the metaphor of the network, each protest is positioned as a node among others, and the influence of other protests is evident, but not direct or linear.

By using the metaphor of the network to conceptualize rhetoric's recurrences across time, I join a growing list of scholars that includes Jenny Rice and Laurie Gries who are interested in how rhetoric circulates beyond an original rhetorical situation. Jacqueline Jones Royster and Gesa E. Kirsch frame social circulation as a feminist concern because circulating rhetoric necessarily complicates the "separate spheres" framework that has constrained the spaces where researchers have looked for evidence of women's rhetorical contributions. Tracing socially circulating rhetorics, they argue, leads researchers to locate women in a "more fully textured sense of what it means to place these women in social space" (24). Yet, Royster and Kirsch's charge to researchers also includes following rhetoric's circulation across time, not only backwards but forwards. I take up that charge, and in so doing, join the contributors of the recent anthology *Feminist Circulations: Rhetorical Explorations Across Space and Time*, to understand how rhetoric's circulation can advance or stall on nonlinear timeframes. In a network, the route from one point to another is not linear, and there may be multiple paths that lead to the same place.

Thinking about networks as expanding across time helped me to reflect on my motivations for taking up this project. This book was motivated in part by my interest in understanding more about the lives of women like those in my family who worked in Chicago's garment industry for generations, whose lives intersected with global market trends and the rise of organized labor. Through the research process, my interest in family history deepened, and by conversing with family members and looking through census and newspaper records, I learned what I could about the women in my own family who immigrated from Poland to Chicago's northwest side. Deepening my personal connections to this project made me rethink Royster and Kirsch's charge to feminist rhetoricians to attend to the "things that we absorb even without conscious awareness rather than a static sense of direct inheritance" (23). My interest in my own family history was seemingly the opposite of what Royster and Kirsch were suggesting; I was researching "direct inheritance" (23). Yet, a detailed labor history of women in my family was unknown to me or many of my living relatives. It remains largely unknown. I have learned, though, about the texture of my ancestors' lives by taking up this parallel project of inquiring into the rhetorics of women on the west side of the city, living at the time approximately four miles away from my great-great grandmother and her two young daughters. Despite the four-mile geographical distance between them, I found that the west side women who are the subjects of this book and my ancestors had their lives shaped by similar work opportunities, technologies, fashion trends, and the pull of American progress narratives that led countless women to employment in the garment industry.

It is not always possible to find documentation about how historical rhetorics circulated. In addition to triangulating sources and identifying patterns, my own experiences in the locations I write about allowed me to imaginatively reconstruct ephemeral rhetorics in circulation. Chicago is much changed since the late nineteenth and early twentieth centuries; nevertheless, being on location allowed me to imagine how spaces may have served as rhetorical resources for and constraints on solidarity. The original Hull House mansion and its separate dining hall now constitute a museum on the University of Illinois Chicago campus. Houses that could be classified as tenements still line west side neighborhood streets, though many have been torn down in twentieth century slum clearance projects; the Field Museum of Natural History owns textiles that were once displayed in Hull House Labor Museum exhibits. I made many trips over several years to these locations and others as part of my way of taking up critical imagination, a skill Royster defines as "a commitment to making connections and seeing possibility. So defined, imagination functions as a critical skill in questioning a viewpoint, an experience, an event, and so on, and in remaking interpretive frameworks based on that questioning" (83–84). My observations of contemporary places gave me insight into the materials and built features of environments I read about in historical texts. I gained a sense of room dimensions, wallpaper colors and textures, proximity of houses to streets and saloons, and the relation of streets and buildings during protests. These details, together with more traditional kinds of research based in archival and published texts, gave me a better understanding of the contexts in which the subjects of my study circulated rhetoric.

By writing through the lens of labor rhetorics, with a feminist focus on solidarity, I hope to instill appreciation for the ways that negotiating labor requires access to the space and time needed to invent and deliver arguments. Even with necessary space and time, women labor rhetors in industrializing American cities had to build on existing traditions and practices to invent new ways to come together across differences and gain power in their unity to create change. Along the way, the women I focus on in this study sometimes thwarted opportunities for solidarity by deploying arguments for keeping labor traditionally divided along gender, ethnic, and racial lines. By noting these instances, *City Housekeeping* offers insight into the classist and racist roots of debates over whether women can "have it all" and traces longstanding ambivalence to policies intended to aid women in laboring outside the home. I also feature moments when women embraced possibilities for reimagining gendered labor and made room for others, in their moment and across time, to see that the boundaries between home and work, men and women, and domestic and foreign, are not so fixed after all.

1 Settlement: Claiming Cosmopolitan Space

If the union could only meet here.

—Mary Kenney O'Sullivan, unpublished autobiography

In 1891 Jane Addams invited bookbinder and union organizer Mary Kenney to a dinner party at Hull House. When Kenney arrived at the newly opened settlement house, she was awed by its "furnishings and large rooms" (63). In an unpublished autobiography written decades after this first visit, Kenney recalled how she had been seeking a place to organize women workers who were excluded from joining the all-male craft unions in Chicago. Women workers had reported to Kenney that when they attended union meetings held in saloons, their moral character was called into question by coworkers and family members. Though Kenney initially thought Addams and other guests at the party "were all rich and not friends of the workers," her impression changed after Addams offered Hull House as a meeting place free of charge and paid for and distributed circulars (63). Over the next three years, Kenney organized garment workers, bookbinders, cab drivers, retail workers, laundry employees, and more, and helped establish Hull House as a center for women's labor organizing in Chicago.

Despite their differing social worlds, access to resources, and work experiences, Kenney and Addams mutually recognized that for women to organize, they must first find a space to do so. West side women's access to large assembly space was almost nonexistent, and women hesitated to organize because doing so implied identifying as a wage worker, a role at odds with the domestic ideal of a white woman who performed unpaid labor in a middle-class household. Nonwhite and immigrant wage-earning women were positioned further from this ideal and risked not only sexist but also racist responses from employers and white wage earners when seeking to organize. Even Kenney and her fellow workers of Irish descent could not always claim the categories of whiteness and Americanness. What did Kenney see in Hull House's "furnishing and large rooms" that made her consider new possibilities for labor organizing (63)?

Kenney saw an interior that Addams and Starr had decorated with a cosmopolitan, or nationally diverse, aesthetic. They had filled parlors, dining rooms, a library, and more with art and furnishings meant to reflect the traditions and interests of their immigrant neighbors and to invite neighbors to convene in solidarity alongside Hull House's residents. The diverse foreign art and furnishings were not only decoration; they were central to a project of expanding the places where women might claim speaking authority to include both domestic and foreign geographies. The cosmopolitan aesthetic overtly signaled an embrace of national diversity, but I am interested here in arguing that it also communicated a labor politics. By decorating Hull House with art and furniture imported from diverse international locales, the founders conveyed their knowledge and authority as consumers in a global market. Through savvy consumption, they established an anti-industrial stance toward the mass-produced domestic goods—food, fabric, furniture, clothing—manufactured in cities such as Chicago at this time.

My goal in focusing on Hull House's design and décor is to reveal the possibilities and perils of women claiming cosmopolitan space for labor rhetoric. The cosmopolitan settlement sent conflicting messages about its inhabitants' labor politics and allegiances. While the international artisan wares Addams and Starr displayed were meant to demonstrate solidarity with immigrant and exploited workers, they also communicated additional, less inviting messages. Hull House's interior provided evidence of its founders' impressive power as white and wealthy US consumers in the global capitalist system they were seeming to challenge. Historian Kristin Hoganson, tracing the wider phenomenon of nineteenth-century women's cosmopolitan consumption, notes that for many women in this era, ownership of international domestic goods was meant to signal appreciation for the cultures of Europe and Asia, and reflect the owners' openness to the wider world. But, argues Hoganson, purchasing was also an act of "imperial buy-in" (11). This chapter takes the settlement as its central organizing space to acknowledge that Hull House's founders participated in a long history of settlers claiming authority over cosmopolitan geographies and the labor conditions of Black and Indigenous people and communities of color, one that began in Chicago when French traders settled on the homelands of the Potawatomi, Odawa, and Ojibwe Nations. Like settlers before them, Hull House residents who claimed authority to make distinctions among spaces and people they deemed racially and ethnically non-white participated in an imperialistic project.[1]

---

1. Rosalyn R. LaPier's and David R.M. Beck's *City Indian: Native American Activism in Chicago, 1893–1934*, and James B. LaGrand's *Indian Metropolis: Native Americans in Chicago, 1945–1975*, provide more recent histories of Native American people in Chicago and the white settlers who claimed their land.

After exploring how the Hull House founders communicated a fraught labor politics *through* the space of Hull House itself, I turn in the latter half of this chapter to the labor rhetorics occurring *inside* Hull House to illuminate the effects of cosmopolitan space on verbal labor negotiations. Through reading accounts of unionizing efforts by Kenney and Addams, alongside the textual ephemera from their labor organizing, I offer analysis of appeals to garment workers to come together at Hull House across differences of gender, nationality, language, and work histories. Like Kenney, those invited to the settlement had complicated and at times conflicting responses to using a space so thoroughly curated to renounce the industries that employed them. Kenney, in her organizing efforts, focused on appealing to women to meet with men at Hull House by reimagining parlor rhetoric genres to include working-class participants. While Hull House provided new opportunities for women to speak about labor, it was also a space many could not, or did not want to, claim as a resource in seeking labor solidarity. Individual workers had differing levels of access, ability, and desire to claim authority over cosmopolitan space, and the labor rhetorics that emerged at the first union meetings in Hull House both complicated and reinforced hierarchies of power along lines of gender, class, racial, ethnic and national identity.

JANE ADDAMS AND ELLEN GATES STARR: CONSUMING IN A GLOBAL MARKET

A cosmopolitan space, to offer a definition, is one where characteristics of many different countries collide, an effect created by the transnational flow of capital. Under capitalism, industries have a "cosmopolitan character," according to Marx and Engels, because the bourgeoisie shares an economic interest in moving raw materials across borders from rural areas to industrial centers (77). As an adjective that points to how the transnational flow of labor and capital shapes economies, culture, language, and experience, the term *cosmopolitan* can be a useful concept in rhetorical studies for describing the conditions under which people communicate. A person in cosmopolitan space must negotiate economic, nationalistic, cultural, linguistic, and political boundaries. For example, rhetoric and composition scholar Xiaoye You argues powerfully for cosmopolitanism as an alternative framework to multiculturalism, one that better captures realities of English as a language in which local usage is shaped by a globalized economy (15). You explains cosmopolitanism is both descriptive of the conditions under which communication already takes place and a pedagogical heuristic for reframing

English in a transnational, capitalist network. Drawing from a variety of traditions and contexts across millennia, You argues recognizing cosmopolitan English is a pedagogical imperative so writing teachers can support students in becoming "global citizens," a subjectivity that constructs students as aware of and in control over their English in world markets (18). Over a century ago, Addams also recognized potential in calling attention to the global influences on rhetorical engagement. Addams did this outside of a traditional educational space and was especially interested in how the cosmopolitan ideal framed rhetoric for women seeking civic and labor roles from which they were typically excluded. Addams argued that women should be able to take up roles beyond those defined by the "family claim," such as daughter, mother, sister, and wife ("College" 4). Observing that a woman who fulfilled family roles often found herself "in addition, under an impulse to act her part as a citizen of the world," Addams presented Hull House as a place where women might expand domestic roles to include worldly citizenship ("College" 4).

Addams and Starr began planning to open their settlement house while they were students at the Rockford Female Seminary and then traveling companions in Europe. As partners, they brought different resources to the project of settling. Addams, a talented leader and prolific writer, became the settlement's figurehead and articulated its theories and purposes for the public. Starr, quieter though ever-present, initially helped gain social support for the settlement among Chicago's elite citizens by drawing on her aunt's local connections and memberships in women's clubs. With Addams's leadership skills (and inheritance) and Starr's social connections, the two founders secured an Italianate, Victorian-era mansion in the heart of Chicago's garment district with an ever-changing population of Italian, Polish, Russian-Jewish, Bohemian, French-Canadian, Irish, African American, and Chinese neighbors.

The settlement stood out among the tenements and saloons lining Halsted Street. Hull House was ornate. Inside, according to the architect Allen B. Pond, it had the typical "drawing-room, library, dining-room and the other usual apartments of a northern house of the period" (178). Upon moving into Hull House, Addams furnished the interior with expensive, imported furniture and art that she and Starr had purchased the year before when traveling in Europe ("The Art-Work" 614–15). A few reporters who visited Hull House in its early years attempted to give readers a sense of its interior. *Chicago Tribune* reporter Nora Marks (a pseudonym) wrote that "the walls were made of ivory and gold like the Auditorium [Theater]; there were Venuses with broken arms, Apollos, heads of Madonnas, art rugs, oak tables, china, silver, porcelain-lined baths, and the latest improved range" (2). In addition, an unnamed reporter for the *Chicago Times* offered a description of Hull House's expensive décor, some of which was of foreign origin:

> The halls were done in delicate terra cotta tints and the rooms in ivory and gold. The floors were polished and laid with rugs from the orient. There was the music room with its classic simplicity, the dainty piano, and soft etchings and water colors on the walls. The library blossomed forth with rows of books in scented leather bindings and in dusky niches flashed the snowy marble of bits of rare statuary. ("Work of Two Women")

By founding Hull House in a home in a nationally diverse neighborhood and decorating it with expensive and foreign décor, Addams and Starr claimed cosmopolitan space as their own. This space also signaled to others their identities as white, wealthy, college-educated women who were knowledgeable about diverse cultures, languages and geographies.

That a home should express the character of its occupants was commonplace at this time. Historian Gwendolyn Wright notes that writers of domestic literature that circulated in popular periodicals drew extensively from art and architecture theorists John Ruskin and William Morris to support the idea that a home reflected "the owner's occupation and background, as well as the values held in common with other citizens" (12–13). The home as reflection of character remains an idea undergirding the popularity of contemporary home design advice delivered through television and social media. Addams and Starr understood home design as symbolic of character better than most. They were serious students of Ruskin and Morris, and both theorized the settlement as a space where art could reflect the shared values of residents who lived at Hull House and their neighbors.[2] At a moment when the home was powerful in shaping ethos for women, Addams's and Starr's cosmopolitan display was an effort to convey they were citizens of the world.

In describing Hull House's interior as a reflection of its founders' character, I join other feminist scholars of rhetoric in exploring contexts and

---

2. Both Addams and Starr theorized art and labor in their writing. In an 1895 essay titled "The Art-Work Done by Hull House, Chicago," Addams described Hull House as an experiment in making "the aesthetic and artistic a vital influence in the lives of its neighbors" (614). "Art-work" in the essay refers to the pictures on the walls of the settlement and also to the art-related labor the residents undertook on behalf of neighbors. In "Art and Labor," appearing in *Hull-House Maps and Papers*, Starr cites Ruskin and Morris to develop the thesis that a settlement should encourage neighbors to take pleasure in their labor and to create arts and crafts that reflect their role as artisans.

influences beyond an immediate rhetorical event that establish authority. Though Aristotle cautioned audiences against prejudging a speaker's ethos, or character, based on prior knowledge or circumstances outside of a speech itself, feminist scholars of rhetoric more readily acknowledge character as influenced by myriad contingencies (39). Noting that social categories such as gender factor into a speaker's ethos, Nedra Reynolds has argued that ethos is additionally constructed by "the location or position from which that person speaks or writes" (326). The settlement's interior was a key location the founders curated to communicate their worldly ethos, but they also located, on a broader scale, in Chicago's west side garment district, a place that carried additional symbolic meaning for their character. It was unusual for two well-to-do white women to choose to live there. Their choice to settle on the west side invited publicity, and reporters gleefully wrote about the founders' class difference from their neighbors: "They Help the Poor: Jane Addams and Ellen Starr's Self-Sacrificing Work Among the Lowly" appeared as a headline from *The Chicago Times* on March 23, 1890, one that managed to disparage the founders' seeming benevolence and west siders' poverty at once. Compare for a moment Addams and Starr to the fictional Carrie Meeber of Theodore Dreiser's *Sister Carrie*. Carrie arrived in Chicago in 1889, the same year as Addams and Starr, and first lived with her sister and brother-in-law less than a mile from Hull House on Van Buren Street. Carrie lived there because she had no money and nowhere else to go, and her family expected her to find work in a shoe factory. As Carrie climbed Chicago's social and economic ladders and succeeded in acting, she obtained the finest clothing, furniture and consumer goods available to her. Through her rags-to-riches journey, Carrie moved to wealthier and whiter neighborhoods, and eventually to New York. Along the way, Carrie strove to own material objects that signaled she shared the wealth and status of her immediate neighbors. Addams and Starr, in the real world, stayed on the west side. They shared Carrie's interest in consuming the finest goods as a way of demonstrating their social position, but by staying in the west side garment district, their cosmopolitan consumption remained a display for a local audience of immigrant and migrant workers on Halsted Street.

The Hull House founders intended their artisan-made objects from around the globe to not only reflect their personal social and economic values, but also to serve as resources for establishing a common labor politics with neighbors. They theorized that their neighbors, upon encountering art and décor, might appreciate it, identify with its national origins, and potentially extend solidarity to the artisans who made it. In expressing these beliefs, they were interpreting and applying Ruskin's theories. Starr cited Ruskin when arguing the role of the settlement should be to help neighbors recognize that art objects communicated an artist's identity and the labor conditions under which the objects were produced ("What the Artist"). Addams shared Starr's interest in promoting arts and crafts as a political response to the alienation of industry. Addams, for example, centered aesthetic theory when explaining the nursery at Hull House, stating that it is "like others in most respects, differing chiefly, perhaps, in the attention paid to the matter of pictures and casts. The Madonnas of Raphael, in the best and largest photographs, are hung low, that the children may see them, as well as casts from Donatello and Della Robbia" ("Appendix" 165). Hull House, a place where even toddlers could appreciate art and develop distaste for mass-produced goods, was by the early twentieth century headquarters of the Chicago Arts and Crafts Society and home to a manual training school and labor museum that showcased handmade and artisan wares.

In a city fixated on industrial progress, Addams and Starr were preoccupied with the past. They were curious about immigrants' work histories that connected to cultures and traditions they brought with them upon immigrating. Expressing interest in cultures of labor the industrial city seemed to erase might have been a potential first step for the founders seeking solidarity with their neighbors, but Addams's and Starr's labor politics were ultimately enmeshed with stereotypical and demeaning beliefs about immigrants. Underlying their project to form bonds of solidarity with locals was the premise that their neighbors were formerly European peasants who, once working in US industry, were in danger of losing their connection to key parts of their identities and cultures. In one of the most overtly condescending episodes in Hull House history, Addams and Allesandro Mastro-Valerio, editor of the newspaper *D'Italia*, promoted an actual colony for Italian immigrants in Daphne, Alabama, where they could start a farming community and replicate the peasant culture they had practiced in Italy ("Weekly Programme"). While thousands of immigrant neighbors across decades participated in Hull House's programs, many did not share an interest in idealizing a preindustrial economy in which they had worked by hand. Of course, they had had varying work histories, and many had previously held middle-class occupations and had experienced downward mobility upon immigrating. For example, many of the Russian-Jewish tailors I discuss later in this chapter had worked as traders, merchants, and professionals prior to immigrating and learning the tailoring trade in the US, becoming part of the working class in the process. These tailors shared more in common class-wise with Hull House residents than residents fully appreciated.

Furthermore, the founders' artisan wares communicated a racially exclusive politics. Addams's and Starr's white racial identity was apparent in their easy ownership of goods in a neighborhood where so many struggled to buy food and clothing or pay rent for tenement apartments. They owned items such as Italian paintings, German books, East Asian rugs, and Greek theater stage props, and their collection skewed toward products from artisans whose whiteness was not stable in the US in this era. In adorning their space with this select décor, they highlighted the national origins of goods as a proxy for racial difference, further denying whiteness to the immigrant artisans who might identify with items in their space. The founders also excluded by race through absence in their décor. Hull House décor did not reflect the interests of Black neighbors, whose community grew in numbers on the west side over time as many Black Americans left the local economic and cultural systems of the South and hoped to find better conditions in Chicago. If the founders' cosmopolitanism was meant to demonstrate their knowledge about the transnational movement of people and goods under capitalism, then Hull House's failure to represent its Black neighbors, whose lives had been shaped by slavery and its aftermath, was an extraordinary oversight. More likely, the absence of décor for Black neighbors reflected the founders' acceptance of a racist norm in which white women ignored or excluded the contributions of Black workers in their efforts to improve gendered labor relations.[3]

Overall, then, Hull House as a visual text communicated a complicated message. It signaled there was an alternative to the domestic spaces that effectively limited where, with whom, and on what topics women could speak. The founders offered the alternative of a cosmopolitan space and made the products of artisan labor visible and tangible in Hull House. They presented their wares as objects around which to reflect and reconsider industrial labor relations. In theory, speakers could incorporate their surroundings by making use of stages, instruments, artwork, or books to spark reflection on the multinational networks through which goods were produced and circulated. In so doing, speakers could potentially demonstrate their mutual interests across differences. Such a project shares similarities to contemporary labor-based critical pedagogies in the idea that through

---

3. Elisabeth Lasch-Quinn offers an extended analysis of Jane Addams's beliefs and writings about African American communities in *Black Neighbors: Race and the Limits of Reform in the American Settlement House Movement, 1890-1945*. Lasch-Quinn argues that settlement residents' silence about their Black neighbors reflected settlement leaders' racist beliefs about African American culture in which they located the problems of poverty, housing and work within African American culture, one they thought could not be changed through their efforts (11). At Hull House, this understanding of African American culture differed from residents' celebration and idealization of European immigrants' culture that led them to think of their problems of poverty, housing and work as situational.

dialogue about the world around them, participants might come to better understand their own power in a capitalist, global economy. Yet, the objects in Hull House were not drawn from neighborhood workers' everyday lives, but instead from the founders' imaginings of neighbors' lives prior to immigrating. While few local workers beyond union organizer Kenney left records of their interpretations of Hull House's décor, many used Hull House as a rhetorical space. When they did so, they brought with them their own motivations, histories, and traditions, and participated in crafting the meaning of space in the process. Local garment workers began crafting labor rhetorics there after Kenney, impressed by Hull House's large rooms, invited them to use the space.

Mary Kenney: Persuading Garment Workers to Meet at Hull House

I return now to where I began this chapter—in Hull House's parlors—to explain what happened when Kenney collaborated with Addams to organize workers. I return to this scene to move beyond an exploration of the founders' cosmopolitan labor rhetorics conveyed *through* Hull House and toward a critical imagining of the labor rhetorics happening *inside* Hull House. Kenney's persuasive tactics as a union organizer ultimately convinced numerous women and men garment workers to use Hull House, where they forged new ethē, developed trust, negotiated, and (mis)understood each other in the process. Kenney's claim to the settlement for workers in the early 1890s established it as a space where they could unionize even after she left Chicago for Boston in 1894.

Kenney first learned about organizing in her hometown of Hannibal, Missouri, by witnessing a famous 1887 railroad strike unfold. In her autobiography, she described how she watched men working on the Burlington and Quincy Railroad walk off the job for fair wages as part of one of the first national strikes in the United States. Later, upon moving to Chicago, Kenney began organizing women in her printing trade after finding they worked eleven-hour days and were reprimanded for taking time to drink water. Finding space to organize women remained her persistent problem. The saloon, the preferred organizing site for craft unions, was not simply a place of vice that excluded women; it was also the space that women activists in the city were united against. Women reformers in Chicago, led by Frances Willard and the Women's Christian Temperance Union, had largely built public and political ethos by attempting to abolish the saloon. The WCTU's primary aim was to aid women and children who suffered when great numbers of men abused alcohol and committed domestic violence. While the WCTU also advanced women's labor and suffrage causes, it did so while dedicated to arguing alcohol consumption was opposed to religious and traditional family values. Thus, women's moral ground when engaging in political speech in Chicago was built in opposition to the saloon, not from working within it.

Upon gaining access to Hull House, Kenney turned her attention to garment workers, the largest trade group in the neighborhood, whose needs were pressing. Garment workers' wages and hours were declining rapidly in the early 1890s because of recent technological improvements made to electric-powered machinery in the clothing industry. Employers slashed workers' hours and replaced skilled men tailors with inexperienced women workers who could operate electric-powered sewing machines. Unionized men had largely resisted the entrance of women into their industry up to this point because they thought of them as scabs willing to embrace mass production and work for lower wages. Women, meanwhile, often accepted these lower wages to survive. Kenney's initial foray into organizing garment workers across gender lines at Hull House began with cloakmakers, a subset of garment workers who experienced a particularly rapid upheaval in their trade as advances in mass production intersected with demand for a newly fashionable "short coat that hung about sixteen inches below the waist" (Kenney O'Sullivan 102). According to Coat Maker's Union founder and president Abraham Bisno, the demand for this black woolen coat disrupted only the cloak-making industry in Chicago. In New York, Bisno recalled, customers still favored the pricier, hand-sewed cloaks made by skilled tailors (95). Because the Chicago cloaks were mass produced, women garment workers with little to no sewing experience quickly gained entrance to the factory. This rapid shift in the gendered makeup of Chicago cloakmakers spurred men and women in the trade to realize they had a mutual interest in organizing.

Cloakmakers, however, did not easily trust each other, and their differences exceeded the categories of gender and skill level. Writing about the cloakmakers, Addams remarked that the men and women were "separated . . . by every possible social distinction" (142). The men tailors shared a Russian-Jewish identity and the Yiddish language. From their perspective, young women of mostly Irish descent had advantages in the industrializing trade. According to Bisno, they held the common belief that women did not need the same wages as men because women did not support families. Furthermore, women, they thought, were better able to negotiate with local factory owners because they shared American attitudes and the English language (81). Kenney needed to appeal to garment workers not only across differences of gender but also of skill-level, race, ethnicity, culture, and language. Working in an early version of fast fashion, the garment workers were all too aware of the cosmopolitan character of their industry and the divisions it created among workers. Yet, they had not yet established norms around the rhetorical spaces, practices, and modes that could aid in bridging their differences.

Figure 1.1 An advertisement for "Stylish Cloaks" that appeared in *The Ladies' Home Journal* in 1893.

Kenney found women cloakmakers hesitant to organize at Hull House and pointed to gender ideology as the biggest obstacle. Many women, Kenney noted, thought of themselves as only temporarily part of the labor force until marriage. Joining Kenney in this observation were other labor leaders, including the anarchist lecturer and writer Emma Goldman, who in 1914 noted women workers asking, "Why should I join a union? I am going to get married, to have a home" (229). Women were reluctant to unionize because doing so would imply a more permanent shift in understanding their identities beyond family roles and an abandonment of an idealized version of womanhood embedded within domestic discourse.

Kenney's observation about women's reluctance to unionize echoed Addams's argument that society offered women few roles beyond those defined by the "family claim" ("College" 4). That domestic discourse constrained possibilities for women's labor was a point over which Kenney and Addams forged consensus. To persuade women to meet at Hull House, Kenney reimagined the ethos of a union member. Like Addams, who had argued that women needed access to expanded roles still aligned with family ones in creating an exigence for Hull House, Kenney framed unionizing as offering an expansive version of traditionally domestic roles. By holding the meeting at Hull House, Kenney signaled to women that participating in a union meeting could align with working women's aspirational claims to ideal womanhood, as they would be invited into a middle-class home and be among the Hull House residents who already claimed the middle-class identity elusive to working women. Kenney invited both women and men cloakmakers to a "musical entertainment with addresses" ("Musical"). Kenney, speaking at the World's Columbian Exposition in 1893, explained that holding an "entertainment with addresses" appealed especially to women precisely because it promised an alternative to the kinds of rhetorical speech associated with unions (871). "If there is any 'speeching' going on here tonight, I skip," Kenney recalled hearing a woman say upon attending a musical entertainment she had planned in New York (Kenney O'Sullivan 84). As if in response to this attitude, Kenney's invitation went further in offering women workers an opportunity to understand the traditional, feminine ethos as compatible with the role of organized worker. Kenney wrote that the aims of the union were to make each employee "feel that she is surrounded by an association of friends—helping each other and self helping—whose common object is the welfare of all, which cannot fail to elevate her moral character as an individual" ("Musical"). Kenney emphasized that claiming an ethos or "moral character" in a union was a parallel process to claiming one in a family; it was built through relationships with and concern for others.

Settlement: Claiming Cosmopolitan Space 43

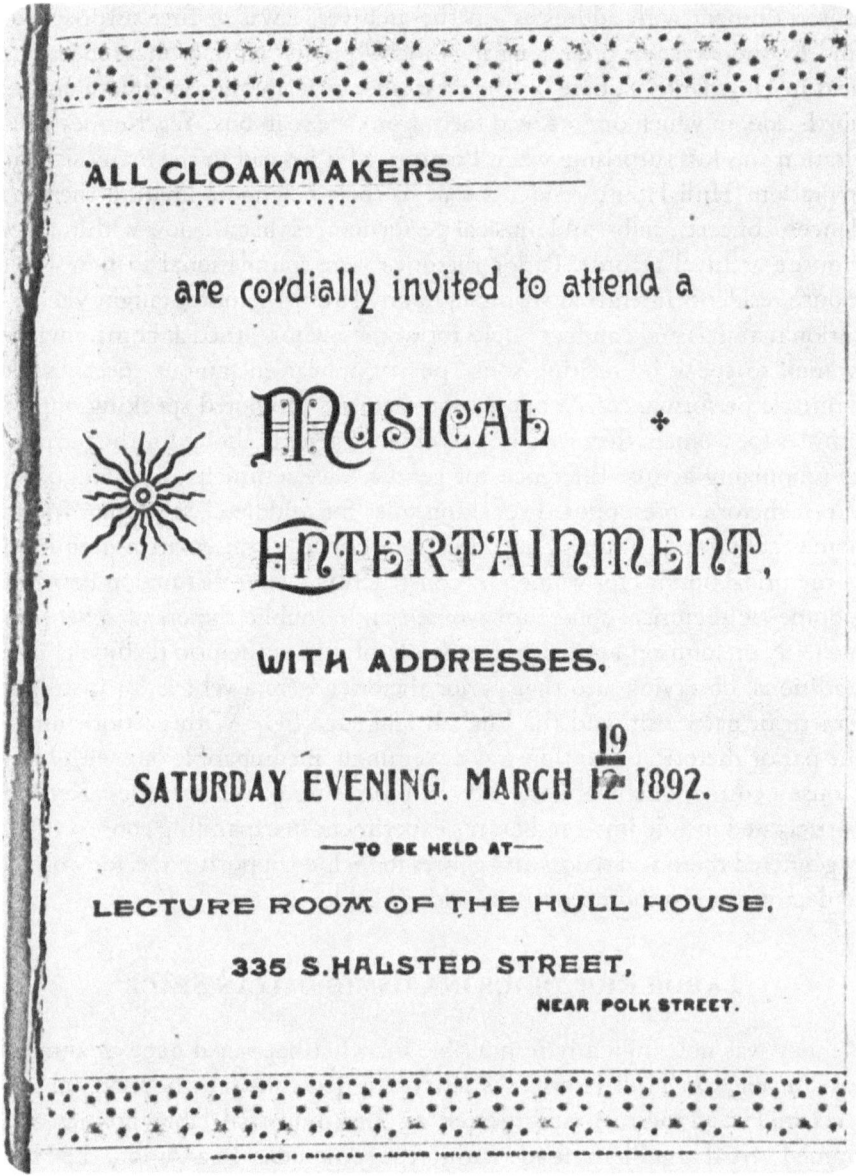

Figure 1.2 Invitation to Cloakmakers to an Entertainment with Addresses in 1892. Richard J. Daley Library, University of Illinois at Chicago.

Kenney's promise of a "musical entertainment with addresses" did more than de-emphasize the possibility of conventional labor rhetorics via speech. Kenney's description of the meeting invoked parlor rhetoric traditions. I want to pause here to offer context about finding Kenney's invitation to an "entertainment with addresses" in the archives. I was at first surprised to find Kenney was not promising the kind of public, outdoor mass meetings held in Haymarket Square on the west side, or in Bughouse Square on the north side, in which orators held forth from the soap box. Yet, Kenney's invitation was less surprising when I compared it instead to the many similar invitations Hull House residents sent to their neighbors inviting them to dances, concerts, clubs, and musical performances that are now within Hull House's archival records. Parlor rhetorics were foundational to how Hull House residents interacted with neighbors. Parlor rhetorics, taught via elocution manuals and conduct books for women who learned at home, invited women to speak by reciting song, poetry, rehearsed famous speeches, or dramatic performances. While parlor rhetorics promoted speaking opportunities for women, they were not an obvious generic choice for the purpose of unionizing across differences of gender, race, ethnicity, and language. Parlor rhetorics presupposed speaking roles for middle-class women whose homes contained parlors. They also "reinscribed a conservative definition of rhetorical options for women by constructing a clear distinction between a domestic rhetorical sphere for women and a public rhetorical sphere for men," Nan Johnson argued in her study of parlor rhetoric textbooks and traditions, observing also that parlor rhetorics were a vehicle for instilling American patriotism and the English language (33). With patriotic aims, the parlor rhetorical tradition was a seemingly incompatible one with Hull House's cosmopolitan project. Yet, in promising parlor rhetorics, Kenney participated in Addams's and Starr's experiment in expanding conservatively gendered rhetorical spaces and genres to include opportunities for women to demonstrate authority over the wider world.

Labor Rhetorics in Cosmopolitan Space

Kenney was not singularly responsible for what happened once cloakmakers convened in Hull House. As I have argued thus far, the material objects in Hull House communicated an anti-industrial labor politics and framed verbal arguments made within the settlement. In addition, the Hull House residents participated fully in organizing workers, their presence complicating the possibility of workers enlisting an easy kind of gender-integrated solidarity over a shared trade. It was the Hull House residents who provided the parlor entertainment at the meetings of garment workers. As at other events in Hull House, residents' parlor rhetorics were more pointed and diverse in content, language, and national origin than those offered in most popular elocution manuals of the time.[4] At one of the first meetings for cloakmakers, two residents—Agnes Sinclair Holbrook, who played piano, and Helen Goodrich, who sang—chose musical selections from composers Rubinstein, Mendelssohn, Schubert, and Paderewski, and demonstrated their familiarity with Russian-Jewish and Eastern European music to their audience of Russian-Jewish men ("Cloakmakers"). Through these selections, Holbrook and Goodrich signaled to their guests that all present shared an appreciation of men cloakmakers' national, cultural, and linguistic traditions. Beginning with a musical performance, however, departed from how men cloakmakers' meetings had previously unfolded. In Chicago in the 1890s, meeting conventions for local craft unions were idiosyncratic until those unions began engaging with larger, more established organizations, such as the American Federation of Labor. Before engaging with the AFL, craft union members invented their own rules through a trial-and-error process. According to historian Wilfred Carsel, cloakmakers' first attempts at meeting in the 1880s had resulted in shouting. By 1888, speakers were awarded "precedence and respect" in union debates "on the basis of their speed as operators," or how quickly they made garments (22). Parlor rhetorics, then, redistributed speaking roles and allowed Hull House women residents to speak first at the union meeting.

Kenney's invitation locates at least one meeting for cloakmakers in a place familiar to men: Hull House's Lecture Room. Neighborhood men were familiar with the Lecture Room in Hull House's newly built Butler Studio Building, a space that doubled as a reading room and public library branch. The Lecture Room held bookcases, tables and chairs "specially designed for the room" and catered to a cosmopolitan readership ("In the Butler" 38). Residents furnished it with periodicals "from different sections of the globe" and "printed in as many different languages, so that every visitor, no matter what may be his nationality, may be supplied with interesting reading matter" ("A Local" 4). A photograph of the Lecture Room featured

---

4. The contents of popular nineteenth-century elocution manuals such as *The Handy Speaker, The Speaker's Garland and Literary Bouquet,* and *The American Star Speaker* support Johnson's thesis that parlor rhetorics were a vehicle for instilling American patriotism and the English language. The speeches anthologized in these manuals focus on American and English history, with virtually no speeches in languages other than English. Parlor rhetorics at Hull House, by contrast, drew from diverse texts. An invitation to an 1892 reception for German neighbors, for example, promised "music and the reading of German literature, or history," noting that "a small German library is at the disposal of the guests" ("Reception" 8). Similarly, at the cloakmakers' meetings, residents introduced musical selections from Russian, German, and Polish composers to appeal to the Russian-Jewish cloakmakers.

in resident Florence Kelley's *New England Magazine* article revealed a space with a speaker's platform and a piano used for musical performances, surrounded by paintings, pottery, statuary, and candlesticks. In the Butler Building, where during previous visits they were offered the role of readers, Russian-Jewish men garment workers were offered the role of listeners to a series of songs by Russian, German, and Polish composers, and were not invited to bring their own music or organizing practices to the meeting. While the performances allowed the Hull House residents to demonstrate knowledge of diverse, international musical traditions, they encouraged the men cloakmakers to identify with their geographic locations prior to immigrating rather than with their current location in Chicago.

It is not surprising, then, that Addams observed that residents' first attempts to establish a cosmopolitan ethos were not appreciated by men cloakmakers. Addams gave a detailed account of the first cloakmakers' meetings in an essay titled "The Settlement as a Factor in the Labor Movement" and wrote that the men thought "Hull-House was a spy in the service of the capitalists" (141). The residents' attempts to display cosmopolitan knowledge were shallow, ignoring the specificity of any particular linguistic or classed identity that the Russian-Jewish men workers were developing as a group living in the US and working in the garment trade. Furthermore, residents did not demonstrate knowledge of prior conventions of cloakmakers' meetings, nor did they attempt to learn about the Russian-Jewish garment workers and their histories by asking questions. The residents did little to inspire the men cloakmakers to trust them.

Figure 1.3. An image of the lecture room in Hull House from Florence Kelley's 1898 article "Hull-House" in *New England Magazine*.

Women cloakmakers, meanwhile, appreciated Hull House residents' authority, though not based on their cosmopolitan knowledge. According to Addams, the women cloakmakers trusted residents because they felt "chaperoned," a feeling that speaks to the age difference between college-educated residents and young women garment workers (141). Women cloakmakers' understanding of residents as chaperones also reflected their history of attempting to meet with men in the saloon and having those experiences deemed socially unacceptable by their families. While Hull House residents took up formal speaking roles via performance, the women cloakmakers were not offered similar speaking roles through which to establish connections or demonstrate authority, though according to Addams they "talked volubly, at least amongst themselves" (142). While women cloakmakers were enticed to the meeting in part because it promised the chance to inhabit the spaces of middle-class respectability, the conventions of the meeting reasserted class distinctions and a hierarchy of rhetorical authority between women residents and women workers.

To their credit, residents found in parlor rhetorics a way to communicate with workers through music during an event in which language barriers largely prohibited spontaneous conversation between groups. Residents and women workers spoke English, while men workers spoke Russian or Yiddish. Addams recounted that a cloak maker attempted to lead a conversation about unionizing by standing between the men and women workers occupying different sides of the room. She called this person an "interpreter," and evaluated him as "somewhat helpless." Addams wrote, "he was clear upon the economic necessity for combination; he realized the mutual interdependence; but he was baffled by the social aspect of the situation" (142). This interpreter, in theory, was an individual who might benefit from occupying a space designed to honor and value differences of nationality, class, gender, language, and ethnicity. Yet, the interpreter, who knew multiple languages and physically stood between groups, failed to translate. The interpreter's failure was partly a failure of the rhetorical space of Hull House to provide him with resources and precedents to construct a trustworthy ethos among all parties.

In a meeting in which speeches were unwelcome and spontaneous conversation was curtailed by parlor rhetoric genres, Hull House residents used the cloakmakers' dress as a proxy for their character. Addams noted that the "American-Irish girls were well-dressed, and comparatively at ease" and concluded that "there was much less difference of any sort between the residents and the working-girls than between the men and girls of the same trade" (141–42). Men cloakmakers, meanwhile, failed to establish a trustworthy ethos with Hull House residents because of their appearance. Addams described them as "ill-dressed and grimy" and "shamefaced and constrained" (141). As Carol Mattingly has argued, dress was and is an important extra discursive means of communication, and nineteenth-century women rhetors were especially attentive to using dress to negotiate expectations about their feminine gender presentation. At Hull House, women workers' dress also demonstrated an ease with presumably consuming clothing and wearing it rather than producing it, contributing to a reversal of how the unionized men cloakmakers' previously established authority during union meetings.

In Addams's detailed account of the first cloakmakers' meeting, Kenney is entirely absent. Kenney's absence from Addams's account is surprising because Kenney gives an overview of her involvement organizing cloakmakers in her own autobiography. While Kenney does not write about specific meetings as Addams does, Kenney nevertheless states that she "was chairman of these meetings" (67). Even if Kenney was not at the meeting Addams recounted, Addams nevertheless excluded Kenney's contributions to setting up the cloakmakers' meeting. Addams excises Kenney from her account, perhaps, because her alliance with Kenney poses a challenge to the tidy lessons about solidarity Addams takes away from these first meetings. Upon reflection, Addams considered workers agitating against employers as necessary but shortsighted and hoped in the future there could be a "larger solidarity which includes labor and capital" (144). Addams pointed out that workers were reacting to employers rather than reimagining more just labor practices, while employers were morally corrupt in their pursuit of profits at the expense of workers' wellbeing. Addams credited her ability to develop this understanding to her position in the settlement, where she was able to take the "larger ethical view" she hoped workers and capitalists would come to appreciate over time (147). Though Addams and Kenney shared an interest in improving women workers' labor conditions, they ultimately had different ideas about who should be enlisted in relations of solidarity. Addams ultimately hoped workers and employers would seek solidarity with one another, but Kenney, a bookbinder who shared ethnic and class identities with the Irish women garment workers she was organizing, challenged this interpretation of solidarity by remaining focused on bringing workers together across differences and in opposition to exploitative employers. Addams did not discuss her collaboration with Kenney as its own act of solidarity because Addams did not understand herself as a worker or a capitalist. Addams positioned herself as an observer, watching class struggle unfold.

Hull House as a Space for Solidarity

While the cloakmakers had difficulty speaking with one another, their very act of meeting in a room together demonstrated a moment of ephemeral solidarity in which they acknowledged their mutual subjectivity as laborers, even though their expression of solidarity did not carry forward into gender-integrated unionizing.[5] I reconstruct what happened during an early cloakmakers' meeting at Hull House to demonstrate that establishing a cosmopolitan space did not alone provide the necessary conditions for sustaining relations of solidarity. The space of Hull House, in fact, presented obstacles. When the founders decorated their settlement with artisan wares of international origin, they flattened national differences and the conditions of individual trades to commodities in the facile service of diversity. Despite founders' hopes that neighbors might be able to claim authority as speakers in cosmopolitan Hull House, neighbors did not talk easily across national differences. Garment workers, for example, were not invited to claim knowledge of multiple languages and traditions like the Hull House residents. When Hull House residents demonstrated their familiarity with foreign traditions and languages to appeal to cloakmakers, they flattened cloakmakers' complicated and emerging identities in the US. During cloakmakers' meetings, residents attempted to preserve or promise ideal identities—a traditional version of white womanhood, for example, or a stereotypical version of a Russian peasant—at the same time they attempted to shift the relations of labor underlying those ideals. The Hull House residents did not have their own theoretical version of intersectionality, a term coined by Kimberlé Crenshaw to describe a framework for understanding womanhood as fundamentally shaped not by a single identity category but by the intersection of gender, race, and other identities that are interanimated and changed through experience. Thus, enveloped in decontextualized, dehumanizing cosmopolitan space, Russian-Jewish men cloakmakers did not view the residents as offering solidarity; they interpreted residents as working in the service of capitalists.

In the decades after this early foray into organizing cloakmakers, Hull House grew into an even larger cosmopolitan space. Its growth made it possible for residents and neighbors to continue to meet together and discuss

---

5. While the cloakmakers did not come together to form a gender-integrated union, women workers developed labor organizing at Hull House as a gender-segregated activity. Hull House's archived programs and bulletins in the University of Illinois at Chicago's Special Collections and University Archives list at least eight different women's unions meeting there in the decade following the first cloakmakers' meetings.

labor. Addams had initially funded the settlement with money she inherited from the successful mill her father had owned, but she was soon joined by powerful underwriters in funding Hull House's growth. Historian Kathryn Kish Sklar examined closely Hull House's account and expenditure records and found the settlement was largely funded by three other women: Mary Rozet Smith, Addams's longtime partner; Louise deKoven Bowen, a wealthy Chicago socialite; and Helen Culver, owner of Hull House and the land surrounding it. Because of these underwriters, Hull House was transformed over the next two decades from a cosmopolitan home into an institution with multiple assembly spaces, crucial for collectives to meet and discuss labor. While the name Hull House fittingly describes the original mansion where Addams and Starr founded the settlement, the name can obscure Hull House's rapid expansion beyond a house to take up an entire city block. By 1907, Hull House was a large complex containing several assembly halls including an art gallery, lecture hall, coffeehouse, gymnasium, and auditorium. This growth was only possible because a group of women had access to capital, an unusual circumstance at this time.

Hull House's financing and growth contributed to making labor a continually tense and pressing subject there and led more neighbors to critique the very institution that made it possible to meet in large numbers. In 1911, a former neighbor identifying as M McG wrote to Addams and said, "I was a neighbor of Hull House when it first started up and I got help in many ways especially where I was a member of the Lincoln Club but since it has to be run by capitalists who can afford to give some of the tainted money they have squeezed out of there [sic] brothers Hull House don't stand for any thing [sic] in pertickular [sic] that counts." For McG, Hull House's funding discounted its residents' efforts to support neighbors in improving their labor conditions. Historians exploring the intersections of women and the labor movement, including Diane Balser, Philip S. Foner, and Annelise Orleck, have responded to critiques such as this one by conceding that class tensions were a hallmark of women's organizing in this era, but highlight the power of women's coalition building at a time when unions were discriminatory and women were excluded from voting. Individuals who met at Hull House to come together in solidarity in 1891 complicate the organizing picture even further, as they were not only negotiating gender and class identities, but also ethnic identities, language differences, and work histories.

What I hope to have demonstrated in this chapter is that the available spaces for organizing and genres for expression also have power in shaping how labor rhetorics unfold. Hull House's cosmopolitan message to workers did not invite them to claim authority in the space, even though the products of workers' labor might have been a resource for sparking a collective labor consciousness under different circumstances. Later, in the twentieth century, strategic consumption of goods became a recognized part of working-class labor politics. Historians Nan Enstad, Dana Frank, and Lizabeth Cohen have all documented the ways that working women in in the twentieth century incorporated consumption into their labor politics, for example, by imploring consumers to buy garments tagged with the union label. Indeed, more precisely than the artisan-made furniture, candlesticks, prints, and books, it was the cloaks the garment workers were making that might have best represented the cosmopolitan character of the industrial economy. The cloaks were manufactured only because Midwestern women who desired European styles wanted coats made quickly and cheaply in Chicago, and were unwilling or unable to pay for one-of-a-kind items like New Yorkers. It was consumers' demand for these cloaks that brought together Russian-Jewish tailors in competition with Irish-American women new to the sewing trades in a cutthroat market increasingly dominated by the machine. Analysis of the cloak might have offered the "larger ethical view" Addams was seeking as the basis for solidarity (147). Such a view would have challenged the garment workers who met at Hull House to acknowledge their interdependence more fully and to be more inclusive in their organizing. Within the production process, the men and women seeking to unionize at Hull House were relatively privileged in the manufacturing chain of production. They worked in factories with machines. Had they inquired into the production process of the cloak, they would have inevitably noticed that after the cloaks left the factory, they traveled to the tenements where sweatshop workers—mostly immigrant women—sewed on buttons and pressed seams before the cloaks were sold to consumers. These tenement-based women workers were excluded entirely from talks at Hull House, despite working on the same cloaks as the factory workers.

In the next chapter, I leave the settlement and trace the network of women's labor rhetorics to where the cloaks were made in the tenement. In the 1890s, when Hull House residents focused their labor reform efforts beyond Hull House and on the tenements, tensions elevated among residents and garment workers regarding who had the power to reimagine the spaces of home and work, and what labor meant in those spaces.

2 Tenement: Publishing Visual Rhetorics

> I wanted to see you in your own homes.
>
> —Frederick Engels
> *The Condition of the Working Class in England in 1844*

The tenement is a space of both home and work, shared by family, friends, coworkers and strangers. The word "tenement," originating in English law, was first used to designate the scenario in which a lord owns land and divides and leases it to multiple tenants. This definition of leased and divided property tracked into nineteenth-century cities where "tenement" referred to a house built originally for one property owner and his family that was divided into multiple units and then rented to two or more families.[1] Hull House was surrounded by tenements, many of which were built with wood as temporary housing after the 1871 Chicago Fire and then moved outside the city center to discourage subsequent fires (Philpott 12–13). For Chicago reformers, the geography of the little wooden tenement perhaps better signified a problem in need of a solution than New York's multi-story brick tenements. Chicago's were obviously intended for a single family, hastily built, temporary, and combustible. Industrial manufacturers further upended domestic norms in the tenement by encouraging garment workers, many of whom were recently immigrated women and girls, to use their tenements as workplaces. In so doing, manufacturers saved money on rent and required less factory space. Without government oversight on the uses of space, safety standards, or work protocols, the tenement kitchen table became a sewing station.

A tenement scene of garment making could look much like the one Hilda Satt Polachek described in her memoir *I Came a Stranger: The Story*

---

1. The *Oxford English Dictionary* traces some of the oldest uses of the word "tenement" to designate owned land that was then leased and divided ("tenement, n."). In the United States and by the nineteenth century, the word "tenement" referred to a leased and divided house. In the early 1900s, the Chicago Building and Health Ordinance Code reaffirmed a tenement's divided and leased status by defining it as "any house or building or portion used as a home or residence for two or more families living in separate apartments" (Civic Federation of Chicago).

of a Hull-House Girl. Polachek recounted how her fourteen-year-old sister Rose, after working in a factory during the day, brought home bundles of half-finished gloves and mittens to sew on the fingertips. "As soon as the evening meal had been eaten and the dishes cleared away, Mother and my sister would take their places at the table and sew mittens until late into the night," Polachek remembered (46). In outsourcing work to tenements, manufacturers exploited workers' space and time. Polachek's sister Rose worked well over forty hours per week by bringing work home. Manufacturers also infringed on tenement dwellers' domestic labor of caring and cooking. Polachek's mother's labor doubled when after completing her daily domestic tasks, she sat down to sew mittens. Across industrializing US cities, manufacturers were benefiting tremendously when women like the Polacheks toiled from the tenement.

Figure 2.1 Tenement houses on Liberty Street from the article "Chicago Housing Conditions, IV: The West Side Revisited" by Sophonisba P. Breckrinridge and Edith Abbott.

At the same time immigrants and migrants arrived in cities in great numbers and sought the affordable housing of tenements, reformers, journalists, photographers and legislators sought new modes and media to best represent the labor problems posed by the tenement. In Chicago, Hull House was the hub of this rhetorical project, and resident and reformer Florence Kelley led the effort to alert the public to manufacturers' uses of the tenement and abuses of women's and children's labor. Kelley recognized the need for housing as a feminist issue; it was not easy for women and children to secure a place to live without depending on men. To do so, women needed to earn money in an economy in which women had a gender pay gap and fewer opportunities to work. Kelley personally experienced the difficulty of securing housing after leaving an abusive relationship. The daughter of a US congressman known for supporting protections for workers, Kelley had moved to Chicago in 1891 immediately after divorcing, bringing her three children with her. Despite an affluent upbringing, Kelley needed to earn money to support herself and her children, so she secured two government positions, one as a slum investigator with the US Department of Labor, and another as the Illinois state factory inspector. She worked in these positions while she lived at Hull House, while her three children lived with journalist and Hull House supporter Henry Demarest Lloyd and his wife Jesse Bross Lloyd in Winnetka an hour-long train ride away. Her residence at Hull House, along with her government-sponsored positions, provided Kelley with opportunities to publish widely on her findings as a labor investigator.

Through using labor rhetorics, Kelley continued her father's protectionist politics and sought to keep women safe from the exploitative effects of industry. She especially advocated for limiting women's work hours and keeping the tenement's domestic uses separate from its workplace uses. This chapter focuses on an ambitious mapping project that Kelley led among Hull House residents that ultimately reflected her Progressive and protectionist approach to labor reform. Kelley, along with resident Agnes Sinclair Holbrook, created maps depicting the weekly wages and nationalities of families in their neighborhood and later collaborated with other residents to write essays about tenement labor conditions to accompany the maps. Kelley ultimately published the maps with essays as *Hull-House Maps and Papers* by the residents of Hull House, an overlooked yet remarkable labor treatise containing both visual and verbal labor rhetorics focused on the west side tenement district. In this chapter, I analyze *Hull-House Maps and Papers* as representative of Kelley's use of visual labor rhetorics to reach beyond local audiences and include viewers with an interest in claiming knowledge of cosmopolitan space.

The maps in *Hull-House Maps and Papers* make public the locations, wages, and nationalities of tenement dwellers. By creating knowledge about where tenement labor was happening and who was laboring, Kelley ostensibly helped protect the public from purchasing potentially inferior products made under conditions of duress. Through publishing, though, Kelley also stereotyped and excluded the very neighbors she was seeking to aid. In the first chapter, I argued that founders Addams and Starr curated Hull House with cosmopolitan and artisan-made wares to create the settlement as a space for in-person and spoken labor rhetorics primarily for neighbors. Kelley did not share the founders' interest in engaging in spoken labor rhetorics to communicate with neighbors. She was especially uninterested in working on labor reform with neighbors who dwelled in tenements, calling them "incapable" of organizing precisely because their location in the tenements kept them isolated (65).[2] Kelley's labor rhetorics elided local tenement-based workers and anticipated contemporary anti-sweatshop campaigns that enlist into labor reform a "purchasing public" with an interest in consuming ethically, thereby influencing industries to produce fair trade goods (65). In addition, the visual labor rhetorics in *Hull-House Maps and Papers* comfort readers by offering racist and xenophobic arguments that white, wealthy, US born people were spatially and categorically different from those who occupied tenement homes, and the threats posed by the tenement, including the inevitable mixing of home and work, and of family and foreigners, were spatially distant and contained.

Visual Labor Rhetorics in the Progressive Era

Kelley's use of the visual mode, along with her efforts to bring about women's labor reform without considering the very women who would be most impacted by these reforms, are part of a Progressive approach to labor rhetorics that has been largely overlooked in rhetorical studies. Communications scholar Cara A. Finnegan, writing about Progressive-era child labor rhetoric, has argued this rhetoric has been overlooked in part because it was delivered in the visual mode rather than in the oratorical one (250). When rhetorical studies focuses on oratory in the Progressive era, it also overlooks women rhetors who were leaders in developing visual rhetorics about women's and children's labor. As I have argued so far, women rhetors were excluded from the city's union halls, saloons, and soapboxes where traditions of labor speech were developing. Even if granted access to those spaces, the subject of women's and children's labor was a historically private topic relegated to the domestic sphere rather than the public one. The visual mode offered an

---

2. My citations of *Hull-House Maps and Papers* are from the 2007 edition published by the University of Illinois Press, though in this chapter I discuss my experience using a first edition of the book owned by the Newberry Library, which is cited separately. The Hull-House Maps are available to view in the New York Public Library Digital Collections via permalink to the digitized Nationalities Map: https://digitalcollections.nypl.org/items/b31f7720-e5d5-0132-f9f9-58d385a7b928, and permalink to the digitized Wages Map: https://digitalcollections.nypl.org/items/bd684a40-e5d5-0132-c38f-58d385a7b928.

alternative to using speech and afforded possibilities for bringing to light the historically private problems of women's and children's labor. As publishing became more widely accessible to both rhetors and readers throughout the nineteenth century, women turned to publishing visual rhetorics to deliver messages about labor exploitation. Publishing overcame the requirement that rhetors and audiences share time and space. In contrast to oratory, published visual rhetorics could circulate across time and space, and bring national, even global attention to women's and children's labor exploitation.

Among Progressives working in labor reform, Kelley was an especially savvy rhetor who published visuals to illustrate the problems of the tenement. Kelley and her collaborator Holbrook first found a model for publishing visual labor rhetorics in Charles Booth's 1889 poverty maps in *The Life and Labour of the People in London*, which had been researched and created by residents of the English settlement Toynbee Hall. In addition, Kelley found inspiration closer to home. Her use of visual rhetorics occurred at a moment in Chicago when there was heightened demand for maps that helped visitors understand the city. Because of the upcoming World's Columbian Exposition, Kelley and the Hull House residents joined the rest of Chicago's citizens in 1892 in grappling with intense interest in their city from a national, even global, audience. Hull House residents joined photographers, mapmakers, and artists in this moment in experimenting with ways to represent social problems as place based.

A nationalities map might seem a less obvious document of visual labor rhetoric than a wages map, but the tenement was a site of Progressive labor reform precisely because it was cast as a foreign space. *Hull-House Maps and Papers'* most well-known precursor was Jacob Riis's 1890 book *How the Other Half Lives: Studies Amongst the Tenements in New York*, which featured images of immigrant men and women using tenements as both homes and garment sweatshops, stoking widespread fear that the immigrants laboring there were now competing with US-born, white men who worked outside the home. The Nationalities Map, together with the Wages Map, made visible Chicago's west side as relevant to the national conversation about recent immigrants remaking labor, culture, and housing American cities. Like Riis's photographs of where the "other half" lived in New York City, the Nationalities Map bounded the foreign, immigrant and working-class space of the west side from the rest of the city.

While the maps are the titular and most spectacular visuals in *Hull-House Maps and Papers*, the book also includes graphs and photographs that visualize relationships between labor and the spaces of factory and settlement. To create *Hull-House Maps and Papers*, Kelley intermixed a traditional method of making visuals in paint with newer methods like photography to represent labor. In so doing, Kelley participated in creating Hull House as a crossroads for visual culture where anti-industrial sentiments intersected with Progressive interest in technology's potential for creating and circulating new kinds of images.

Hull-House Maps and Papers: From Painting to Print

Given the Hull House founders' elevation of arts and crafts as an antidote to the problems caused by industrialization, it may not surprise that the Hull-House Maps were first created as paintings before they were reproduced in print. When Holbrook first painted the original set of two vibrant, full-color neighborhood maps, she asserted the tenement as the focal space for the labor reform conversations that would follow in the book. One map revealed the distribution of weekly wages, and the other revealed the nationalities of families living in each tenement. Each map depicted the same portion of the west side, starting east of Hull House on Halsted Street and stopping before the commercial downtown of Chicago. The major thoroughfares Twelfth Street on the south and Congress Parkway on the north framed the area depicted in the maps. Whereas Booth's poverty maps of London were scaled to reveal the distribution of wealth throughout the whole city, the Hull-House Maps were scaled smaller and based on the mapmaking firm Greeley and Carlsen's fire insurance maps to reveal buildings and lots that could be owned and insured within a third of a square mile.

Their scale, together with the bird's eye view of the neighborhood, revealed the scope of the neighborhood's tenements, which was not apparent from the perspective of a walker on the street. Most tenements were not visible from the street because they were located on alleys behind houses and other buildings. Holbrook argued that from the street, visitors would see the "better tenements of more pretentious aspect," but that "the smart frontage is a mere screen, not only for the individual houses, but for the street as a whole. Rear tenements and alleys form the core of the district" (54). The color codes designating wages and nationalities asserted the primacy of the tenements for viewers who could not see them with their own eyes, while simultaneously downplaying the street and commercial spaces of the neighborhood that remained uncoded. Together, the two maps offered the tenement as the space in which to understand the intersections of domesticity, wage earning, and national difference in the city.

Throughout the process of making the maps and papers, ideological tensions emerged at Hull House surrounding painting and print. As paintings, the maps aligned with the Hull House founders' intent to communicate with local neighbors. Through painting, Holbrook delivered images viewable among those sharing space at Hull House, and the medium of paint communicated an embrace of artisan labor and opposition to the industrial labor workers were undertaking to earn the wages reflected in the Wages Map. The scale and content of the maps very well could have offered locals new perspective on their labor, too. Despite Kelley's grim belief that tenement-based workers could not organize themselves, it is easy to imagine that her maps might have offered locals a broader perspective on their economic standing in relation to other neighbors. The Wages Map, for example, revealed patterns in wage distribution across the tenements. Together with the Nationalities Map, the Wages Map revealed that Italian families consistently earned the lowest wages ($5 or less) of all eighteen nationality groups and suggested manufacturers were systematically taking advantage of Italian workers and suppressing their wages in relation to other workers. If, as Kelley asserted, workers' isolation in tenements kept them from organizing, then they might have looked across the wages and nationalities maps and understood manufacturers were dispersing their wages unevenly across immigrant groups as a first step toward negotiating for better pay and conditions.

Printing the maps in a book would require residents to surrender to the very industrial processes the Hull House founders had previously sought to boycott. Starr expressed trepidation about print ironically by contributing an essay to *Hull-House Maps and Papers*. In "Art and Labor," Starr argued that print could not express an individual's thoughts or artistic vision like painting; the machine had its own message. Starr wrote that "the product of a machine may be useful, and may serve some purposes of information, but can never be artistic. As soon as a machine intervenes between the mind and its product, a hard, impassable barrier—a non-conductor of thought and emotion—is raised between the speaking and the listening mind" (132). In articulating these beliefs about art and labor, Starr was echoing a more widely held, interconnected set of fears that as new machine technologies rendered the skilled work of printers obsolete, the page would begin to reflect a message divorced from human ideas and values.[3]

---

3. In "Unruly Servants: Machines, Modernity, and the Printed Page," book historian Megan Benton explores the topic of nineteenth century print technologies and notions of modernity, arguing fears surrounding print and labor were widely held and appeared in metaphorical debates over whether print was a servant to printers, or was itself the master.

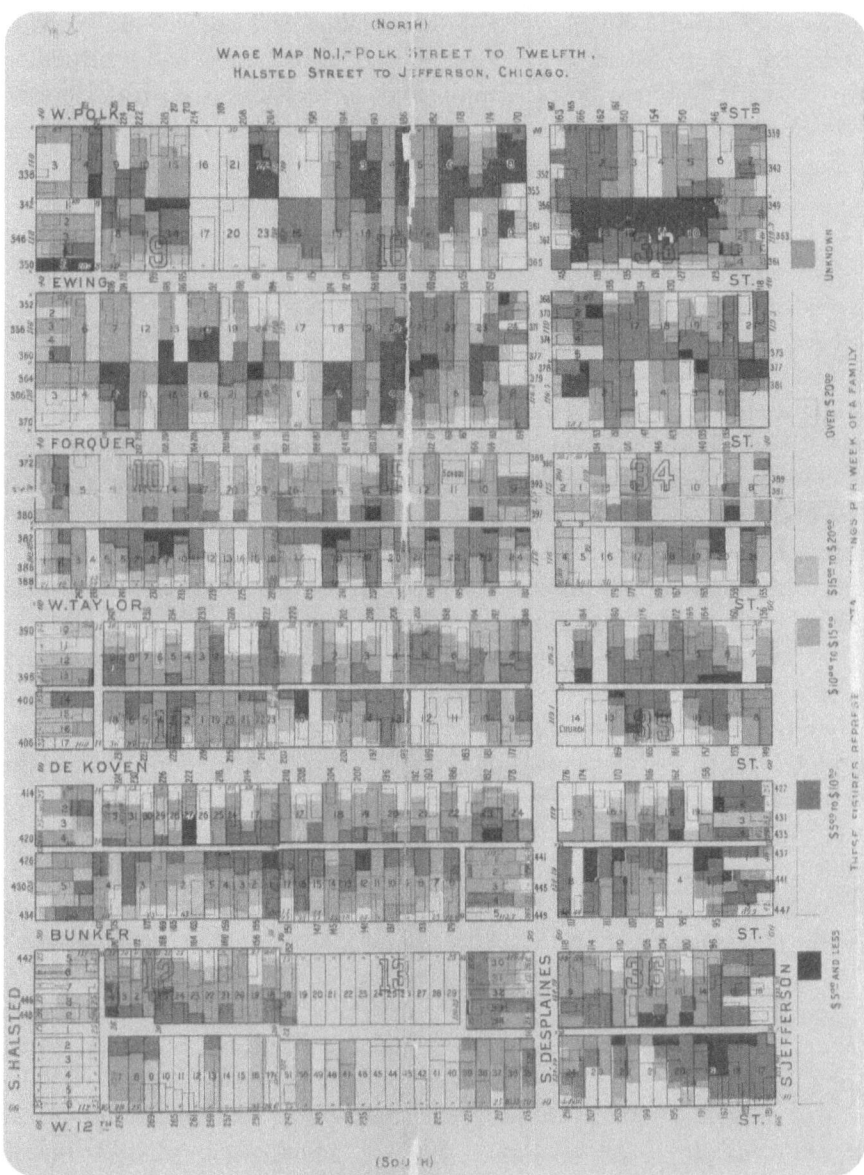

Figure 2.2 A section of the Wages Map from *Hull-House Maps and Papers*.

Kelley's choices when creating the printed maps as part of a book reflected both the politics of art and mass production at Hull House and her own prior experiences with publishing. She had been warned not to give labor theories to workers by her reluctant mentor—German economist, journalist, and textile industry heir Frederick Engels. After earning a bachelor's degree from Cornell University, Kelley had studied law, workers' movements, and European socialism at the University of Zurich, and had returned to the US in 1887 intent on bringing European texts that theorized labor to American workers, whom she had described in a letter to Engels as "in a state of confusion" about their purpose and goals for organizing (31). Kelley convinced Engels to allow her to translate his book *The Condition of the Working Class in England in 1844* into English, though Engels warned Kelley his labor writing was a description of an evolving process rather than a theory that could guide American labor organizing (166).[4] Once at Hull House, Kelley heeded Engels's literal warning not to give labor theory to workers and pivoted to appealing to consumers, a process that she began while at Hull House and culminated once she left Chicago in 1899 and assumed the presidency of the New York-based National Consumers' League.

In August of 1893, Hull House residents joined Kelley in the decision to publish the maps. "Map – Publication – What is to go with the maps," a resident wrote in scribbled, loopy cursive in the Hull House residents' meeting minutes. The minute taker did not explain what had motivated Hull House residents to embrace publication, but the collective decision to publish the maps coincided with a moment when several residents had reached the upper limits of what was possible for circulating their remarks through speech. The World's Fair had given prominent women—including several Hull House residents—access to a new speaker's platform, and residents had occupied some of the biggest stages. Addams and resident Charles Zeublin led the Settlement Congress, a national meeting of settlement and charities workers, during which Starr and resident Julia Lathrop were featured speakers. This Congress had featured a one-day symposium on "The Settlement in its Relation to the Labor Movement" at which Kelley, Mary Kenney, and Addams spoke about labor issues ("Seeking the Truth"). In addition, Addams, Kenney and Zeman spoke about women and domestic labor at the World's Congress of Representative Women. There, they joined some of the most prominent women speakers of the era, such as Hallie Quinn Brown, Susan B Anthony, Elizabeth Cady Stanton, Frances Ellen Watkins Harper, and Lucy Stone. What ultimately went "with the maps" were written versions of speeches Addams, Kelley, Lathrop, Starr, Zeman and Zeublin delivered at the World's Fair.

Kelley made editorial choices for the published version of *Hull-House Maps and Papers* that found a middle ground for the book somewhere be-

---

4. In an 1886 letter to Kelley, Engels wrote, "our theory is not a dogma but the exposition of a process of evolution, and that process involves successive phases. To expect that the Americans will start with the full consciousness of the theory worked out in older industrial countries is to expect the impossible" (166).

tween art object and the hastiest of machine reproductions. In correspondence with the book's editor, economist Richard T. Ely, Kelley insisted Ely publish the maps as "two linen-backed maps or charts, folding in pockets in the cover of the book, similar to Mr. Booth's charts" when he contemplated publishing *Hull-House Maps and Papers* without them because they were so expensive (78). By working with Ely, Kelley placed *Hull-House Maps and Papers* with reference and textbook publisher Thomas Y. Crowell and Co. in a series dedicated to academic texts on economics and politics. In the front matter of the first edition of the book is a list of all the books in Ely's Library of Economics and Politics Series along with their prices. Because the maps were printed in color, *Hull-House Maps and Papers* was a dollar more expensive than the other four books in the series. Ely also offered a "special Edition with Maps mounted on Cloth" for $3.50, or $2 more than the other books in the series. Ely, in a 1910 letter to Addams, rebuked her for publicly critiquing the publisher of *Hull-House Maps and Papers* for declining to print a second edition. Ely snapped that re-printing the book was a question of "profit and loss" and reiterated the "extreme expense" of the maps and insufficient demand for copies during the first print run. Addams apologetically responded that "there are quite often demands for the book, even the Hull-House copy is lost. We are constantly borrowing Mr. Taylor's which he keeps at the School of Civics and Philanthropy." Addams's reply not only sought to appease Ely but demonstrated the problem of Kelley's attempt to find a middle ground for *Hull-House Maps and Papers* between an artisan ware and fast reproduction. The expense and rarity of the book is what made it less available and useful.

Kelley's decision to place *Hull-House Maps and Papers* with an academic publisher also avoided repeating with Addams a debacle that had ensued with Engels over the politics of publication. When attempting to publish Engel's *Condition* in the US, Kelley had collaborated with her friend Rachel Foster, the corresponding secretary of the National American Woman Suffrage Association, to pay for and distribute *Condition* through the channels of the Socialist Labor Party. Such a plan would have aligned with Kelley's earlier intent to provide labor theory directly to American workers. Engels, however, objected to this plan, arguing that asking a labor organization to publish his book would rob his and Marx's work of an ethos of independence and would be interpreted as coaxing "workingmen out of their hard-earned pennies" (151). The wealthy Foster changed course and paid for the book's publication and distributed it through suffrage organizations, an ultimately unsatisfying compromise for Engels. While Kelley's intent to give American workers theory to guide their organizing was classist and patronizing, she at least did not share Engels's belief that producing knowledge about labor was a neutral act and that he might be able to stay independent within the political rift between labor and capital. What Kelley had found in Addams was another figure equally dedicated to being descriptive of labor conditions and to apparently remaining politically neutral in the process. But *Hull-House Maps and Papers* required labor, materials, and technology to produce, and as a product it reflected residents' contradictory interests to wanting to elevate arts and crafts as an anti-industrial stance in solidarity with workers, and to embracing the opportunities the industrializing city and its technologies afforded them as white, well-connected women to take up positions of authority and circulate their own messages widely.

As the center of the arts and crafts movement in Chicago, Hull House was a meaningful setting in 1901 when the architect Frank Lloyd Wright famously gave a lecture there critiquing those who still reproduced paintings with new, mechanized print technology rather than inventing new forms of art that took advantage of industrial technologies. I thought of this critique the first time I viewed a first edition of *Hull-House Maps and Papers* at the Newberry Library in Chicago and better understood the maps as hypermediated objects that drew attention to their material form, and thus their ambivalent message about publishing. They were unwieldy and difficult to use because they were not thin enough to fit neatly into a book with the rest of its pages and were not scaled to fit on book pages. I separated the linen maps from the rest of the book by taking them out of their pocket, unfolding them, and laying them out on a reading room table under a desk lamp. As paintings at Hull House, the maps had been inaccessible and only viewable to those who shared space and time with them. In print, the maps had been remade in a seemingly more accessible form. After all, print was meant to circulate, and their place at Newberry was evidence they had indeed traveled several miles north of Hull House and had circulated at least among vetted patrons like me. Yet, the maps are still a protected art object for a small audience in this private library. The maps remained vibrant and beautiful after more than a hundred years, but only because Kelley had refused a less expensive and less labor-intensive reproduction that would have allowed for easier use and wider circulation. The Newberry Library is not an art gallery, but as a space that houses an exclusive, heavily-surveilled, non-circulating collection, it may as well be. I concluded the maps' continued vibrancy and beauty, along with their inconvenience and inaccessibility, was precisely the point.

Maps of a West Side Midway Plaisance

Because of Kelley's exacting demands for the book, the publication of *Hull-House Maps and Papers* was delayed until 1895, and it was only published then because Addams intervened in October 1894 and implored Ely to complete the printing before the maps' data no longer accurately reflected the populations living in the fast-changing neighborhood. Addams's intervention is a reminder that the maps were meant to reflect conditions in Chicago of 1893. At this time, the World's Fair shaped the daily lives of all in the city, and its influence is evident throughout *Hull-House Maps and Papers*. As a collection containing maps of Chicago and revisions of World's Fair speeches for print, *Hull-House Maps and Papers* served similar purposes to the textual ephemera published for World's Fair visitors. Souvenir maps and guidebooks, for example, delivered information about space to tourists needing to orient themselves to an unfamiliar place and provided material evidence of visitors' encounters with a cosmopolitan city. For World's Fair attendees, traveling to Chicago was a significant and costly event in their lives, and souvenirs provided purchasable and easy-to-carry evidence of their wealth, time to travel, and contact with national, racial, and ethnic difference. As evidence of encounter, attendees saved souvenirs long after arriving back home. They were saved, for example, by Texas resident Mamie Crozier, a daughter in the town of Lebanon's (now Frisco's) first white family. Today, her 1893 World's Fair souvenirs are displayed near where I lived for a time in Texas at the Frisco Heritage Museum. While the greater Frisco Museum is dedicated to narrating the provincial origin story for this Texas town, Crozier's souvenirs—a red diary in which Crozier documented her trip and a heart-shaped ornament engraved with "World's Fair 1893"—represent evidence that through her travels, she connected the rural outpost of Lebanon to the wider world. Like these souvenirs, *Hull-House Maps and Papers* was a visual and material object that both provided information and communicated the cosmopolitan values of its owners to others.

While Kelley and Holbrook cited Booth's London poverty maps as an influence, the Nationalities Map also resembled maps made closer to home in Chicago. It looks like maps of the World's Fair's Midway Plaisance, the carnivalesque portion of the fair and display space where tourists could appreciate foreignness and consume foreign goods, food, and culture. The honkytonk Midway was a space juxtaposed with the main World's Fairgrounds, called the White City because the buildings were created in a neoclassical revival style and spray-painted white. The two spaces of the Fair—the White City and the Midway—worked in concert to communicate an imperialistic vision: the White City represented white, civilized progress since Columbus's supposed discovery of the Americas, while the Midway represented the foreign, nonwhite, and primitive communities left outside the progress narrative. Historian Robert Rydell has argued for the strong possibility the Fair's Department of Ethnology, in concert with museum curator G. Brown Goode, planned the fairgrounds to juxtapose White City and Midway, civilized and savage, and modern and primitive (65). In depicting the Midway, souvenir maps spatialized the arrangement of foreign and primitive communities next to each other on square or rectangular lots and created knowledge for tourists about what they could expect to encounter during their visit. Hermann Heinze's 1893 souvenir map, for example, guided visitors walking down the Midway past an Irish village, a Turkish village, a Moorish palace, and a street in Cairo, interspersed among amusements like the very first Ferris wheel and a tethered hot-air balloon.

The Hull House Nationalities Map cast the west side of Chicago as a kind of Midway Plaisance. Like Midway maps, the Nationalities Map appeared to represent the work of experts on national difference, but upon closer inspection it presented a questionable combination of national, racial and ethnic categories that highlighted differences that helped further a narrative of American imperialism. Because the US Department of Labor's schedules from which Kelley pulled her data are included within the text of *Hull-House Maps and Papers*, it is possible to see these schedules did not prompt enumerators to record tenement dwellers' nationalities; instead, they prompted enumerators to solicit information about race, place of birth, and the languages individuals could read, write, and speak. Holbrook suggested the Nationalities Map was more accurately a birthplace map; however, Kelley did not offer tenement inhabitants the possibility of identifying as US born (55). As an alternative, Kelley offered a language category, "English Speaking, Excluding Irish." In "excluding Irish," Kelley also offered "Irish" as its own foreign and racialized category. In the absence of a US-born category, Black Americans might have fit into the "English Speaking, Excluding Irish" category, but instead Kelley labeled Black American households as "Colored." Such a racial categorization upsets the purported logic of a nationalities map, but by highlighting the identities of Black Americans alongside foreign-born inhabitants, Kelley— like the designers of the Midway—protected whiteness both within and beyond the space depicted in the maps.

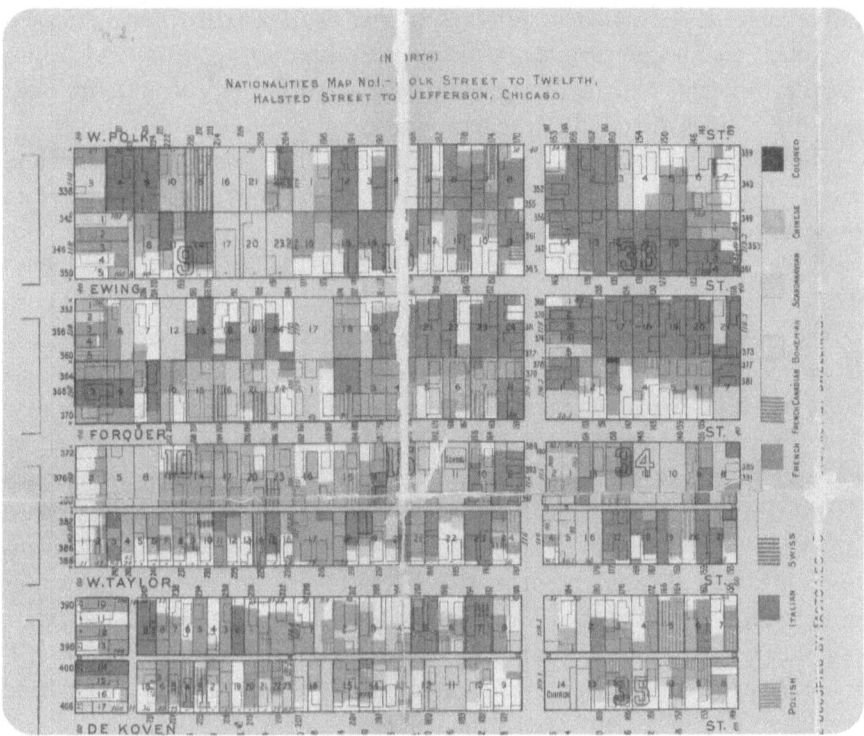

Figure 2.3. A section of the Nationalities Map and its key from *Hull-House Maps and Papers*.

By locating Black families in the Nationalities Map, Kelley spatialized how these families remained segregated from foreign-born families. While on the Nationalities Map foreign-born families are largely interspersed among one another, allowing viewers to understand this neighborhood as diverse or cosmopolitan, Black families are segregated and living close to the rail lines depicted in the map. Joseph Kirkland, in 1892's *Among the Poor of Chicago*, described the housing policies that led to this early spatial segregation even before city-wide redlining policies took effect in the 1920s. Speaking of Black homeowners, Kirkland wrote that "there are impediments to any accumulation such as their white neighbors engage in. For instance, suppose one of them were to invest his savings in a 'Building Society,' he would find, when his lot was ready for him, that he would be unwelcome to his neighbors of lighter skin. Even as a renter he is only acceptable in regions devoted to his race" (198). Black families' spatial segregation on the west side from white and racialized immigrant communities ran parallel to how Black Americans were excluded from representation in both the World's Fair's White City *and* on its Midway, where Blackness was coded as foreign rather than as American. The Nationalities Map revealed that Chicago's city planners and government officials were supporting white and immigrant families in creating a segregated and exclusive city by way of racist housing politics mirrored in the temporary city of the Fair.[5]

The Wages Map layered a working-class identity alongside national and racial identities to mark tenement inhabitants as multiply different from those beyond the boundaries of the maps. The key to the Wages Map, for example, denied possibilities for families depicted on the map to claim wealth or earnings that were not paid weekly. It also bounded and contained working-class space from the city's middle-class and wealthy spaces. If viewers saw the maps as extending Kelley's project to protect consumers from participating in exploitative industries through purchasing, they may have also been comforted by seeing that labor exploitation represented by low weekly wages was contained and distinct from the spaces white, middle-class and affluent people occupied. The maps disconnected the west side from key spaces of consumption, such as the city's commercial downtown just east of the river, or to the World's Fairgrounds to the south, or even to Hull House to the northwest and left off the map. The Wages Map, together with the Nationalities Map, offered white consumers the possibility to know themselves as different and distant from foreign and racialized producers of goods who lived in the tenements.

To be sure, wage earners were also consumers, and in 1893 west siders who lived in tenements were using their purchasing power to visit the World's Fair like other tourists. Yet, readers were not invited to think of west siders as fellow consumers in the pages of *Hull-House Maps and Papers*. In "Art and Labor" Starr reminded that consuming tastefully was a matter of class privilege, and the recently immigrated should be discouraged from purchasing cheap consumer items. In a passage describing a visit to an Italian man's home, Starr reflected that "the peasant immigrant's surroundings begin to be vulgar precisely at the point where he begins to buy and adorn his dwelling with the products of American manufacture. What he brings with him in the way of carven bed, wrought kerchief, enamel inlaid picture of saint or angel, has its charm of human touch, and is graceful, however childish" (132). Starr's racist, sexist, and classist assertion that an Italian working-class man should stay away from consuming the products of American manufacture aligned her closely with Kelley's view of him and

---

5. At the time of the World's Fair, journalist Ida B. Wells circulated a pamphlet at the Fair to point out and protest Black Americans' exclusion. In the pamphlet, Wells also contests the Fair's progress narrative about labor, pointing out that the US's historical progress and achievements had relied on enslaved people's labor, a fact that Fair architects ignored (1).

his home on the maps: he was best identified, for both Starr and Kelley, as Italian and part of a cosmopolitan and working-class community rather than as an American and white consumer.

Hull-House Maps and Papers' delayed publication prevented it from being useful to the 1893 tourists seeking in-person encounters with difference, but its authors were nevertheless responding to the tourist discourse about the west side at the time that had cast the neighborhood as a vice district. Chicago guidebooks printed in anticipation of the World's Fair promoted the spectacle of west side women—especially poor, working-class and nonwhite women— as part of the commodified tourist experience of encountering difference. Rand McNally & Co's *Handy Guide to Chicago and the World's Columbian Exposition* coaxed tourists to take a "nocturnal ramble" in one of the city's west side vice districts to view women on the street, in brothels, and dance halls (105). Responding to the west side's reputation as a red-light district, Kelley and Holbrook explained their Wages Map offered only a view of wages earned from labor sanctioned in the formal economy and excluded the wages of women who worked in brothels. Holbrook explained she did not calculate wages for women working in brothels because "it would be unfortunate to confuse them with laboring-people by estimating their incomes in the same way" (62). The Hull-House Maps, though, lost this veneer of moral high ground by portraying the west side's diversity as part of its commodified draw. In *Chicago and its Environs: A Handbook for the Traveler*, author Louis Schick cast immigrant women's everyday domestic labor as a tourist spectacle by encouraging tourists to visit streets on the west side east of Hull House on Sunday afternoons when "almost all the inhabitants are to be seen out of doors and the variety of costumes and the diversity and brilliancy of color fully make the scene worth witnessing." Schick singled out Italian women caring for their children as a colorful scene, one that looked like "a rainbow," an image that, like the maps, used diverse colors to represent cosmopolitanism (106). By offering a bird's eye view, the Hull-House Maps simply provided a different perspective from which to appreciate diversity that was unavailable in other tourist literature.

The maps continue to be an object that, once purchased, speak to their owners' interest in claiming knowledge of cosmopolitan space. While seeking a first edition copy of *Hull-House Maps and Papers* outside of the Chicago area and closer to where I lived and worked in Texas, I encountered one for sale on the website *Etsy* for $10,000 and considered what it would mean to buy it. The book's seller marketed the book as "very rare" and claimed the maps were the "only complete set for sale worldwide" (VintageClothing-Dream). The book's seller, in highlighting it as singular, unique, and expensive, reiterated the values Hull House residents sought in consumable objects in their own time. *Etsy* is a fitting place to find *Hull-House Maps and Papers* for sale because the website markets itself as a "global online marketplace" that highlights the work of makers "in a time of increasing automation" (*Etsy* About Page). Etsy, modernizing the discourse of cosmopolitan consumption for the Internet, promised that I was connected to sellers from around the world and that through purchasing, I could participate in supporting the book's owner, a discerning collector, in eschewing automation. *Etsy* allows a wealthy consumer today to buy *Hull-House Maps and Papers*, in part to gain knowledge from the book, but also to reinforce an identity of savvy purchaser who helps artisans from around the globe. Today, as in 1893, the concrete effects of purchasing artisan wares to help producers of goods working in increasingly automated industries remains unclear.

WOMEN AND CHILDREN BEYOND THE MAPS

While the Hull-House Maps explicitly spatialized national, racial, ethnic, and class-based categories, they did not represent gendered categories. There was no gender map guiding viewers to locate women and men. Though the maps of tenement homes implied women on the scene, the very idea of a wages map subordinated and obscured the traditionally feminized labor and unpaid domestic tasks of women, such as cooking, cleaning and caring for children and family members. Women are absent, too, from the six photographs of the interior Hull House spaces of parlor, art studio, music stage, library, men's club, and nursery within *Hull-House Maps and Papers*. Photographs could have revealed perhaps better than maps the gendered locations and conditions of women's exploited labor. Later, from Hull House in 1910, photographer Lewis Hine took up Riis's project of photographing tenement interiors through a series revealing women simultaneously parenting children and conducting piecework from kitchens that were also bedrooms. These photographs communicated that when the space of the tenement collapsed home and work, women and children suffered. While making *Hull-House Maps and Papers*, Kelley considered publishing photographs of child laborers who should have been at home or school, but were instead in the factory, in the service of labor reform: "We are weighing and measuring factory children at a great rate and shall publish photographs of deformed children found in the cutlery trade," Kelley relayed in an 1893 letter to Henry Demarest Lloyd, with whom her own children lived while she resided at Hull House (69). Ultimately, Kelley did not include these photographs in *Hull-House Maps and Papers* and instead the weights and measurements of factory children appeared in visual form as charts within the book. These charts communicated that factory children were underweight and underdeveloped compared to school children. Kelley's photographs of factory children would have been sensational and exploitative, and even though it is no doubt for the best she did not publish them, I am left wondering why she made this choice. Instead, she published charts, along with maps and photographs without women and children. One answer to this question is that publishing exploitative images of women and children would have been at cross purposes with protecting women and their authority in the home. Photographing women and children, especially in tenements, might have exposed the abuses of industry, but it would also have offered up for public scrutiny women's labor in domestic spaces that Kelley ultimately sought to keep private.

Kelley's Protectionist Politics

While I emphasize here the maps' power to keep private where women were located, they certainly also had the power to spark conversations about lived experience and women's paid and unpaid labor within the tenement. Kelley and Holbrook began this conversation in the pages of *Hull-House Maps and Papers* when exploring the implications of the maps. For example, in analyzing the intersection of wages and nationalities, Kelley noted that Italian families' low wages in comparison to other nationality groups had a gendered component, as the "home finishers" earning the lowest wages were "the wives and daughters of the streetsweepers and railroad gang hands" (66). This written interpretation of where and how women featured in the maps was necessary because the Wages Map, aggregating the total wages a family earned, did not indicate where wages were earned or who in the family was earning them. As Holbrook's and Kelley's insights demonstrate, the maps implied the presence of women and children on the labor scene of the tenement, even though the maps protected this scene from view.

Overall, though, Kelley's verbal labor rhetorics in *Hull-House Maps and Papers* furthered the project of protecting women's and children's labor and domestic spaces. Kelley discussed her work as the Illinois factory inspector, a role in which she drafted and then enforced the 1893 Illinois Factory and Workshops Bill. Expanding on her congressman father's protectionist politics, Kelley's bill aimed to provide women with the protections she believed they could not procure themselves via organizing. The law's first clause restricted the use of living spaces for industrial work purposes, stating, "no room or rooms, apartment or apartments in any tenement or dwelling house used for eating or sleeping purposes, shall be used for the manufacture, in whole or in part, of coats, vests, trousers, kneepants, overalls, cloaks, shirts, ladies' waists, purses, feathers, artificial flowers or cigars, except by the immediate members of the family living therein" (99). In seeking to protect bedrooms and kitchens from the intrusion of industrial labor, while also limiting women's working hours to eight per day, the law codified a "separate spheres" division of space and labor that had until then been enshrined only as a social contract rather than as a legal one.

In one way of looking, by determining where, when, and how women in tenements could labor, Kelley was hypocritical. Hull House was effectively a tenement by the strict definition of a home originally built for one family now occupied by many living outside the bonds of traditional familial relationships. Residents, Kelley included, worked for pay from within Hull House to support themselves. In addition to protecting neighborhood women from public view, the visuals in *Hull-House Maps and Papers* protected Hull House residents, too. The maps, for example, did not represent the geographic area that included Hull House, allowing residents to avoid reporting their weekly wages for readers to see. The photographs of various rooms in *Hull-House Maps and Papers* did not feature women working from home even as they conducted investigations, taught classes, curated an art gallery, managed a kindergarten, and more, all from inside the house. Instead, most of the six photographs depict empty exhibit spaces and parlors, except one of the men's club that includes men playing pool and one of the nursery that contains toddlers. Women do not appear.

In addition, the photographs obscured the ways Hull House's inhabitants were regendering their spaces by using them for domestic and for work purposes. For example, the photograph of the library in Hull House does not necessarily suggest its multifunctional uses as a reading room, a parlor for receiving guests, and as a classroom. While a photograph that withholds this information about the library's mixed uses may seem benign, it also withholds a larger understanding of the way residents used Hull House like a tenement. The room-level scale of the photographs avoided a display of Hull House as a whole; no bedrooms or kitchens appear, space that might have suggested the unconventional living arrangements at Hull House. The photographs, by obscuring a sense of how residents used their spaces, did not reveal the ways that residents subverted traditional domesticity through daily living. What all six of the photos have in common is that they are images of rooms heavily decorated with Hull House's cosmopolitan art collection. The photographs are like the maps in that they are reproductions of paintings. They invite viewers to appreciate Hull House residents' knowledge about and authority over cosmopolitan space. They do not, however, invite viewers to understand those residents' uses of space.

Figure 2.4 The library in Hull House, an image from *Hull-House Maps and Papers*.

The absence of women residents in the printed photographs of Hull House is even more striking when compared to their willingness to appear in painted scenes. In 1895, the Hull-House Maps enjoyed a kind of second reproduction in paint when accomplished painter and Hull House affiliated teacher Alice Kellogg Tyler displayed a watercolor titled "Miss Holbrook Painting the Hull-House Maps" at an exhibition in Hull House's Butler Art Gallery. Kellogg Tyler's painting—of Holbrook painting the Hull-House Maps—was featured in a larger collection of "water color sketches of Hull-House residents and co-workers" in the acts of making, doing, and living. The group included another by Kellogg Tyler ("Miss Turner resting"), and three by Enella Benedict ("Miss Fryer Bathing Baby Wallace," "Sig. Allessandro Mastro-Valerio in fencing costume," and "Miss Goodrich at the piano") (Hull-House Exhibition). Collectively, the paintings revealed residents occupying the space of Hull House and using it like a tenement in which many live and work together.

Through paintings, artists Kellogg Tyler and Benedict created a feminine visual rhetorical style that authorized them to publicly represent other people's labor. This style was comparable to what Hull House residents had accomplished on speakers' platforms of the World's Fair. There, Addams and other residents had adopted what Karlyn Kohrs Campbell has called a feminine speaking style that centered women's lived experiences and craft learning rather than formal academic training (13). Addams, for example, had claimed rhetorical authority based on her experience of observing other people's labor and managed the seeming paradox of taking up the masculine position of public speaker by reaffirming she valued traditionally feminized domestic spaces and roles in the substance of her speech. One of her topics was exploring why working-class women preferred factory work over domestic service, and she argued that because factory work offered women shorter hours and higher wages than domestic service, it allowed women workers more time to attend to their own families rather than to their "employer's family claims" (629). In making this argument, Addams authorized her role on the speaker's platform by endorsing women's supposedly traditional interest in caring for family members. In parallel, Kellogg Tyler authorized herself as painter by representing women in the acts of painting, bathing, and playing piano, traditionally feminized kinds of labor. In other paintings, residents were engaged in activities that were decidedly not labor, like resting. Kellogg Tyler's subject matter of a woman resting was perhaps the most potentially transgressive of the collection because in it she reimagined the subject of a woman at home beyond a relationship to any kind of labor. Her painting of Holbrook painting the Hull-House Maps was more representative of a feminine visual rhetorical style. In this painting, Kellogg Tyler revealed a woman using a home as a space of production, but Holbrook was *painting* and thus participating in manual, artisan labor rather than mechanized industrial labor. Through her watercolor, Kellogg Tyler elevated the maps to fine art objects and redoubled Holbrook's dedication to the medium of paint.

The existence of these paintings highlights that in *Hull-House Maps and Papers*, Kelley did not attempt to re-create a comparative feminine visual style in print. Yet, the feminine speaking style had translated for Addams and other residents from the podium to print. Collectively, residents' papers provided what Addams called "recorded observations" that were of value because they were "immediate, and the result of long acquaintance" in her prefatory note to the papers. Within the pages of *Hull-House Maps and Papers*, residents used their authority based in experience and observation to leverage a comprehensive critique of industrial capitalism, explain the garment trade, explore the living conditions of the Bohemian, Italian, and Jewish communities, and describe the role of Hull House and other institutions in supporting neighbors and the labor movement on the west side. The absence of women in published visual labor rhetorics may highlight that carrying out a feminine visual rhetorical style may require a labor rhetor adept at anticipating audience expectations surrounding gender. Through painting, and by circulating work at an exhibition in Hull House's art gallery, Kellogg Tyler and Benedict had some reassurance that a sympathetic audience would participate in collaboratively making meaning from their texts. In writing, Addams and other residents could explain at length their authority based in traditional domesticity to discuss labor. Addams's emphasized her feminine style and intent for *Hull-House Maps and Papers* to provide observable knowledge, or to "simply record certain phases of neighborhood life with which the writers have become most familiar," in the book's prefatory note. Perhaps because the printed maps and photographs met viewers in individual rhetorical situations without explanation, Kelley could not anticipate response to visuals of women laboring in the same way. Through the absence of visuals of women, Kelley continued her larger project of protecting women and children.

Tenement Inhabitants: Protecting Their Own Privacy

Kelley was not the only one with an interest in protecting labor from view. Neighbors had significant motivation to avoid participating in a project of making visual representations of their labor. Under Kelley's eight-hour law, overturned in 1894 because it was so unpopular among Illinois citizens, many women working in Illinois industries experienced reform as a return to traditional gendered divisions of labor. By singling out women for eight-hour protections, women could no longer compete with men who could work for pay for longer hours. The law effectively restored employers' demand for men workers. The law Kelley participated in writing had made women's acts of paid labor beyond eight hours illegal, and her neighbors surely did not want to make public their now illegal labor. Holbrook's and Kelley's own accounts of their investigation concede neighbors resisted attempts to represent them. Holbrook hinted at neighbors' resistance when admitting to "the painful nature of minute investigation, and the personal impertinence of many of the questions asked" (58). Kelley was even more forthcoming about neighbors' resistance to her inquiries when writing about her experience as factory inspector during a smallpox epidemic. In 1894, the connection between the Midway Plaisance and the tenement district on Chicago's west side was strengthened by the widespread belief that smallpox had originated on the Midway and had spread through the west side tenements where people could not avoid living in close quarters. During the epidemic, Kelley began a special investigation based on the unproven belief that garments made in tenements in which there were cases of smallpox would carry and then transmit smallpox to purchasers (65). This unproven belief adapted a popular, racist theory that immigrants carried germs with them when they immigrated and thus posed a danger to the wider population, one used to stoke nativist fears and support restrictions on immigration from eastern and southern Europe, China, and Japan (Kraut; Shah).

By networking together the Midway Plaisance and the tenement district with this germ theory, Kelley reified racial discrimination and conflated working people's homes with spaces that were unsafe and dangerous. Kelley wrote that in response to her investigation of smallpox in tenement homes, neighborhood people evaded her inquiries by ignoring her visits when she knocked on the door. Parents attempted to conceal children who had smallpox. I quote Kelley at length here to give a sense of neighbors' urgency to protect their children and their homes from Kelley's view:

> Among the reasons for concealment, the chief are the fear of the pest-house and financial loss. Parents dread to see suffering little children carried away to a pest-house where 70 per cent of all the patients die, and they resort to extraordinary measures, such as hiding sick children in coffee sacks, locking them in water-closets, or smuggling them away to remote suburbs wrapped as bundles of coats and transported in streetcars filled with unsuspected fellow passengers. In some cases an entire flat has been darkened and locked for days together, the parents coming and going in the small hours of the night, while they nursed their children through the plague, and neighboring tenants upon the same floor believed that the whole family had gone away. In other cases, doors and window were barricaded as well as locked and bolted, and the health officers were obliged to break down the doors. The afflicted families found steadfast allies in their struggle for concealment among the neighbors whose interest in the matter coincided with their own." (40)

For some tenement inhabitants, protecting their homes from Kelley's view was a matter of life and death. As factory inspector, Kelley had the authority to send children to the hospital where "70 per cent. of all patients die" (40). Others avoided her because she had enormous power to enforce the Factories and Workshops Bill and shut down the shops located in their tenement homes. Hiding from Kelley was not enough; she and the employees under her supervision could and did break down the doors of tenements. Thus, while Hull House residents and their neighbors had mutual interest in protecting their labor from public view, they had unequal ability to do so. Kelley was both Hull House resident and a government official policing her neighbors.

In *Hull-House Maps and Papers*, the tenement is made visible, but it is not represented as occupied by women and children laboring, and the various stakeholders had different motives for keeping labor private. Kelley's graphs and maps kept women absent from view and aligned with her interest in protecting women's domestic labor from becoming public and paid labor, even as she used the state to enforce this protection. One of Kellogg Tyler's paintings of a Hull House resident could have been included in the book and could have served as the basis for discussions about women's labor conditions. Such a visual could have communicated not only the kinds of spaces, but also the kinds of labor that some women shared and some did not share, a first step to creating solidarity between the subject of the image and the viewer. Yet, the Hull House residents who contributed to the book declined to visually represent women's labor—including their own labor. Finally, tenement dwellers had every reason to refuse to make themselves visible in Kelley's research. Her appearance at their door could have disastrous consequences for their lives and labor.

The Power in Publishing

When US industrial development occurred at an uneven rate and was geographically concentrated in northern cities, print had the power to circulate the message that industry abused and exploited workers to readers who lived further from cities and who nevertheless participated in producing and consuming from afar. New print technologies allowed journalists, photographers, and reformers like Kelley to potentially communicate across languages and give viewers a sense of immediacy about industrial labor exploitation. Throughout this chapter I have explored what followed from Kelley's premise that solidarity was not possible among tenement-based workers: an embrace of publishing for the consumer-minded reader and viewer. Working from this premise, Kelley led Hull House residents in collectively publishing *Hull-House Maps and Papers* and created new possibilities for Hull House residents to circulate their labor rhetorics widely. In so doing, she helped to shift the settlement's audiences for labor rhetorics beyond the west side of Chicago.

Through these efforts, Kelley was reimagining Engels's transnational publishing project. Where Engels had published about the condition of the working class in England for German audiences, Kelley was publishing about the working class in Chicago for American audiences. While Chicago's working class is obviously part of the US, Kelley considered those she wrote about as foreign and represented them as such. Her nationalities and wages maps and their keys perpetuated xenophobic, racist, and classist stereotypes about workers and their homes, urging consumers to see tenement-based workers as foreign, contained and separated from the rest of the city. Kelley, like Engels, offered readers/viewers insight on a foreign place as a cautionary tale about the effects of industry for her home country. In addition to Engels's influence, Kelley was responding to the exigencies provided by the Chicago's World's Fair, a pinnacle event celebrating the US as an imperial power. Like the literature printed for the Fair, *Hull-House Maps and Papers* addressed readers and viewers as white, American consumers and offered them a chance to see themselves as spatially and categorically different from the foreign producers of their goods. Kelley and Holbrook represented space with clear boundaries in which the consumer and producer did not share the tenement, city space, or even a nation.

While *Hull-House Maps and Papers* was not a translation project like the one she had undertaken for Engels to make his German accessible to English language speakers, Kelley's use of visuals opened up possibilities for understanding labor rhetorics across languages. She made publishing choices that ensured the visual maps remained the focal point of the book, especially by negotiating their printing in color and on paper designed to last. Her printing standards also made the book expensive, delayed its publication, and likely limited possibilities for its circulation. In these printing choices, Kelley was responding to an ambient anxiety at Hull House about producing a text in print meant to circulate. With the maxim "the medium is the message," communications theorist Marshall McLuhan pointed out that media communicate not only content, but also that the machine technologies used to produce content restructure social relations, work, and the patterns and rhythms of daily life (1). McLuhan was writing at the height of fears about the effects of television on society; in the 1890s, Hull House was a hub of anxiety about modernity and the machine, and residents feared publishing meant participating in the very exploitative industries they were seeking to reform. The maps' journey from painting to print reflects Hull House residents' ongoing suspicion that industrial modes of production diminished producers' authority and control over their processes and products.

In publishing, Hull House residents joined neighbors in the labor of manufacturing a product. However, residents kept their status as laborers obscured in the visuals within the book that did not depict women engaged in the variety of work they took up from the settlement. In addition, the photographs obscured the status of Hull House itself as a kind of tenement, a space where home and work mixed. In so doing, the photographs, together with the maps, obscured where women's embodied acts of doing, making, and being took place. If they had produced visual representations of women working, Kelley and the Hull House residents might have reimagined the tenement as a space for solidarity where the labor taking place within it was a shared geography between residents and the other laboring people of the neighborhood. Instead, residents asserted themselves as more powerful authorities who could create knowledge about other people's homes and withhold knowledge about their own home.

Publishing was and is resource intensive. It requires not only the space and time to create a text, but also access to editors and publishers who can print and circulate it. Given the need for these resources, tenement-based workers' ability to publish their own accounts of their labor was not equal to the power Hull House residents had. Kelley's assessment that tenement-based workers faced monumental challenges to organizing themselves was accurate, and part of the challenge was gaining access to delivery systems like print for circulating their messages. While garment workers in the factory were able to organize in part because they worked together and could speak to each other, those in the tenement were more isolated and could not so easily organize. Spatial separation along the chain of production meant that factory workers lacked opportunity to enlist tenement workers in organizing campaigns because they did not often cross paths, even when employed by the same manufacturer at making the same product. On top of these challenges to collective action, workers' access to the time, space and capital required to publish was scarce. In 1906, a Russian printer who set type for a newspaper publicly resented the intrusion of investigators who came to his house, stating that the "next time a party of them comes to my house I am going to ask each member where he lives and tell them that I am coming with a party of my friends, to their houses to make an investigation of my own" ("Ghetto"). The printer's comment was no empty threat. As a printer, he had the specialized knowledge of printing and access to the means to make his hypothetical study public. Such an imaginary study is helpful for noticing that neighborhood people could have participated, but were not included, in Hull House residents' composing of neighborhood studies.

To follow the lead of the Russian printer for a moment, I want to imagine other possibilities for publishing visual rhetorics that Kelley might have created had she been operating in pursuit of solidarity. To build solidarity, Kelley might have chosen, instead of a book, to make a vernacular object more connected to the everyday lives of those around her. In the twentieth century, Hull House became a space for this kind of object making when it supported Mexican American pottery making.[6] Or, Kelley might have

---

6. Cheryl R. Ganz and Margaret Strobel created an edited collected titled *Pots of Promise: Mexicans and Pottery at Hull-House, 1920-1940*, that explores Hull House as a space for Mexican immigrants who made pottery as a form of creative expression and symbol of ethnic identity. While the 1920s are beyond the scope of this book, the story of Hull House as a sponsor of Mexican pottery making also extends the story I tell about its investment in cosmopolitanism. On one hand, Hull House and its residents supported Mexican immigrants in creating pottery as a practice of finding mutual benefit in cross-class and cross-cultural interaction. On the oth-

recognized reciprocal relations with neighbors by listening to and learning from how they, like the settlement residents, were addressing the problems of space, sanitation, epidemics, and gender relations at work and home through building social centers and making architectural choices to communicate their solutions to the problems of city life. She might have mapped the vernacular architecture of neighborhood social centers and explored the meaning of the sokols built and used by Czech immigrants as social hubs and gymnasia, institutions imported from Europe and suggesting the functions of home could be collectivized. A vernacular architecture study might have focused on the visual design of Italian and Bohemian Catholic churches for how they reflected ideas about gender, power, authority, and immigrant identity. It might have included Hull House itself, a social center with an ever-expanding architectural plant signaling women were taking up more space and roles on the west side. Or perhaps Kelley could have worked toward solidarity in the mode of print, the Russian printer's threat to go to the homes of the social workers could have been, in another configuration, an invitation to collaborate. One might imagine a radical mapping project built as a true partnership between neighbors and Hull House reformers, with both groups taking the risk of inviting viewers into their homes. Kelley shared with the Russian printers of the neighborhood a general interest in Marxist theory. A collaboration that resulted in mapping of homes and businesses as private property could have been a radical one, a first step toward knowing what spaces to socialize for the uses of collectives. Had Kelley found a way to pursue a solidarity agenda in print, she might have rethought her publishing venues to include the myriad foreign-language newspapers that could have circulated findings about the neighborhood. There are many ways to imagine Kelley making more solidaristic visual rhetorical choices about process, product, audience, or publication venue. They begin with an approach motivated by an interest in seeking reciprocity and a willingness to question her own class-based and race-based privileges.

Rather than build power among workers, Kelley harnessed what power she could from the state to protect workers. In this case, Kelley's power to publish about labor relations was state sponsored through her roles as enumerator and factory inspector. This power to publish was not the same as the power granted voters and legislators to reimagine labor conditions. In his influential meditation on the value and meaning of art in an age of mechanical reproduction, the cultural critic Walter Benjamin was concerned that fascist governments were giving people "a chance to express

---

er hand, they did this at a time when Mexican immigrant pottery and Mexican inspired furnishings were becoming valuable commodities that white American women might claim expertise over and among middle-class consumers (x).

themselves" without giving them actual rights or opportunities to redistribute wealth and property (19). His concern offers a lens onto Kelley's publishing projects. Kelley was a reformer uncommonly well-connected in the political sphere, and her verbal and visual rhetorics were made possible by the Illinois state government, which encouraged her to make tenement conditions known to the public. She even drafted the first eight-hour women's labor law while serving as Illinois state factory inspector. Yet, the government at no point granted her, along with other women, the right to be part of the legislature or vote for the bill she drafted. Also excluded from voting were the many recently immigrated, non-US citizens impacted by the eight-hour labor law. Without access to state mechanisms that could redistribute wealth and property, Kelley invoked a "purchasing public" when writing about tenement conditions and urged them to participate in capitalism differently by consuming mindfully when they bought products, and in the process she prioritized containment and othering of neighbors in pursuit of reform (65).

I want to end by offering a view of the tenement as a space for solidarity beyond Kelley's gaze. In her smallpox investigation, Kelley admitted neighbors were organizing, at least informally, to resist her power. Tenement-based sweatshop workers recognized a mutual interest in protecting themselves from Kelley and government intervention and were "steadfast allies in their struggle for concealment" (40). When seeking to keep their labor private from Kelley and other government officials, neighbors expressed the alignment of their labor interests via reactive, unplanned, and spontaneous organizing. Their organizing for concealment did not overcome Kelley's project to set legal limits on their labor, but they disrupted her efforts. In the next chapter, I explore the space of the labor exhibition that included replicas of west side tenements, where meaning-making required collaboration between reformers, neighbors, and the public. Together, sharing space in real time, neighborhood people had the opportunity to unsettle the planned representations of what women's labor should look like and where it should happen. As I will discuss, through embodied and disruptive labor rhetorics at the exhibition, neighborhood garment workers further created the tenement as a potential space for solidarity.

3 Exhibition: Contesting Progress Narratives

Women have always worked.

—Banner at the 1907 Chicago Industrial Exhibit

During the Progressive Era, social reformers created exhibitions to communicate messages about labor rhetorics and solidarity. To do so, they drew from a long tradition of exhibition making that both celebrated and reflected the anxieties about industry's impact on domestic and craft-based labor. The first world's fair, the 1851 "Great Exhibition of the Works of Industry of all Nations" held in London, was an event William Morris thought so garish he dedicated his career to refining the taste of his peers through his design theories (Ellis 619). By the early 1890s, women philanthropists and reformers were using the exhibition as a gendered arena for celebrating fine and domestic arts and crafts in response to industrialization's role in further separating the home and paid workspace, devaluing domestic labor in the process. The Washington, DC, chapter of the Daughters of the American Revolution was one of the first women-led groups to open such an exhibit to colonial-era decorative arts. In Chicago, the philanthropist and socialite Bertha Palmer and a Board of Lady Managers curated the 1893 World's Fair's Woman's Building with works that highlighted women's contributions to art and labor from around the world. In Boston in the early 1900s, Isabella Stewart Gardner helped design and curate a museum featuring both fine and decorative arts. In Chicago, beginning in 1901, Addams led the process of creating the Hull House Labor Museum as a memorial to women's artisan craft making and challenged the idea that industrial progress benefited women. Later, in 1907, Addams and other Hull House residents participated in creating the weeklong Chicago Industrial Exhibit, which was overall more celebratory of women's entrance into industrial and factory spaces. In each of these instances, the exhibition was a space that brought together women with diverse perspectives and experiences around labor progress narratives using multiple rhetorical modes.

In this chapter I explore the linked Chicago exhibitions that created and contested progress narratives about industrialization in the early twentieth century. An affordance of exhibits is that they can travel, and each display of an exhibit meets the demands of a new rhetorical situation while building narrative momentum from previous instances of display. The two exhibitions I consider at length here—the Hull House Labor Museum and the Chicago Industrial Exhibit—were linked by their creators and their content. Addams and the Hull House residents were among the group of collaborators who created both exhibitions, and both featured tableau displays of west side working-class women performing their labor of textile making for the public. The two exhibitions, though, communicated distinct messages about women's labor progress, with the labor museum contesting the value of women's entrance into industrial life, and the Chicago Industrial Exhibit celebrating it. While networking together these two exhibitions, I attend to how and why they had distinct messages even as they contained some of the same content.

In the ephemeral and ever-changing space of an exhibition, the power to shape narrative is distributed. In the Chicago exhibitions, power was distributed (albeit unevenly) among elite reformers, working women and men, unions, manufacturers, and the public. This chapter explores challenges to progress narratives made by a variety of stakeholders collaborating and challenging one other. Industrial workers—especially immigrant women whose interests were supposedly represented in exhibit displays—critiqued home-to-work narratives in real time. By looking back through archival records and historic newspaper accounts of these exhibits, I recover the stories of workers who had initially agreed to demonstrate their labor in tableau scenes and who publicly contested the meaning of the exhibits they participated in. I consider these moments when participants contested, interrupted, and complicated the progress narrative as hopeful ones that potentially provided opportunity for reflection and solidarity.

The exhibitions I discuss in this chapter are notable for centering the stories of women's labor; they also participated in granting and withholding whiteness. Key to the exhibits' communicating racial and ethnic hierarchies was their representation of primitive time. Exhibits memorializing supposedly primitive labor especially highlighted the ethnic, racial, and immigrant identities of the women performing in these scenes, while exhibits to modern labor were performed by white women. Through examining the temporal dimension of the exhibits, I hope to highlight the word "primitive" developing classist and racist meanings and conflating whiteness with modernity. For Marx, primitive had referred to the "prehistory of capital," yet through the ethnographic and anthropological discourses in which exhibits participate, the word also related to the study of people in pre-industrial societies, portrayed as simple and existing at a cultural deficit (875). In exhibits labeled as primitive, organizers displayed pre-industrial, foreign, and racialized tableau performers, withholding whiteness from them and the people they supposedly represented.

In what follows, I first explore the Hull House Labor Museum and the challenges both women residents and neighborhood women workers posed to progress narratives that minimized the meaning and value of women's craft labor. Then, I turn to exploring the 1907 Chicago Industrial Exhibit's embrace of industrialization as progress, along with the disruptions to this progress narrative via workers' spontaneous, unplanned work stoppages. In recovering workers' protests, I contribute to theorizing the strike as an important rhetorical tactic that disrupts capitalistic space and time.

THE HULL HOUSE LABOR MUSEUM: INVENTING A COSMOPOLITAN PAST

The Hull House Labor Museum commemorated and idealized a past during which women had always worked. Its exhibits represented a supposed history of women's artisan labor that had taken place in the home through cooking, weaving, bookbinding, metalwork, and woodwork. Addams collaborated with the residents and artists Mary Dayton Hill and Jessie Luther to initially create the museum. When Luther left Hull House in 1903, Addams became the museum's director. Addams argued in her *First Report of the Labor Museum at Hull House, Chicago,* that the museum was a learning space that supplemented schools' omission of labor history. "Educators," Addams argued, "have failed to adjust themselves to the fact that cities have become great centers of production and manufacture, and manual labor has been left without historic interpretation or imaginative uplift" (2). Addams's goal was to shift authority over labor not only across gender but also across age, so older neighborhood people "would have an opportunity, at least for the moment, to assert a position in the community to which their previous life and training entitles them, and would be judged with something of an historic background" (1–3). Addams hoped younger people, in turn, would begin to question the notion that industrial labor was superior to manual labor.

The labor museum, though, was additionally about Addams and her colleagues reclaiming authority and standing over social reform efforts through Hull House as the city encroached on their territory. From the vantage of the labor museum, I want to revisit the argument from Addams's speech given at the 1906 NAWSA Conference that I previously discussed in the introduction of this book. In the speech Addams argued that "most of the departments in a modern city can be traced to woman's traditional activity; but, in spite of this, so soon as these old affairs were turned over to the care of the city, they slipped from woman's hands, apparently because they then became matters for collective action and implied the use of the franchise" (6). As the city offered more services to its citizens, Addams theorized that the public forgot that most of these services had been provided by women, and women continued to perform them without the benefit of suffrage. When Addams argued the city was taking historically domestic affairs "from woman's hands," she was talking not only about a general process of industrializing, but also about her personal experience (6). The city was overtaking Hull House's functions by, for example, opening its own west side library branch and its own nearby post office, making Hull House's versions of these services less needed. The labor museum physically manifested a history that backed the claim women in general, but Hull House residents in specific, were ideal city housekeepers. Organized into departments of wood, metal, grain, textiles, and paper, the labor museum offered a kind of metaphorical version of city departments, and reminded that it was Hull House for a time had provided the main supports for immigrants and their labor rather than the city itself.

Compared to the original Hull House mansion, the labor museum was a much bigger cosmopolitan space. In 1902, Hull House dedicated a three-story brick building with forty thousand square feet to the museum. The design was panoptic. Addams explained the museum made private labor public via windows "purposely planned for the convenience of the spectator who might be attracted by the 'show' elements of the museum and the casual passerby" (8). In the five departments, residents displayed a variety of manually made art and artifacts for the public on Saturday evenings (2). During these evenings, neighborhood women were featured in tableau scenes and made artisan wares. In the textile department, women performed "Syrian, Greek, Italian, Russian, and Irish" spinning techniques (*Hull-House Bulletin* 12). The editor and author Marion Foster Washburne visited the museum in 1904 and wrote a detailed account of her visit for the art and architecture magazine *The Craftsman*. In this account, she described the diverse, foreign display from varying places and time periods in the textile department. She recalled the following:

> Embroideries in gold and silk from Germany of the seventeenth century, beautiful Norwegian embroideries and fringes, Nuremberg and Italian embroideries, all manner of modern weaves, Mexican serapes, Venetian velvets from the fifteenth century. Resplendent in gold, red, green and yellow, upon a cloth-of-gold background, and even a framed fragment of mummy-wrapping. (577)

The generalized diversity of the exhibits created a cosmopolitan space and alluded to a past in which foreigners had made handcrafted goods over several centuries.

In addition to reimagining space, the exhibits in the labor museum also reimagined time in ritualized fashion. Through the exhibits displaying items across several centuries of handicraft, residents communicated the idea that women had always worked to a public they thought was at risk of forgetting the enduring value of women's domestic labor. As it was expressed by the museum, the idea that women have always worked was inflected with imperialist meanings. By inventing a specifically cosmopolitan past to juxtapose with the industrialized present, Addams and the other residents involved in organizing the museum participated in what anthropologist Renato Rosaldo has called "imperialist nostalgia," a term that names when the "agents of colonialism long for the very forms of life they intentionally altered or destroyed" (107–08). Rosaldo argues that agents of colonialism express the feeling of nostalgia to demonstrate their innocence in perpetuating relations of inequality under imperial conditions. By valorizing immigrant women's preindustrial labor, Hull House residents were forestalling critique of their own participation in perpetuating colonialist discourse. The reformers making the exhibits I discuss in this chapter were not trained in anthropology, nor were they aspiring to join the profession. Still, they participated in anthropological discursive strategies in their representations of the past. The rhetorician Risa Applegarth has argued anthropology was a branch of science more inviting to amateur women in the late nineteenth century because women had access to domestic spaces foreclosed to men and could create knowledge about humanity from observing those spaces (26). While the women anthropologists Applegarth researched found alternatives to perpetuating the colonial outlook of the profession, the women exhibit makers led by Addams created exhibits-as-texts that expressed deeply colonial messages by inventing a cosmopolitan past.

An imperialist nostalgia for white American women's authority over the wider world had local roots. That the Hull House Labor Museum was a manifestation of nostalgia for the prior decade was most obvious in its artifacts first displayed at the World's Fair in 1893. The Field Museum, opened to memorialize the World's Fair, loaned a large textile collection to the labor museum in 1902. When I contacted the Field Museum to find out if they had any record of this loan, they sent me a Microsoft Excel File that listed 2,184 items it had loaned to Hull House.[1] At first, the volume

---

1. Though the Field Museum kept a list of every scrap and tassel it loaned to Hull House in 1902, the meticulous record keeping stopped there and then. In 1924, the director of the Field Museum, D.C. Davies, wrote to Jane Addams asking to

of items astonished me, but upon closer inspection the number of items potentially overstates the scope of the loan. Bobbins, tassels, doilies, and fabric scraps are itemized on the list, though listed are also larger items, like spinning wheels, hats, and rugs. The provenance of the items listed was diverse, though vague. Some were listed as from a continent (i.e. Asia, North America), while others had national origins (i.e. Turkey, Sweden, Japan). While the provenance of individual items remains vague, they were all brought together at a specific location within the World's Fair. These were not the textiles first displayed in the Woman's Building to celebrate women's arts and crafts from around the world, nor were they from the carnivalesque Midway to emphasize foreignness as spectacle and show. The loan was from the Department of Anthropology. In accepting this loan, Hull House residents reasserted Hull House as Chicago's current authority over foreign people and culture.

Addams and other residents involved in the museum connected the cosmopolitan past to the industrial present through written reports and articles. In addition, Hull House hosted a speakers series in which speakers gave lectures that connected labor museum displays to modern industry. For example, in the winter of 1902 *The Hull-House Bulletin* advertised lectures on "The Evolution of Industry," the "Industrial Life of Primitive Man," "The Evolution of Tools," and "The Evolution of Textiles" (1). In all these instances, Hull House residents and speakers maintained the privilege to place displays in chronological context and to narrate their meanings and relationships to the present, setting residents and the public in conversation and apart from the women workers on display. These women performers were rendered instead as objects rather than as rhetorical subjects who could invite solidarity from the public in their present labor struggles. Overall, the labor museum denied women in the tableau scenes what the anthropologist Johannes Fabian has called coevalness, or the sharing of time (30). Fabian argues that anthropologists deny their research subjects coevalness by using discursive strategies to temporally distance themselves when communicating ethnographic knowledge, and, in so doing, foreclose their subjects the ability to communicate this knowledge for themselves. Residents engaged in a similar process by creating an exhibition that largely obscured individual immigrant women's present-day labor conditions in favor of celebrating their labor history, outside the US and prior to immigrating, while not

---

recall some of the materials, and she wrote back stating that the Art Institute had taken "the best textile exhibits" several years prior. In the Excel file the Field Museum sent me of the items it had loaned to Hull House in 1902, there is a column to make note of the items' current locations, but most items are vaguely described in that column as "possibly deaccessioned."

offering them verbal opportunities to make connections between the past and present.

WOMEN WORKERS' CHALLENGES TO A COSMOPOLITAN PAST

In response, through the act of performing in tableau, women textile workers became subjects who intervened in narrating their own labor histories. Washburne, writing about her visit to the museum, quoted the performer Honora Brosnahan's discussion of her work as she demonstrated Irish spinning techniques. Brosnahan, who according to Washburne was "too respectable and too modern to look her part," told the following narrative (577):

> Yes, we all spun and wove in the old country. It is not many of them that keeps it up now, except perhaps an old granny in a tucked away corner that does it for the love of it; but when I was young, we dressed in flannel and linen from the skin out, and grew it all and made it all ourselves. (579)

When Washburne asked Brosnahan what she did when she arrived in the US, Brosnahan replied, "I begged on the streets, dear" (579). In this exchange, Brosnahan's narrative confirmed that immigrant artisan labor—in this case textile making—was devalued in the US industrial economy. Nevertheless, Brosnahan contested nostalgia for a cosmopolitan past by telling a specific narrative that included her history pre- and post-immigration. In addition to begging on the streets, Brosnahan described struggling with her husband's alcohol abuse and coping with two of her ten children contracting spinal meningitis. Brosnahan's performance at the museum further complicated nostalgia for a cosmopolitan past because the museum remade her spinning skills relevant in the moment. Brosnahan was not only performing spinning for a large audience; she was also teaching spinning to a young woman sitting beside her (580). This specificity and scope of Brosnahan's narrative and performance challenged the museum's general indifference to immigrants' lives and labor post-immigration.

Washburne also spoke to Mrs. Sweeney, who was not an official performer, but an actual employee of the museum who served as an unofficial tour guide. In Washburne's exchange with Sweeney, "a neighborhood woman, employed in keeping the museum clean," Sweeney refused to embrace a cosmopolitan outlook. Sweeney, looking at displayed artwork, remarked that she recognized the "Irish lady spinning" in a picture on the wall: "I'd know her, big or little, in all the world" (576). Washburne believed Sweeney's interpretation of the picture was too narrow, writing that "perhaps she overlooks a little the Kentucky spinners, whose picture hangs next, and disregards their blue and white quilt, which makes a background for the pictures" (576–77). Washburne thought Sweeney was missing the connections between spinners across national boundaries. Sweeney and Brosnahan were both interested in spinning as a reflection of an Irish national past, not a cosmopolitan one, and meaningful to their present. In the present they were both embracing and making visible new kinds of work. Within the museum, they were not only Irish and familiar with spinning as a form of craft; they were also Irish-American and performing new kinds of labor. Brosnahan was a teacher and Sweeney a custodian and tour guide.

The Hull House Labor Museum, which focused on tableau scenes of women creating textiles, placed women artisans at the center of a capitalist history in a neighborhood surrounded by garment factories. The links between past textile making and present garment making were obvious, though what conclusion visitors might draw remained implicit. These were not, for example, exhibits supporting revolution, or efforts to collectivize labor and form communist utopias, though one might have glimpsed such a display if they had seen Hull House residents living their daily lives in the collective housing and working experiment that was the settlement. To encourage visitors' interests in a revolutionary future might have also led them to question Hull House residents' middle-class and affluent status and complicity in perpetuating class inequality and imperialist ideologies. Residents, though, could not control how visitors interpreted and made use of the past offered by the labor museum. Beyond Washburne, other visitors contested the meaning and value of a cosmopolitan past. For example, when Washburne encountered an old loom imported from Syria, she overheard two neighbors discussing that Hull House had paid forty-five dollars to import it and that it had arrived damaged from shipping. The loom, they agreed, was worthless: "I'd burn it up for kindling if I had it," one of the neighbors commented (577). This instance of talk challenged the value of a cosmopolitan past as a useful one for building a cosmopolitan future, and hints at the possible alternative to burn it all down.

An Insider's Refusal to Labor

In my search through the archived and published materials about the labor museum, I have not encountered evidence of a Hull House resident explicitly challenging the cosmopolitan ideologies of the museum. When I consider the possibility residents might have objected, I think about Harriet Rice, Hull House's first Black occupant and a medical doctor, and wonder what she would have thought about the labor museum project. Rice began objecting to the whole Hull House project soon after she arrived there in 1893 by refusing to work as a doctor and instead taking on less specialized Hull House roles like library worker and cashier. Upon her arrival, Rice was paired with the white doctor Josephine Milligan to run the Hull House medical clinic, but after Milligan left, Rice declined to take over the clinic (Knight 740).[2] Addams wrote in February 1895 to her partner Smith that Rice had left residents "indignant by her utter refusal to do anything for the sick neighbors even when they are old friends of the House. I am constantly perplexed about her." While Rice did not leave records explicitly discussing the motive behind her refusal to practice medicine and Addams's letter suggests Rice did not verbally discuss her motive, the refusal itself communicated. Given the broader context in which Rice was the only Black occupant living among white residents and mostly white immigrant neighbors, it is difficult not to wonder whether Rice experienced racial discrimination in her encounters with patients and at the same time felt silenced in a discursive space that celebrated cosmopolitan diversity while ignoring Black/white race relations.

Again, to be clear, there are no records tying Rice's refusal to work as a doctor to a critique of any particular aspect of the settlement, nor are there records that speak to Rice's thoughts about the labor museum or its expression of imperialist nostalgia. Decades later, though, Rice wrote a letter to Addams that suggested the US South, rather than the geography of US empire, could help make sense of the racial dynamics that had devalued her labor in Chicago. In 1928, after learning that Addams had been in Boston near where Rice lived in Rhode Island, Rice wrote, "I'd have been so glad to see you once more – although I hardly imagine that you would have been the least glad to see me. I've never forgotten once hearing a southern doctor tell about seeing again his old 'colored Mammy' and how glad she was to see him; but on his side there seemed to be nothing." On its face, Rice's analogy figures Addams as the white male Southern doctor, a person with social standing and racial privilege that contributes to an attitude of indifference to a Black caretaker. Rice in this analogy is figured as the "colored Mammy," a stereotype rooted in the history of slavery of an un- or underpaid Black female mother figure who cared for white children. In her letter, Rice places quotation marks around the term "colored Mammy" to signal it is an identity the Southern doctor is giving to his former caretaker, not an identity the caretaker would give herself. Rice is also suggesting that Ad-

---

2. I draw details about Rice and her life from the biography written by the historian Louise W. Knight that appears in *Women Building Chicago, 1790-1990: A Biographical Dictionary*. In her biography of Rice, Knight describes in detail Rice's family background, educational history, and various roles at Hull House.

dams saw Rice through this stereotype. Rice's encounter with the Southern doctor, though, inevitably reminds us that it is Rice who was the medical doctor, not Addams. In the role of doctor Rice had cared for Addams in 1895 when she diagnosed Addams with typhoid fever, a diagnosis overruled by a white male doctor who incorrectly diagnosed Addams with appendicitis and then operated on her. Given how Rice's expertise was ignored by Addams and others in this situation, it is easy to imagine that neighbors of Hull House did not recognize or value Rice's medical expertise. The analogy about the Southern doctor and "colored Mammy" is further interesting because Rice had never lived in the US South—she had always lived in the Northeast and the Midwest—yet her letter suggests her work in Chicago finds historical context in the South and might best be compared to the devalued labor of care that Black women in the South extended to white people during the period of slavery and afterward.

Addams either had limited insight into the racial dynamics that shaped Rice's experience or was privileged enough not to have to interrogate them. Addams wrote to Smith in the same letter explaining Rice's refusal to work that Rice "has not the settlement spirit." From Addams's perspective, Rice was struggling to fulfill what Addams asked of all residents, which was to craft one's own purpose for living at Hull House and then follow through with a self-directed project to serve neighbors. Addams must have been hopeful Rice would thrive at Hull House. Rice had been the first African American graduate from Wellesley College and one of only 115 African American women to hold a medical degree in 1896 (Knight 740). In these achievements, Rice far exceeded Addams's academic record of graduating from the two-year Rockford Female Seminary and then dropping out of the Women's Medical College of Pennsylvania after a semester. Addams, by framing Rice's problem as one of her spirit, akin to something like personal will or motive, ignored the impact racism would have played on Rice's experiences interacting with Hull House's immigrant neighbors. That Addams had reported to Smith in her letter that she was "perplexed" and did not have a theory to explain Rice's refusal beyond thinking about it as one of individual spirit squares with her focus on a selective and global understanding of diversity rather than a national one. The complicated gender and racialized labor dynamics playing out for Rice at Hull House found no sufficient historical context in Hull House's cosmopolitan ideologies or in its labor museum. The idea that women's labor relations in Chicago could be best understood within a cosmopolitan, agrarian, and largely European history did little to explain the failure of white patients to reciprocate dignity and respect to a Black doctor.

The Chicago Industrial Exhibit: Embracing the Progress Narrative

In 1907, the Hull House Labor Museum displays were repurposed to illustrate a period of so-called "primitive" work for a Chicago industrial exhibit. Unlike the labor museum, the industrial exhibit celebrated the modern, working-class woman and argued electrified factories were the ideal space for women to conduct paid work. It occurred at a moment of optimism about women's place in industry right before a national economic crash that checked the Progressive spirit and spurred a cultural shift in which women workers seized an opportunity to represent their own labor interests through organizing. Held at public theater house Brooke's Casino from March 11–17, the Chicago Industrial Exhibit was a collaborative effort by the city's leading settlement houses, women's clubs, and labor organizations. According to the exhibit's handbook, Addams chaired the executive committee planning the event, and although she and other Hull House residents participated in creating the industrial exhibit, it was ultimately led by Ellen Henrotin, a Chicago philanthropist and national president of the Women's Trade Union League (WTUL). Through tableau scenes, charts, posters, and displays of model equipment, the exhibit visually and verbally represented different kinds of work—food production, garment making, candy wrapping, boot making, and printing—through three distinct temporal stages: women's "primitive," domestic-based craftwork; tenement-based sweatshop labor; and factory-based labor (Program). By presenting women's labor in three stages, Chicago's reformers hoped the exhibit's visitors would reconsider women factory workers not as new to industry, but as laboring at the previously domestic tasks they had always performed (McDowell 322). In so doing, the exhibit put a positive spin on the maxim "women have always worked" by revealing the modern woman was a factory worker, a sign of progress.

"As you entered the hall your eye caught this legend in large print," wrote social reformer and University of Chicago Settlement founder Mary McDowell, describing seeing a "women have always worked" banner while moving through the industrial exhibit (319). The banner responded to the perceived public fear that women newly working in industry threatened a traditional, gendered division of labor in which men, not women, worked for pay outside the home. McDowell explained that many people had not noticed women working "until suddenly they were found in large numbers coming into the industrial life competing with men for a living" (322). The phrase is stereotypically Progressive in its assurance and sweep of history, but useful for refuting the idea that women's work was somehow new. Because of its usefulness, the phrase has remained in circulation in feminist discourse, a reminder that women have endured in working through time to counter the numerous and recurring attempts to devalue women's labor.

In 1981, historian Alice Kessler-Harris addressed feminists and historians by publishing *Women Have Always Worked: A Historical Overview*, a book that recovered histories of wage-earning women. Her title called more feminist historiographers to take notice of a seemingly forgotten women's labor history. Likewise, bell hooks reminded feminist readers that Black women "have always worked. From slavery to the present-day black women have worked outside the home, in the fields, in the factories, in the laundries, in the homes of others" (133). She made this point in response to white feminists in the women's liberation movement who had identified motherhood and a lack of childcare as obstacles to entering the workforce, whereas Black women, who had always worked outside the home, identified racism and exploitive industries as keeping them from more humanizing work inside the home, caring for family (133). Poet Adrienne Rich, though, reminds readers to be generally wary of sentences that begin with "women have always . . . " because the "'always' blots out what we really need to know: When, where, and under what conditions has the statement been true (214)?" The makers of the Chicago Industrial Exhibit subordinated questions about the specificity of labor conditions in an attempt to visually represent the historic sweep of women working. In so doing, they resorted to stereotypical and condescending representations of working women's history.

In this new exhibition space, the "primitive" exhibits displaying an agrarian and peasant past were framed as a necessary but intermediate era of labor along women's path to embracing industrial progress. Resident Edith de Nancrede, alongside typographer and artist Frank Hazenplug, directed the primitive labor exhibits, on loan from the labor museum. Under the title "Process Exhibits of Women at Work," Hull House neighbors "illustrated the grinding and preparing of food by the Indians, the manufacturing of cloth—processes from sheep shearing to the finished fabric—by Greeks; pottery by Japanese; tool making in stone, bone and wood, by Esquimaux; barter in an Arab market place, and character writing—the forerunner of printing—by Egyptians" (44). Three nights during the week, these process exhibits were accompanied by performances of "tableaux and songs" (*Handbook* 8). Whereas at Hull House these displays had been the main attraction and emphasized a cosmopolitan past, at the Chicago Industrial Exhibit these displays were subordinated in the service of creating a lineage for elevating women's modern, industrial work.

The day after the exhibit opened, the Chicago-based *Polish Daily News* featured front-page photographs of two of the displays on loan from Hull

House, one representing Native American food grinding and one depicting Greek cloth making ("From the Industrial Exhibition" 1). At the Industrial Exhibit, these displays furthered a colonialist narrative, underscored by the inclusion of the Native American exhibit that harkened to a supposed time before Indigenous people had contact with industrialization and Western civilization. The *Polish Daily News* did not name the participants, the place, or the era being represented, nor did the *Handbook of the Chicago Industrial Exhibit*, which served as the event's program and otherwise explained each of the displays in detail. These tableau scenes, representing a multiplicity of cultures and nationalities together in primitive time and idealized domestic space, suggested the maxim that "women have always worked" was global and universal.

Like the labor museum's, the industrial exhibit's depiction of women's labor was in conversation with displays at the World's Fair. In 1893, Henrotin, writing about the Woman's Building at the World's Fair for *Cosmopolitan Magazine*, had described prominent murals, one titled "The Primitive Woman" by Mary MacMonnies and the other titled "The Modern Woman" by Mary Cassatt (561). Fourteen years later, MacMonnies's mural could have fit in at the Chicago Industrial Exhibit in depicting primitive women's labor in a general and idealized past in which work was completed by hand. While its representations of primitive women looked much the same as they had in 1893, the industrial exhibit's modern woman departed drastically. In Cassatt's 1893 "The Modern Woman," women in an allegorical scene of the Garden of Eden picked fruit from the tree of knowledge, implying modern woman was from an affluent background and work included attending college or becoming an educator. The industrial exhibit's modern woman, in contrast, was *working class*, shown toiling in garment and baking factories. The exhibit's executive committee and local labor unions found common ground in creating the factory displays featuring modern, working women, as both groups hoped the factory would provide cleaner and safer work conditions.[3] The Bakers' and Confectioners' Union, for example, created the exhibit of the modern, sanitary bakery, which was shown in contrast to both the old-fashioned, "insanitary" bakery in a sweatshop and the tableau scene of manual food grinding (*Handbook* 11, 17). The primitive, sweatshop, and factory displays worked together to create a temporal and spatial progress narrative and to suggest working-class women in factories were

---

3. Factory work was not always safer. Although the Industrial Exhibit organizers promoted factories as safer than sweatshops, factories often presented new hazards for workers. In 1911, for example, 146 garment workers in the state-of-the-art Triangle Shirtwaist Factory in New York City perished in a fire because of blatant workplace mismanagement (Hapke 51).

modern, yet still performing the same kind of work historically located in domestic settings.

The exhibit's labor progress narrative was further complicated by the inclusion of sweatshop scenes. The word "sweatshop" is difficult to define, and its history is intertwined with the tenement house. Historian Laura Hapke notes the sweatshop is a notoriously tricky geography to study, as it was a term that referred to, between the 1840s and early 1900s, the homes of workers who brought extra work home with them to complete at night, a workshop in a home, a shop in a former dwelling place, and the factory where subcontractors conducted piecework (38–39). In addition, "sweatshop" was not just a geographic location but an ideological one infused with ever-evolving fears of immigrant and women's labor competing with US-born male workers. Because of its shifting meaning, I pause here to offer more context about the Chicago sweatshop, as well as its relation to the tenement in this time period.

In the exhibit's *Handbook*, Chicago's chief sanitary inspector Perry L. Hedrick acknowledged that while "sweatshop" can refer to other workplaces, the term "is usually taken to mean the place where articles for public sale are manufactured in the home under questionable conditions" (21). Chicago's reformers were especially concerned about sweatshops located in wooden, one-story tenement homes on Chicago's west side. Although Chicago sweatshops increasingly migrated to brick, two- and three-flat homes on Chicago's northwest side in the early twentieth century, it was the one-story, wooden "typical Chicago frame tenement" that reformers displayed in replica at the exhibit. This kind of tenement was used as a stage for sweatshop workers to demonstrate garment-making, nut-picking, and flower-making (Taylor 40). The exhibit displayed wooden tenements in part because they were locally known to Addams and her colleagues from Hull House, who led the effort to create the full-scale reproductions based on actual west side tenements inhabited by their neighbors. The residents of Hull House recruited sweatshop workers from their neighborhood to perform in the exhibit, and sweatshop workers brought their furniture and work supplies with them to the replicas ("Labor Troubles"). The display of the kind of sweatshop that existed in a wooden tenement reflected the exhibit's purpose to show conditions as they existed in Chicago and Illinois and perhaps complicated visitors' expectations that sweatshops were solely located in the multistory, brick tenements that Jacob Riis had photographed two decades earlier for *How the Other Half Lives*.

Figure 3.1. A reproduction of a Chicago tenement from Graham Romeyn Taylor's essay on the Chicago Industrial Exhibit.

Though the sweatshops were reproductions of actual homes, in the narrative of the exhibit, they represented industry's midpoint, a space of labor temporally located between home and factory. By the twentieth century, according to historian Youngsoo Bae, it was fashionable to argue that tenement labor was passé, while clean, bright, electric-powered factory work was the better, more sanitary and hygienic way to manufacture (70). Sweatshop laboring, though, was not an obsolete practice as suggested by the exhibit; it was part of workers' present lives. "Home finishing" and sweatshop working were wholly interconnected to factory production in what was known as the sweating system (*Handbook 32*). Chicago's industrialists made their great wealth by outsourcing labor to homes and sweatshops, reducing their need for rental space while underpaying workers. Exhibit organizers included tableau scenes of sweatshops to condemn them and to promote the factory as an alternative. Addams and the exhibit's organizers temporally distanced sweatshops from modern factories by suggesting they were old-fashioned, dirty, and unsafe for the health of workers and consumers. For example, organizers described one of the tenement reproductions as an "insanitary tenement sweatshop—old fashioned foot-powered shop," highlighting the sweatshop was not powered by electricity, a marker of industrial modernity (*Handbook* 10). Calling the sweatshop "insanitary" also suggested a metaphorical, temporal distance from the clean, modern factory. With these descriptors, organizers denied sweatshop workers coevalness.

Despite including actual items from workers' homes, the sweatshops were not reconstructed for accuracy. The *Chicago Inter Ocean* noted that the "society matrons" in charge of the exhibit filled the sweatshops with debris and curated them with "carefully selected grime" ("Workers Strike" 3). *The Chicago Chronicle* called one sweatshop replica a "make believe hovel" ("Stared at; Strike" 6). The term "insanitary" implied not only dirt but disease. In a photograph of a sweatshop reproduced along with minister and reformer Graham Taylor's essay about the exhibit, the caption says, "in a room such as this the factory inspector found a child with scarlet fever sleeping on a pile of sweat shop clothing" (40). Such a description highlighted the sweatshop as a domestic space that included family members (children) taking part in domestic activities (sleeping) and experiencing illness (scarlet fever). Given a view of these conditions through the exhibit, members of the public were invited to protect themselves from contamination by declining to purchase sweatshop-made goods, and in so doing, promote safety and regulation for workers by encouraging production in factories. The argument about the tenement sweatshop as insanitary was the same argument that resident and factory inspector Kelley had furthered in 1893–1894 to keep manufacturing out of bedrooms and kitchens and enforce an eight-hour labor law for women. Residents who curated the tenement sweatshops displays reimagined Kelley's protectionist argument in exhibit form. As I discussed in the previous chapter, underlying arguments about sanitation were built on racist fears that immigrants carried germs, and the tenement sweatshop displays furthered this racist belief.

Print materials about the exhibit pointed out sweatshop workers' immigrant, ethnic, and racialized identities. The exhibit's *Handbook*, for example, informed readers that the sweatshop displays, the examples of unmodern and unclean workplaces, had been modeled after Italian immigrant workers' tenement homes (10–11). Historian Thomas A. Guglielmo notes that although Chicago Italians were generally accepted as white, they nevertheless faced racial discrimination and prejudice that could not be reduced to ethnic identity as its sole source (7). A writer for *The Chicago Chronicle* referred to sweatshop workers participating in the exhibit as Russian, marking them as part of the large group of Russian-Jewish immigrants who also worked in the sweating system and faced racial discrimination ("Stared at; Strike" 6). Although print materials by and about the exhibit highlighted sweatshop workers' national and ethnic identities, they did not remark on the racial identities of women workers performing in factory displays, implying through this absence that the ideal, modern worker was a white woman.

In addition to their idealizing of primitive labor and disparaging sweatshops, exhibit organizers made another racist rhetorical choice by excluding Black women's labor from its narrative of gendered progress. To include Black women's labor history would have presented a challenge to a narrative in which women's historical domestic labor was the precursor to the labor valued in modern workplaces. Enslaved Black women had not owned their labor in the past and, in 1907, their labor was not valued in the modern factories displayed at the exhibit. In representing factories, the Chicago Industrial Exhibit's executive committee had replicated the discrimination of Chicago's employers who contributed to a segregated labor market by denying Black women positions in manufacturing. The 1922 Chicago Commission on Race Relations synthesized statistics revealing the scope of this racial segregation in the first decade of the twentieth century. The commission found that Black women were restricted in their possibilities for work, with only 11 percent employed in manufacturing and mechanical industries, while 78 percent were employed in domestic and personal service industries (379). The laundry, childcare, and household maintenance for which Black women were paid in the domestic and personal service industries remained invisible at the industrial exhibit in part because it was work that remained in the home and did not fit within the exhibit's elevation of the factory as the modern woman's workplace. The WTUL, of which Henrotin was president, had some Black women members from the meatpacking industry, but this industry was excluded from the industrial exhibit's home to sweatshop to factory narrative (Foner 313). Had the slaughterhouse been depicted, it would likely have multiplied the racist representations of space rather than created a space for solidarity for women across racial lines. One need only look to Upton Sinclair's *The Jungle*, published in 1906, for another text that responded to the fear that white men had competition for work, this time not from women, but from Black men. Sinclair offered racist depictions of Black characters as strikebreakers, a role that located a labor problem in the moral character of Black American men from the Southern US who agreed to take jobs from strikers, rather than placing blame on employers exploiting workers, the racist unions that excluded Black workers, or society at large for widespread racial discrimination.[4] The Chicago Industrial Exhibit did not explore spaces like the modern household or the slaughterhouse,

---

4. Two articles that offer in-depth analysis of racism and racial conflict in the Chicago meatpacking industry are John H. Keiser's "Black Strikebreakers and Racism in Illinois, 1865–1900," and William M. Tuttle Jr.'s "Labor Conflict and Racial Violence: The Black Worker in Chicago, 1894–1919." In "It Ain't Your Color, It's Your Scabbing": Literary Depictions of African American Strikebreakers," Mark Noon analyzes racist literary representations of strikebreakers, including Sinclair's.

instead keeping narrow focus to maintain the logics of a spatial and chronological narrative of gendered and raced progress as women moved from home to sweatshop to factory, and closer to whiteness.

CONTESTING PROGRESS NARRATIVES THROUGH THE STRIKE

Chicago newspapers reporting on workers striking for higher wages, safer conditions, and shorter workdays was widespread in the early 1900s.[5] In the early twentieth century, meat cutters, garment workers, and teamsters all launched major strikes against employers. During the week in which the Chicago Industrial Exhibit took place, major daily newspapers were already covering strikes called by the unions for electrical workers and shipbuilders in the city. Once workers performing in the exhibit came to understand that the exhibit itself reinforced discriminatory beliefs, they began striking. Throughout the exhibit's week-long run, Chicago's daily newspapers reported on workers striking in protest of conditions within the exhibit and beyond. This reporting, although typically sensationalizing in its portrayals of women and workers, nevertheless relayed workers' firsthand accounts and reporters' observations of the exhibit.[6]

---

5. Like much reporting in the Chicago major daily newspapers at the time, accounts of striking workers almost always appeared without a byline, so it is unfortunately not possible to identify the individual writers who undertook this reporting work.

6. When searching for newspaper stories that recorded responses to the Industrial Exhibit, I tried to be comprehensive. To find out which newspapers were printed daily in Chicago, I looked to N.W. Ayer & Son's *American Newspaper Annual* of 1907, a historic catalog of all American newspapers indexed by state, city, and circulation. I was able to locate archived copies of Chicago's English-language daily newspapers with the largest circulations in March 1907. These papers were *The Chicago Record-Herald, The Chicago Inter-Ocean, The Chicago Daily Tribune,* and *The Chicago Chronicle.* Chicago's proliferation of newspapers beyond the major dailies in the early 1900s reflected a multilingual and segregated city in which many of the papers invoked specific ethnic and racial communities as audiences. Although I identified ten foreign language daily newspapers circulating in March 1907, I was only able to locate archived copies of *Abendpost* and *The Polish Daily News* during the timeframe of the exhibit's run. In addition, I sought to include *The Chicago Defender*, published weekly, in my corpus of newspapers because of its coverage of and influence on Black life and culture in Chicago. My search for *The Defender* in archives containing Chicago-based papers, assisted by archivists at the Newberry Library and Carter G. Woodson branch of the Chicago Public Library, did not turn up any copies from 1907. Ultimately, I found twenty-five news stories about the exhibit in *The Chicago Record-Herald, The Chicago Inter-Ocean, The*

On the first day of the industrial exhibit, the striking Electrical Workers' Union No. 134, a local branch of the International Brotherhood of Electrical Workers, disrupted the showcase of electrical machinery intended to convince manufacturers to purchase it for their factories (Breckinridge 657). Electrical workers "refused to make the necessary connections for the Western Electric Company's exhibit of motors and other heavy electrical machinery, and, as a result, the various contrivances lay 'dead' all day" ("Labor Troubles" 3). Through their refusal to connect machinery, the electrical workers disrupted the exhibit organizers' argument that electric-powered machinery purchased by manufacturers would make women's labor safer and more efficient. The strike instead refocused attention on the ability of unions to negotiate for improved wages and hours while also communicating the exhibit was not separate from workers' everyday struggles. That the exhibit was a site of tension between workers and manufacturers was reinforced to the visiting public through the presence of "walking delegates from the union" who were ready to call a general strike if strikebreakers attempted to connect the machinery ("Electrical Workers" 3). Although they briefly considered it, the exhibit's organizers decided against hiring non-union men to install electric machinery ("Labor Troubles" 3). The electrical workers' strike, then, convinced the exhibit's organizing committee to side with the union over the Western Electric Company. The strike in this case proved effective as a tactic for inviting solidarity among the all-male Electrical Workers' Union, women workers who were the subject of the exhibit, and the exhibit's organizers, in efforts to gain higher wages, shorter work hours, and improved workplace conditions. The bigger, city-wide Electrical Workers' Union strike was settled during the second day of the exhibit, and workers agreed to make connections for Western Electric's machinery ("Real Strike" 7).

On the second day of the exhibit, women workers and their family members recruited to perform in the sweatshops began their own strike by refusing to take part in tableau scenes. Sweatshop workers—identified as Mr. and Mrs. Guiseppe Berlulucci, their two children, Mrs. Maria Josnini, Mrs. Guiseppi Seminara, and Ida Rossi—declined to participate because they were humiliated upon realizing their tableau scenes were being used as examples of poverty and squalor. The *Chicago Daily Tribune* covered the sweatshop workers' protests as a kind of consciousness-raising moment in which they came to understand, first individually, and then by talking with one another, that their displays "did not compare favorably with the

---

Chicago Daily Tribune, and *The Chicago Chronicle*. I also located six stories about the exhibit in Chicago foreign language dailies.

prevailing neatness outside" and were being offered up as a "horrible example" ("Labor Troubles" 3). These sweatshop workers then spontaneously reimagined the tableaus by rearranging them to reflect more accurately the conditions in their real sweatshops. In one display, workers removed "a bed, a broken-down oil stove, several mattresses and blankets, and an indefinite amount of broken china and rubbish" (3). Henrotin and McDowell objected to workers changing the displays, calling their rearrangement "hopelessly neat," but ultimately workers were successful in reorganizing the sweatshop exhibits (3). In so doing, they disrupted the progress narrative in which sweatshops represented old-fashioned and insanitary workplaces. The *Inter Ocean* reported that, in addition to cleaning the displays, the Berluluccis, Josnini, and others reimagined the occasion altogether by beginning to host members of the public as visitors to their tenements, drawing attention to the use of the tenement as a home rather than a sweatshop. Taylor observed that the members of the public visiting the exhibit were "plain folk," two thirds of whom he estimated were trade unionists interested in seeing their work reflected in the exhibit, though more affluent clubwomen, society people, and reformers also visited (39). Many visitors who came to see themselves in the exhibit's displays may have been just as offended by the original sweatshop scenes as the workers performing in them. The tableau performers invited the public to view their relation to each other not as one of exploited producer and savvy consumer as was intended, but through the frames of host and guest. By inviting the public into their homes, workers countered the ethnic and racial stereotypes about immigrant homes and sweatshops as dirty and unmodern. For the exhibit's second day, sweatshop workers had come back in "their best attire, not their worst" to greet the public ("Workers Strike" 3). Whereas clothing displayed in the sweatshop tableau scenes was supposed to represent fast fashion and potentially diseased product, workers who put on their "lace and finery" signified to the public that they, too, valued well-made clothing (3).

The power of the strike to reimagine relations among stakeholders was highlighted again in the model factory bakery that was shown in contrast to the sweatshop bakery. Throughout the weeklong exhibit, members of six different women's clubs were slated to pose as unionized waitresses. This posing seemingly began as clubwomen's attempts to demonstrate solidarity with workers when the clubwomen gained the consent of the waitresses' union to serve from the bakery without actually becoming union members. Once this plan was executed, according to *The Chicago Tribune,* clubwomen wearing caps and aprons and practicing a "lunchroom dialect" only highlighted distinctions between themselves and workers ("Club Women" 7). The Chicago Women's Club, who served in the bakery the first day, highlighted distinctions beyond clothes and language when they appropriated the action of the strike, and in so doing mocked it. Instead of actually serving lunch at the exhibit from 3–6 p.m. as planned, clubwomen stopped working at 5 p.m. and asked some of the sweatshop workers to fill in for them ("Urge Need" 7). Their stopping work emphasized their usual roles as clubwomen who faced no risk of losing employment when striking, a luxury not afforded actual waitresses. Inviting the sweatshop workers—nonunionized workers, no less—to fill in for them further mocked the power behind striking because it replicated the dynamics of the sweating system, suggesting that the work of unionized waitresses could be easily outsourced. In response to clubwomen's appropriation of the strike, the baker in charge of the model bakery stopped clubwomen from serving after the second day and invited unionized waitresses back to work ("Club Women" 7). By barring the clubwomen, the baker communicated that restaurant work was not mere performance and highlighted the skilled labor of waitresses. Like sweatshop workers reimagining their tenements against the wishes of the exhibit's organizers, the baker disrupted the intended performance by halting work and then reimagining it for the public.

The daily newspapers in Chicago went beyond describing workers' spontaneous strikes to critiquing the entire conflict between the executive committee and workers by using derisive humor. For example, the *Chicago Daily Tribune* called into question the committee's expertise over labor they had never previously performed when members of that committee clumsily attempted to herd sheep down Wabash Avenue to Brooke's Casino for a shearing and textile-making demonstration. The *Tribune* described this episode in detail under the headline "Sheep on Strike" (6). By positioning this episode as one more in a series of strikes taking place within the exhibit, the *Tribune* not only pointed out the organizing committee's lack of knowledge over labor, but also undercut workers' dignity by suggesting that sheep—an animal well-known for following along—could strike as well.

At the end of the week-long exhibit, the *Chicago Record-Herald* ran a front-page cartoon by artist Ralph Wilder lampooning the exhibit's progress narrative about sweatshops. Under the headline "An Exhibit at an Industrial Show of the Future," the cartoon depicted a group of men uniformly dressed in coats and hats heading to work by crowding onto a trolley car on a city street. The trolley exhibit is set on a stage and surrounded by a stunned crowd, and captioned, "Historical Section Exhibit A14. Going to Work—Before the Passage of the Traction Ordinances. A Horrible Example of Insanitary Overcrowding" (1). By showing middle-class men as objects of a historical exhibit, Wilder's cartoon denied those with privilege coevalness, reversed the gender and class dynamics of the industrial exhibit, and revealed the absurdity of its portrayals of sweatshop workers. Singling out sweatshop workers as a remedy to capitalist inequality was unfair, the cartoon suggested, when middle-class men and their work conditions of "insanitary overcrowding" could be called into question in the same way (1). The cartoon further undermined the argument that factories would solve the problems of sweatshop "insanitary overcrowding" by showing that people faced crowded conditions when they left their homes and traveled to work, too (1).

Although electrical workers, sweatshop workers, bakers, and waitresses agreed with the exhibit's directors in seeking to regulate time and space for women's labor, they objected to the directors' means for arguing for better work conditions by representing sweatshops as old-fashioned, dirty, and insanitary. Work stoppages were not pre-planned or coordinated—the electrical workers used the opportune timing of an existing strike to reimagine the purpose of the exhibit, sweatshop workers stopped performing and renovated their tableau displays after they were offended by portrayals of the sweatshop, and the baker refused to allow clubwomen to appropriate the action of the strike. These spontaneous actions altered the exhibit's messages to the public. Electrical workers who refused to connect equipment disrupted the message that manufacturers who purchased this equipment would improve conditions for workers. Sweatshop performers brought into focus that tenement sweatshops did not represent the past of women's labor so much as they functioned as present scenes of work and domestic life. Finally, the baker's refusal to allow clubwomen to pose as waitresses revealed that the clean, modern bakeshop ran well not because it was new, but because skilled women worked there.

LABOR RHETORICS IN EXHIBITION

Labor exhibits around the turn of the twentieth century were spaces where the power to communicate and challenge progress narratives about women's labor and whiteness was distributed, though not evenly or fairly. In Chicago, progress narratives in exhibit form were first promoted at the World's Fair, refashioned afterward and elsewhere to comment on working-class women's relationship to industrial employment. Hull House residents participated in creating these exhibits at their Labor Museum where they reimagined the arts and crafts exhibition to include their women neighbors and challenged women's exclusion from progress narratives that valued men's industrial and city-based labor. Within this challenge to progress narratives, Hull House residents perpetuated colonialist narratives in which they expressed nostalgia for idealized domestic labor taking place prior to both colonization and industrialization.

Hull House residents also participated in making the 1907 Industrial Exhibit, which idealized primitive domestic-based work, critiqued sweatshop work, and elevated factory work for women. That exhibit was novel among exhibits for its representation of tenement-based, sweatshop labor, which complicated the argument that women's labor progressed spatially on a continuum from home to factory. Although women have always worked, the exhibit argued, sweatshop labor was a passé kind of labor that turned homes into workplaces and brought about conditions of exploitation, overcrowding, and the potential to spread disease to both workers and consumers when they purchased sweatshop-made goods. Though manufacturers in the city relied on sweatshops to produce goods, sweatshops were represented at the exhibit as old-fashioned, placed between primitive and modern labor. While organizers curated the exhibit to promote women's factory work under unionized and safer conditions and to highlight the exploitative conditions of sweatshop labor, they put forth a narrative of modernity and progress that denied craft and sweatshop workers temporal equality with the public who came to see their spaces of labor. The exhibit cast those who conducted work from homes and sweatshops as nonwhite, factory workers as white, and entirely excluded Black workers, rendering their labor invisible. This erasure of Black women reflected Chicago reformers' racist idealizing of immigrant women's labor history and dismissal of Black women's labor history. While organizers viewed immigrant women's supposedly preindustrial, domestic-based labor prior to immigrating as fitting neatly within a home-to-workplace narrative, they elided Black women's labor history in their progress narrative and thus forestalled acknowledging a women's labor history connected to slavery and an ideology of white supremacy that continued to shape Chicago's segregated economy.

Across the various labor exhibitions, there were points of convergence among women organizers and women workers whose interests were purportedly represented. The affluent reformers managing and working women performing in the exhibits generally shared goals in seeking higher wages, fewer hours, unionization, and safer workplaces. Yet, their shared gender identity had obvious limits as a basis for labor solidarity. As hooks argues, the basis of solidarity must be a sustained acknowledgement and interrogation of "women's varied and complex social reality," not an insistence on the sameness of experience (44). Reformers speaking for working women and positioning them as representative of a cosmopolitan past was a continuation of Hull House's project of claiming cosmopolitan space and offering that space to immigrants to express their idealized identities as foreign craftspeople. Such a view of neighbors denied their present identities and ability to narrate their own kinds of progress. In exhibitions, working women gestured toward this kind of critique by disrupting reformers' narratives. In the Hull House Labor Museum, performers, museum employees, and visitors used the museum to connect their past and present. Washburne, along with Brosnahan and Sweeney, for example, added historical specificity to stories about women's labor through conversation, and they questioned and debated the value of artifacts. Especially at the Chicago Industrial Exhibit, west side neighbors challenged their place in a progress narrative by physically altering the displays. When Hull House residents participated in setting up tenement displays as representative of an unhygienic past, performers cleaned up. They also used the tactic of the strike to assert the dignity and value of their work. Their strikes drew the public's attention to the dimensions of both chronological and metaphorical time, as workers called the public to notice their exploitation in the contemporary capitalist system that required them to conduct piecework with ever-increasing speed over long hours *and* to the exhibit's rendering of time in which women were modernizing their labor and becoming white. Through these challenges, performers made the space of the exhibit reflect a present in which workers had a voice in public conversations about labor. These disruptions gave rise to ephemeral moments in which all parties recognized an alignment of interests across differences of gender, class, ethnicity, race, and national affiliation.

The 1907 Chicago Industrial Exhibit had an "unexpectedly large attendance" (Commonwealth 357). Because of its popularity, organizers publicly declared plans to turn the exhibit into a permanent museum of labor, but this permanent site never took shape.[7] While it is unclear why a permanent site was never established, the industrial exhibit took place during the final weeks of unprecedented economic growth before an unexpected, nationwide financial panic that would have dampened employers' interest in purchasing new machinery and safety equipment for the factory and consumers' interest in purchasing union-label goods to ensure fair wages for workers. While future exhibits depicting women's labor did not materialize, elite and working-class Chicago women continued to collaborate as well as challenge each other's labor politics. The unexpected popularity of the industrial exhibit, together with continued and widespread economic depression that limited job opportunities, catalyzed the cross-class activism

---

7. McDowell relayed plans for the permanent Exhibit in "Industrial Show to be Permanent" in *The Chicago Tribune*; Breckinridge discussed future plans to make a permanent exhibit with the *Women's Industrial News* in an article titled "Chicago Exhibit."

of the members of the WTUL as they held a simultaneous, multi-city conference in Chicago, New York, and Boston that called together the "women of organized labor" four months after the exhibit's close (Steghagen and Henry 11). Soon after the conference, immigrant women workers took the lead in public demonstrations by using the strike as both spontaneous and planned rhetorical tactic, beginning in New York in 1909 when women garment workers left en masse from their shops to protest low wages, harassment from employers, and a ban on collective bargaining. Women garment workers in Chicago led their own strike the following year, supported by Hull House, the WTUL and other organizations. In the next chapter, I follow women garment workers to the street where allyship was primarily demonstrated through appearing together in stasis or motion, thus extending embodied and performed calls to solidarity glimpsed within the space of the exhibition.

4 Street: Allying Across Differences

> In that long procession of factory workers, each morning and evening, the young walk almost as wearily and listlessly as the old.
>
> —Jane Addams, *The Spirit of Youth in the City Streets*

Labor requires the body in motion. When workers want to signal protest to labor conditions, some move their bodies contrary to the logics of productivity valued by industry. A strike, for example, halts production and creates a visual spectacle of bodies at rest rather than in motion to communicate protest. In this chapter, I examine labor protest signified by bodies in relation to the street, a conduit for moving from one place to another. Addams was adept at understanding what bodies on the street could communicate. In her 1906 speech to the American Woman Suffrage Association, she used the procession as a trope to illustrate how the street offered women literal routes away from the home and gendered labor roles within the family, disrupting social roles and norms. In that speech, Addams featured a procession of women traversing from home to the American Biscuit Company to note that when women entered the factory, they gave up authority over the hours and conditions of their work. By 1909, simultaneous to the beginning of the massive, women-led Shirtwaist Strike in New York City, Addams returned to the trope of the procession, this time describing an even gloomier scene. In *The Spirit of Youth in the City Streets*, she noted that the monotonous and repetitive bodily motions required by the factory now extended to the street, and her concern shifted from gender to age as Addams observed both old and young walking to work. Addams had a near decade-old labor museum in which elders modeled artisan and peasant labor traditions for youth as an alternative to factory labor, yet Addams was pessimistic that young west siders could continue to look to their elders as models who performed fulfilling and artistic labor. By the time she published *Spirit of Youth*, Addams hardly saw distinctions between workers across age. In factory workers' bodily dispositions on the street, Addams remarked that the "young walk almost as wearily and listlessly as the old" (107–08). Industry, she thought, was flattening time and space between generations.

By the fall of 1910, the rest of Chicago's citizens would join Addams in observing how bodies on the street communicated the detrimental effects of factory work. In September, garment workers from across the city began a months-long strike in which they occupied the streets to communicate they could no longer live with unsparing conditions in the garment factory. After the 1907 nationwide recession deflated demand for ready-to-wear clothing, manufacturers had begun pressuring garment workers to produce more for reduced wages (Bae 89). In addition, workers were aggrieved by unpredictable reductions in their pay, unexpected charges for using materials such as needles, threads, and soap, and increased outsourcing and division through the chain of production. By 1910, garment workers were no longer willing to accommodate manufacturers' demands. At this time, the clothing industry was the largest employer in Chicago, and half the employees were women. The strike, begun and led by women workers, ultimately included an estimated forty thousand strikers who first ceased work in the factory and then united in walkouts and marches on the street ("Garment Workers"). By focusing here on walkouts and marches as instances of embodied and mobile labor rhetoric, I aim to reveal these labor rhetorical traditions as regendered when women workers led them.

In early twentieth century Chicago, women moving their bodies outside the home and through the streets could challenge divisions of labor on an everyday basis. For example, a common term for a woman sex worker, a streetwalker, is a pejorative intended to discipline the idea of a woman on the move. A woman moving through the streets was both a dangerous figure and considered in danger when she traversed boundaries, upended normative sexual relations, and labored outside the official economy. Chicago in the early twentieth century was the epicenter of a moral panic over "white slavery," which named a supposed scenario in which white girls from the country were coerced into prostitution when they arrived in the city.[1] The white slavery panic revealed not only widespread fear about women challenging the official economy and moral norms by selling sex, but about the value of whiteness itself, in danger of commodification from sex traffickers who had no interest in protecting whiteness if instead they could profit from it. These sexist, racist, and classist fears about women's appearance on the street made women garment workers' early 1900s street protests all the more meaningful. When women claimed the right to move on the street in ways that did not produce value for someone else, they challenged the streets'

---

1. Communications scholar Leslie J. Harris explores the rhetorical and mobile dimensions of the white slavery controversy in her article, "Rhetorical Mobilities and the City: The White Slavery Controversy and Racialized Protection of Women in the U.S."

meaning as an economic distribution channel that moved people and goods and reasserted the right to negotiate the value of their labor.

By taking up the concern of meaning-making during collective, embodied labor protest, this chapter prioritizes the stories of workers and subordinates the stories of Hull House residents. In addition, in analyzing collective mobile action, I go beyond a focus on women and toward an account of workers across gender lines coming together in pursuit of more inclusive labor rhetorics. Judith Butler, in discussing the connections between her work that theorizes gender with her study of alliances, argues alliance requires recognizing that rights for any particular group, such as women, needs to be tied to a broader struggle for justice, even when alliances among groups are difficult to make and maintain (70). What brings groups together across differences, Butler argues, is a shared condition of precarity that transcends identity markers. During moments of street protest, participants in the Chicago garment strike who joined walkouts, pickets and marches demonstrated alliance by coming together across multiple, intersecting differences. Male garment workers, reformers, and members of the public joined female garment workers, demonstrating alliance across differences through visual and aural cues. In the multigenerational and multilinguistic garment industry, these differences exceeded gender, ethnicity and class to include age, skill level, language, and varying degrees of literacy across modes.

Alliance is a common term used in contemporary social movements to refer to individuals or groups who come together for a time to support another group facing discrimination or crisis. Alliances are premised on the need for union despite differences existing between the people involved. In analyzing the rhetoric of coalition building, Karma Chávez prefers the term coalition over alliance. Coalition, Chávez argues, does the similar work of describing a temporary union, but does not have alliance's entanglements with the discourses of national sovereignty, and in its earliest usage, with heterosexual marriage (154). I stick with alliance here because its associations with national identity and heterosexual constructs are also part of the baggage of the street, a privileged site for (white, male) citizens. While allies might recognize themselves as part of a broader struggle, allying does not necessarily redistribute or share the power concentrated in whiteness, masculinity, or citizenship.

Before discussing the broader alliances that formed on the street, I highlight the actions of women workers who led the strike and to whom others were lending support. Women garment workers sparked the months-long strike by walking out of garment factories in Pilsen. In leading the walkout, women claimed authority to use the forms and traditions that had developed in male-dominated labor organizing for generations. After discussing the walkout, I then explore Hull House residents' material and rhetorical support as crucial to sustaining the strike and Hull House as a necessary and stable gathering space that served as a foil to the ephemeral motion of the streets. Finally, I turn to recovering the mobile alliance of thousands of garment workers who came together for a march through the streets of Chicago. Throughout the months-long Chicago Garment Workers Strike, varying combinations of garment workers and their allies participated in the labor rhetorical traditions of the walkout, picket, and march, using their bodies to make visual and aural appeals to others to notice them disrupting conventional meanings of the street.

Women Walking Out

Though women garment workers in New York and Philadelphia led strikes the year prior in their respective cities, it was not until 1910 that women in the Chicago garment industry sparked a massive and months-long labor protest. For manufacturers and union leaders in Chicago, it was unthinkable that unorganized women garment workers could lead an industry-wide strike until they were in the process of doing so. Factory owners lacked the imagination to anticipate a women-led strike in part due to their absence from their own factories and disinterest in talking to workers about labor conditions. Meanwhile, local and national leaders of the United Garment Workers (UGW) were unprepared to lead a strike led by inexperienced women workers and failed to understand the breadth of workers' grievances. Rather than formal, verbal deliberation between manufacturers and unions, the strike began with direct action in which women walked out, amassing on the street to communicate their grievances and to invite fellow workers to join them.

On September 22, 1910, eighteen-year old Hannah Shapiro and sixteen fellow women workers walked out of a garment factory and into the street, sparking the citywide strike. Shapiro, the instigator of the walkout, was a Jewish immigrant from Ukraine who worked in shop number five of the clothing firm Hart, Schaffner & Marx (HSM). She was joined in starting the walkout by Bessie Abramowitz, a twenty-one-year-old Russian-Jewish immigrant who would later co-found the Amalgamated Clothing Workers of America with her spouse Sidney Hillman. Shapiro's and Abramowitz's roles in the walkout were not fully known until more recent historiographic research placed them at the scene. Historian Rebecca Sive-Tomashefsky recovered Shapiro's part in the walkout in 1978 when she interviewed Shapiro. Shapiro recalled that she was motivated to walk out after the managers in her factory cut the pay rate for piecework. Shapiro brought the issue to the attention of her supervisor, but he refused to reverse the pay cut. A few days later, Shapiro led the walkout. Historian Karen Pastorello identified Abramowitz, employed at HSM under a pseudonym because she had been blacklisted for prior organizing efforts, as one of the women who walked out with Shapiro that day (23–24). Sive-Tomashefsky argued that Shapiro never received the attention from historians that Abramowitz did for her role in garment strikes because she never pivoted to using the modes of writing or speaking in her labor organizing efforts. Sive-Tomashefsky's claim highlights historiographers' broader privileging of written labor rhetorics, which can persist on their own while evidence of more ephemeral mobile labor rhetorics remain only when documented through written and verbal accounts and photographs (938).

This is not to say that mobile labor rhetorics do not have material effects. Extradiscursive rhetorics communicated through actions like a walkout, Triece has argued, are effective in part because workers' absence from the workplace has material consequences for employers. When Shapiro's verbal complaint was ignored, she created a spectacle that gained the attention of her employers and halted the factory's production. By stopping production, walkout participants disrupted the factory owners' understanding of the workplace they had created. Factory owners Harry and Max Hart had thought of their factories as modern and progressive and were proud their factories were not sweatshops. They were one of the first manufacturers to end the practice of subcontracting to tenement-based manufacturers by bringing all of their workers into "large, clean, and well lighted" factories (Hart 137). Factory owners like the Harts could proceed with this understanding of their shops as modern only because they were not present in them on a day-to-day basis. Though all stages of the garment making process were done in house at HSM, shop managers had recreated the practices of the sweatshop by continuing to promise retailers garments at impossibly low rates and pushing their employees to work harder and faster. After Shapiro, Abramowitz, and fellow strikers walked out, the Harts could no longer hold onto the fiction that their shops were model workplaces.

Just as spoken rhetoric had limits for gaining the attention of shop managers and owners, it too had limits for enlisting the support of fellow garment workers in bids for change. Under the best of circumstances, building alliances with fellow workers through talk usually requires long-term planning and opportunities to engage in spaces outside the workplace. The contemporary Laborers' International Union of North America, for example, recommends one-on-one conversations with colleagues to build solidarity, but outside of work time and off company property to follow labor laws and to avoid tipping off management who may overhear plans (11). Nor is writing always an alternative. Today, writing that could reach all in a workplace is often mediated by platforms and technologies owned and controlled by employers. When seeking private channels, organizers may find generational divides in literacy and access surrounding social media platforms, email, or text messaging. Writing, then, presents barriers to access and understanding and can be even riskier than speaking, as it is easier for writing to endure and circulate out of the control of workers and into the hands of their employers.

The use of spoken and written labor rhetorics, in addition, require that employees share a common language, and Chicago garment factory workers did not always share one. By 1910, the garment industry in Chicago employed approximately 38,000 garment workers from Italian, Russian Jewish, Polish Catholic, and Bohemian backgrounds (Weiler 239). In an oral history, fellow HSM employee Jacob Potofsky recalled a scene that evoked the diversity of employees under one roof. Potofsky remembered "working right next to a girl who was a Bohemian girl, on one side; on the other side was a Polish girl; and opposite me was a girl working on a button hole machine. She was a Jewish girl. And again on the other side of me was an Italian. So we were a veritable United Nations" (4). In the HSM factories, the most inexperienced immigrant workers, often newly in the US, were not separated by national affiliation and language as they had been in tenements. A nationally diverse and polyglot workforce, though, was not only reflective of immigration patterns at this time. Some factory owners sought employees who did not share nationalities and languages because it helped them suppress wages and labor organizing efforts. Clara Masilotti, a walkout participant who later became a leader in the WTUL, recalled her boss describing this employment strategy by saying, "these greenhorns, Italian people, Jewish people, all nationalities, they cannot speak English and they don't know where to go and they just come from the old country and I let them work here, like the devil, and those I get for less wages" (Coman 425). Mobile and embodied labor rhetorics constituted a way of showing solidarity that could overcome the obstacles to communication imposed by this management strategy. By walking out of the factory, Shapiro and Abramowitz found an effective alternative to speaking or writing to communicate with fellow employees who did not share a common language and pushed back against employers' exploitation of workers' diverse backgrounds.

Shapiro's account of shop conditions motivating the walkout corroborated Potofsky's recollection that HSM employees had immigrated from diverse places and spoke several different languages. Her account also invites reconsideration of Addams's claim that industry flattened differences between young and old; for Shapiro, there were nuanced generational differences in workers' labor politics. Young women HSM employees, like the young, Irish American women workers in the 1890s I discussed in chapter one, were willing to risk more than older workers because they were not married and did not have nuclear families to support. Shapiro recalled that older and married workers were not willing to join the walkout because they had more to lose and were willing to take pay cuts (937). Yet, older workers and those who remained in shop number five and other HSM shops revealed their sympathy by refusing to take up the work left by the strikers. In her oral history account Shapiro remained critical of the older workers' refusal to walk out with her. They were, in Shapiro's words, "like glue" (938). Yet their refusal to move became an asset after the walkout disrupted the movement of garments through the factory's chain of production and older workers contributed to the work stoppage by refusing additional work from within the factory. The walkout offers a kind of rebuttal to Addams's version of procession. During the walkout, younger workers are on the move, reimagining new possibilities for their labor, and older workers are reacting and following the lead of the young.

Butler reminds us that for an appearance on the street to carry political significance, it "has to be registered by the senses, not only our own, but someone else's. If we appear, we must be seen, which means that our bodies must be viewed and their vocalized sounds must be heard: the body must enter the visual and audible field" (86). After Shapiro and her fellow workers left shop number five, they were indeed seen and heard, joined on the street by two thousand other strikers, many of whom were women from nearby garment shops. In the summer of 2022 I visited the site of shop number five in the Pilsen neighborhood to better understand how the spaces of the street and factory played a role in the walkout. Before visiting, I struggled to understand how the strikers had drawn the necessary attention to themselves to gain the large number of strikers who followed them to the street. I pushed my two-year-old daughter in a stroller down Halsted Street on a summer weekday morning looking at the old factory buildings with the same addresses they had had since 1910. Standing on an empty sidewalk next to a street with minimal traffic, I could see that this section of Halsted Street had never been the site of people's homes, nor would it be used for residences in the future. The only other people I encountered were construction workers retrofitting the factories into office and gallery spaces, the neighborhood now more unfit for housing because of the nearby major interstate highway created when the tenement district I have discussed throughout this book was bulldozed in the 1960s. The factory building that housed shop number five at 1922 South Halsted has been torn down, but its location is marked with an unassuming plaque now mostly graffitied over. The warehouse buildings next to the empty lot are now populated by art galleries. After standing on Halsted Street, I better understood that garment workers in the factories had good sightlines to the street because of the loft buildings' large windows. I thought back to the Hull House Labor Museum's design. There, the large windows allowed people on the street to look in. Here, on Halsted Street, the large windows, designed to let light in to make garment making possible, allowed people in the buildings look out. In 1910, these windows had helped workers in other factories see the walkout developing below.

In East Pilsen, many workers would have understood what to do upon seeing the walkout developing. Garment workers, brewers, lumber shovers, carpenters, tractor assemblers, railroad workers, and meat cutters all labored in Pilsen, transforming the water, wood, food, and other raw materials into industrial products. The whole neighborhood occupied less than two square miles and was cordoned off from the rest of the city: to the west were cattle stockyards; to the south and the east, the Chicago River framed the neighborhood; and on the north side, a raised rail line bounded Pilsen from Hull House's immediate neighborhood. This diverse population of industrial workers sharing a small space made Pilsen a pressure cooker for labor unrest. Pilsen's raised rail line, for example, had been the site of the Battle of the Halsted Street Viaduct, one of the biggest street fights in American labor history. There, in 1877, thirty strikers were killed and one hundred wounded while participating in the same nationwide railroad strike that union organizer Mary Kenney had witnessed from her hometown in Missouri. Pilsen's McCormick Reaper Works, the massive farm equipment production company, was the site of the walkout and march that preceded the deadly 1886 Haymarket Strikes. Shapiro and Abramowitz's walkout, a seemingly spontaneous expression of protest, gained traction because their neighbors shared a long history of local labor conventions.

Their shared conventions extended beyond the visual and into the aural mode. Strikers from shop number five also used sound to gain the attention of fellow workers at other factories. They blew whistles. The whistle is a conventional signal, for example, in transportation contexts, and can be heard above street noise and alerts one to know someone or something is on the move. It was conventional, too, in the factory setting because it carried over the din of loud machines to let workers know when to start and stop work.[2] Strikers appropriated the use of the whistle in both transportation

---

2. The shops were loud. The opening lines of Morris Rosenfeld's poem "In the Factory" captures his experience of the sound: Oh, here in the shop the machines roar so wildly, / That oft, unaware that I am, or have been" (7).

and factory contexts to hail others to join them. Describing her first walkout in 1898, glovemaker and WTUL president Agnes Nestor remembered that upon hearing the whistle signaling workers should return to their sewing stations after lunch, the glovemakers left the building instead (32). Garment worker Masilotti remembered anticipating hearing the whistle during the 1910 garment workers' walkout. She taught her fellow workers what to do: "the first whistle we hear in the window that means for us to strike. You cannot work for twelve cents a coat, and I cannot baste thirty-five coats in a day, and we will all go on a strike" (Coman 427). The whistle—arhythmic, atonal, attention getting, loud—signaled a labor protest across languages.

As Shapiro and Abramowitz sewed seams into pants in shop number five, they were part of an unprecedented number of industrially employed women in the US. Driven in part by technological changes allowing industry to produce more goods under theories of scientific management, the number of employed women had doubled between 1890 and 1910, reaching over eight million nationally (Foner 222). By walking out, Shapiro, Abramowitz, and two thousand other women were updating gendered possibilities for labor protest.

Their walkout, initially enlisting two thousand, sparked a much larger and longer strike. By the end of September, forty thousand garment workers from across the city were on strike. In the next section, I turn to exploring how news of the strike circulated beyond Pilsen. In a poem about Pilsen titled "Blue Island Intersection," Carl Sandburg begins, "six street ends come together here. They feed people and wagons into the center" (37). Sandburg positioned the street as the subject of his sentences, an actor who moved people and goods. It is accurate—poetically and geographically—to understand Sandburg as saying the streets move people and wagons into the center of Pilsen. It is also the case that Pilsen's streets moved people and wagons beyond the neighborhood and into a different center, Chicago's center. As people and product moved into the center of the city, so too did word of the strike.

Settlement Allies

The street as the conduit by which news of the strike traveled, though, is partial explanation, and my account of how women communicated and circulated labor rhetorics during the garment strike would be incomplete if relegated to analysis of bodies in motion on the streets of Pilsen. While the walkout demonstrated that strikers could use visual and aural cues to communicate labor rhetorics to others on or near the street in real time, these spontaneous, embodied labor rhetorics were no match to the modes of speech and writing necessary in coordinating the resources needed to sustain the ongoing, collective labor actions that happened at massive, citywide scales or the negotiations between stakeholders that would eventually end the strike. Typically, union leaders coordinate through speech and writing; however, during the first weeks of the garment strike the labor leaders from the UGW, who had the material and rhetorical capacity to do so, were reluctant to negotiate on behalf of workers. They stalled in part because the women workers leading the strike were unorganized, and the union leaders who became involved were reluctant to fully support women who were also the most inexperienced workers in their bid to join unions. Six weeks after the initial walkout, the *Chicago Evening Post* reported the following on the involvement of the UGW and its president Rickert: "men who had investigated and acted as arbitrators in many strikes declared, after surveying the situation, that the strike was the strangest and most intangible affair in their experience. It had come into existence almost in spite of the union, which tried to check it for a week and has not yet succeeded in assembling its organizers" ("Garment Workers"). To union leaders, the strike was incomprehensible. Left unspoken in this quotation are the gendered and hierarchical reasons why. Rickert and his colleagues were disturbed they were not the ones leading the strike and they were not interested in working with women leaders. They also did not want to invite purportedly unskilled workers into the union.

In the absence of union support for women and unskilled workers, Hull House and its residents allied with strikers. The two founders led the effort. Addams offered strikers space in Hull House for planning and deliberation. She also attempted to settle the strike by negotiating an in-person meeting between HSM owners and Rickert, and serving as mediator. Starr, meanwhile, joined strikers on the street and publicized instances in which police abused strikers by speaking to newspaper reporters. Strikers eventually found robust support through a diverse coalition that included not only Hull House, but the UGW, the WTUL, the Chicago Federation of Labor, churches, suffrage organizations, women's clubs, and private citizens. This coalition was crucial to strikers' ability to continue withholding their labor through the winter without the wages that allowed them to purchase food, clothing, and shelter. A joint strike conference board eventually funded the lengthy strike through a fund that offset strikers' lost wages ("Labor Protests" 4).

Hull House, though, was able to support strikers' material needs in unique ways. First, Hull House was nearby. It was geographically central to strike activity. Crucially, residents had the infrastructure that could support spontaneous mass gatherings to gender-integrated crowds and had relationships with west side workers who counted on Hull House to offer space and resources. Early in the strike, Addams provided Hull House as an assembly space where garment workers could meet and plan. Potofsky remembered 500–600 people meeting in Hull House a few days after the walkout (4). After the meeting, he convinced his own HSM shop to join the strike. Potofsky does not mention where in Hull House they met, but by this time Hull House had several large assembly spaces. One of its largest, Bowen Hall, could hold 750 people (*Twenty Years* 431). This early meeting of several hundred garment workers was crucial to their ability to circulate word of the strike across the city. Twenty years after its founding, Hull House remained the gender inclusive alternative to the union hall.

Women philanthropists closely associated with Hull House acted quickly and made gender-based appeals to fundraise on behalf of strikers. Mrs. Joseph T. Bowen, for whom the large assembly hall had been named, spearheaded a milk fund for babies with Ellen Henrotin. Bowen argued that no matter how citizens felt about the strike, "surely we can agree that the children should be fed" ("5,000 Babies" 2). This appeal was savvy because it allowed potential donors to sympathize and give funds regardless of whether they personally sympathized with strikers, but it appealed by reinforcing a traditional gender role for women foremost as mothers rather than as workers. It also positioned Bowen, Henrotin, and the Hull House residents as seemingly neutral in the disagreement between labor and capital, but supportive of families and children. Bowen's and Henrotin's effort to support strikers while claiming an air of neutrality was a possible position for well-to-do women who were not asked to account for their own sources of wealth or participation in capitalist exploitation. In her discussion of sisterhood and the failures of the feminist movement to confront differences, bell hooks offers vocabulary to describe Hull House's version of alliance. Distinguishing between solidarity and support, hooks writes that support "can be given and just as easily withdrawn" (67). This comment synthesizes hooks's discussion of instances when bourgeois women offer monetary support to working-class and poor women. Through such gestures, hooks writes, a bourgeois woman is "not repudiating class privilege—she is exercising it" (60). Addams, Bowen, and Henrotin were responding to the circumstances of the strike and fulfilling the immediate needs of women strikers. They were supportive. Theirs were resources they could have withdrawn at any time, though they did not. At its core, though, the garment strike was a call for the redistribution of wealth, and Addams, Bowen and Henrotin were not supporting the larger purpose or risking their own status and property interests. As acts that communicated differences among women, their offering of space and funds reasserted their class differences rather than rebuke them and highlighted the need for the strike in the first place.

By October of 1910, Hull House's support extended to visiting strikers in their own homes to learn more about their demands. Sophonisba Breckinridge, for example, drew from the labor rhetorical strategies for gathering and circulating information that had developed at Hull House through many years of investigating labor conditions through canvassing and interviewing methods. Breckinridge was the resident who had carried forward Florence Kelley's legacy of gathering statistics about labor and housing to make public arguments. She used these methods to gather information about garment factory conditions across the city. In October of 1910, organizational leaders supporting the strike formed an independent citizens committee to investigate the strike. Breckinridge headed a subcommittee tasked with understanding strikers' grievances and authored the report that articulated those grievances to stakeholders. Her committee's report was comprehensive and included interviews with employees from seventeen different clothing firms and thirty-one of HSM's forty-nine shops (3). In the report, Breckinridge explained strikers were most aggrieved about fines and wage deductions for lost or damaged spools, bobbins and needles. More generally, she found that strikers were troubled by employers who were increasing the speed and complexity of their work without offering additional compensation (4–5). Breckinridge's data collection and findings were important for countering UGW leaders' sentiments that the strike's goals were strange and intangible.

In early November, Addams played her familiar role as seemingly neutral negotiator between labor and management. Since first inviting women to unionize at Hull House in 1891, Addams had secured a reputation as a labor arbitrator and had participated in the infamous 1894 Pullman Strike and a 1905 Teamsters' strike (*Twenty Years* 129; 133). Now, Addams attempted to secure an agreement between Harry Hart and Rickert to end the strike. The agreement would have welcomed all employees back to the factory and set up a committee to address their concerns. Yet, because HSM owners would not agree to allow all workers to join a union, workers angrily rejected the deal. While Addams's deal did not secure workers' interest in joining unions, she at least forestalled Rickert's eventual mishandling of the strike. In February 1911, Rickert called off the strike without consulting workers or any of the organizations involved. In the final negotiation, HSM employees were welcomed back, but the thousands of employees working at other firms, who had joined the strike over the prior months, received no promise of similar welcome.

The two Hull House founders—Addams and Starr—worked across a diverse repertoire of oral, written, and visual modes in support of strikers. To further evaluate the founders' allyship, I locate them where they delivered their labor rhetorics. Their proximity or distance from the street often served as a proxy for the metaphorical relation between their own gendered, classed, raced, and aged bodies and those of the garment workers they were supporting. Through all of Addams's involvement in the strike, she did not publicly join strikers on the street. Whereas walkout participants communicated alliance by sharing the same space of the street through bodily presence, Addams remained absent from the street and relied on spoken labor rhetorics to negotiate. The meaning of her absence, though, is complicated. Addams certainly avoided taking the bodily risk involved in occupying the street, yet, as Butler argues, "not everyone can appear in a bodily form, and many of those who cannot appear, who are constrained from appearing or who operate through virtual or digital networks, are also part of 'the people,' defined precisely by being constrained from making a specific bodily appearance in public space" (8). Addams, throughout the first crucial months of the strike, was dealing with serious and painful dental complications in the fall and winter of 1910 that limited her mobility and ability to appear in public. In November, Addams wrote to her partner Mary Rozet Smith that she was staying away from Hull House and remaining on the north side of the city to be near medical care while her wound from a dental procedure required daily dressing. She explained she was "sorry and ashamed to be so far out of the strike," but did not want to risk coming back to Hull House "while Halsted St is being repaved," presumably because the repaving project would make it more difficult to travel in and out of the neighborhood for medical care. Though impossible to know whether Addams would have joined strikers on the street under different circumstances, her case reminds us that a condition of appearance in the street is a healthy, mobile body, and during the garment strike, the placement of healthy, mobile bodies on the street rather than in the factory was the visual evidence strikers were withholding their labor. In her negotiations, Addams relied on Breckinridge's first-hand interviews with strikers about their grievances instead of her own observations from the street. Addams, despite her illness, was networked with the street through asynchronous communication.

It was Hull House co-founder Starr who appeared on the street with strikers when garment manufacturers began hiring police to disperse crowds. There, Starr and the residents Rachel Yarros, Anna Wilmarth Thompson, and Laura Dainty Pelham used their privilege and relative fame in the city to protect strikers. Starr became a public face of the strike picket. In contemporary labor discourse, a strike picket is a term that refers to a group of people whose bodily presence dissuades others —other workers, or patrons—from entering a place of business. It is a term with militarist roots, as it refers to a guard out front, someone who watches from a stationary position in readiness of attack ("picket"). On the street, Starr's presence was a demonstration of allyship, but she did not move. Her stationary role set her apart from ordinary strikers, and in her stasis Starr's privilege remained visible even while she took the risk of appearing on the street.

In her verbal remarks, Starr, too, simultaneously defended strikers while highlighting her privilege. The *Chicago Daily Tribune* published a letter from Starr in which she described how the police and a group of men prevented her from picketing. Starr recounted that an officer told her to cease picketing or risk arrest. She wrote that he was "insolent and brutal and absolutely outside his rights, as I was entirely within mine" ("Men Fight" 3). When police asked Starr who she was, she responded that she was a "citizen of the United States;" a "settlement worker;" and a "descendent of a revolutionary soldier, an American from 1632" (3). These three identity claims that supported her right to appear on the street were ones many strikers could not similarly claim. "Citizen" set her apart from many immigrant strikers, especially immigrant women who lacked sufficient motive to apply for US citizenship while unable to vote. Through "settlement worker," Starr at least identified herself as a worker, but the title gave her an authority over the street distinct from the average striker (3). As Hull House cofounder with Addams, Starr had not only claimed a right to be on the street, but to remake it. In 1892, Addams had argued for the value of settlement houses by enumerating the problems of the street, writing, "the streets are inexpressibly dirty, the number of schools inadequate, sanitary legislation unenforced, the street lighting bad, the paving miserable and altogether lacking in the alleys and smaller streets, and the stables defy all laws of sanitation. Hundreds of houses are unconnected with the street sewer" (29). This list not only captures the overwhelming experience of the street in sight, sound, and smell, but articulates the exigence for creating a settlement house as a space to make arguments, raise money, and put women in position of power to enforce street paving, install streetlights, ensure regular garbage collection, and connect toilets to sewer lines. Starr had participated in enforcing, surveilling, and inspecting the streets along with other residents for twenty years to make it a cleaner, safer place. Finally, in claiming an identity as a "descendent of a revolutionary soldier, an American from 1632" Starr seemed to be referencing two different ancestors in each clause: William Starr who fought in the Revolutionary War, and Comfort Starr, co-founder of Harvard who was her first ancestor in the US. Together, her lineage provided evidence of her deep family history of protesting injustice. It also implied her whiteness without overtly mentioning race. Whiteness was a key privilege, valuable and thus protected on the streets. Shapiro, Abramowitz and their fellow shop employees at HSM were not US born, English was not their first language, and, as Jews, their whiteness was not a given. Without civic, racial, and linguistic privileges, the bodily mode of communication was effective though risky. When Starr challenged police on the street, she engaged in an act of protest that average strikers could not risk. In visual, spoken, and written formats, Starr extended her privilege to ally with strikers, but nevertheless claimed her right to occupy the street through privileges that others could not claim.

Overall, Starr and the others working from Hull House embodied a sense of allyship in which members of privileged groups extend their privilege, at least for a time, to others under duress. Bowen and Henrotin managed the milk fund that helped garment workers sustain their strike for several months. Addams gave strikers free use of the settlement and used her connections and reputation to broker a negotiation between the manufacturer and the union that ultimately did not succeed. Starr risked her own bodily safety and used her privilege to publicize the cause of strikers through newspapers. No other organizational allies were able to respond as quickly and thoroughly as Hull House, yet residents' acts of support had limits as acts of solidarity. These limits are highlighted in their absence from collective, mobile alliance on the street, a space where individuals' identities were subordinated and the collective was elevated. Hull House founders and supporters, in contrast, sought to assert change as individuals and their efforts highlighted their individuality and privileges of class and whiteness. In the next section I examine the rhetorical dimensions of mobile labor rhetorics, which settlement workers could not or would not participate in. By moving together, garment workers demonstrated their alliance across multiple categories of difference.

Mobile Allies

To theorize the different rhetorical modes necessary to create alliances, Gloria Anzaldúa acknowledged that speaking and writing are both necessary to do things such as set ground rules, create a meta language to discuss alliance, and establish participant roles. During the garment strike, speech was helpful for circulating news of the strike across the city and planning large scale actions with thousands of participants. Addams, Starr, and their fellow residents, too, demonstrated how speech and writing could pointedly name grievances and make demands in ways that visual, embodied, and mobile rhetorics could not. But, Anzaldúa writes, a "symbolic behavior performance" can go deeper because "ritual consecrates the alliance" (229). For the garment workers, walkouts and marches established alliance by making use of space, movement, and proximity among participants who connected, associated, got close. These embodied performances allowed participants to demonstrate their willingness to risk bodily safety and connect to a longer history of ritual in which others moved in similar ways.

By December 1910, strikers consecrated their alliance with a march. By this time, they had not received pay for more than three months, Chicago was becoming bitterly cold, and there had been frequent violent clashes between strikers and police. Despite these serious challenges, garment workers came together across differences to show unity toward the goals of creating better working conditions for all through an agreement that would allow them to unionize and force manufacturers to hire unionized employees. Manufacturers refused to agree to these demands and the Chicago Mayor Fred Busse began to issue calls to end the strike ("Plea" 3). On December 7, at least twenty thousand and possibly as many as fifty thousand strikers gathered on the street for a labor march that culminated in a rally.[3] This march showcased the street as a space for ritualized movements that signaled workers' alliance, appealed to the public to side with labor instead of capital, and challenged the involvement of the state as embodied by the police who had repeatedly attacked strikers.

The December garment march began on Jackson Street between Ashland and Halsted. By lining up along Jackson Street, an east-west thoroughfare within Chicago's grid, strikers made use of the long sightlines of the street to demonstrate their numbers. Newspaper photographers circulated images of strikers. Strikers are pictured wearing winter outerwear: women are wearing long, fitted coats with puffed sleeves over skirts and men are wearing looser, formal overcoats.[4] Their differing clothing styles helped demonstrate alliance across gender differences. That strikers were wearing coats in winter would be unremarkable on the everyday street and was perhaps unremarkable to individual strikers, but I think it is worth noting what coats communicated in this instance because the strikers were the people creating these garments and the conditions under which they were creat-

---

[3]. The *Chicago Daily Socialist* reported the march included forty thousand garment workers and ten thousand supporters ("Police Told" 1). Articles in *The Chicago Daily Tribune* and *The Chicago Inter Ocean* estimated the number of marchers was closer to twenty thousand ("Strikers Parade" 3; "20,000 Strikers" 3).

[4]. Photographs of marchers appeared in *The Chicago Daily Tribune*'s "Strikers Parade to Show Number," and *The Chicago Inter Ocean*'s "20,000 Strikers in West Side Parade."

ing was the subject of the strike. Reporters, on the street alongside strikers, certainly took marchers' clothing as evidence of their poverty ("20,000 Strikers" 3; "Strikers Parade" 3). Because it was so cold, reporters noted the material of some strikers' garments was thin, and some men marched without overcoats. While reporters overlooked the gendered dimension of the garments as commonplace, the gender-specific garment styles were overt and thus effective in making a visual spectacle of gendered alliance in black-and-white newspaper photographs. These same photographs, for example, did not capture strikers' stylistic choices to create visual unity through wearing red "ribbons, sashes, and neckties" to signal their revolutionary intent, though these choices would have been apparent in person ("Strikers Parade" 3). Demonstrating alliance across gender lines was important because the trade was gender-integrated and the participation of both women and men signaled collective opposition to employers. This gender integration was also important as a response to the UGW's initial and continued resistance to allying with unorganized women workers.

Garment workers began their march along Jackson Street where many of the garment factories were located. One obvious route for the march would have been to move east on Jackson Street toward the downtown, passing by more garment factories and disrupting the commerce on a thoroughfare that connected the garment workshops west of the river to the downtown offices of the clothing firms east of the river. Such a march would have reimagined Addams's procession of west side workers who crossed the river daily to work in factories and demonstrated workers taking back control over their time and conditions of labor from employers. Earlier in the strike, in November, strikers had requested the city allow them to march east, but Busse declined their request. When strikers tried to march east into the downtown commercial district anyway, police used the geography of Chicago's downtown, which is cordoned off by the Chicago River, against the strikers and blockaded the bridges where they would have needed to cross ("Strikers Barred" 1). For this December march, strikers were again denied a permit to enter the downtown, inspiring at least one striker to create a banner that read, "We are allowed to slave in the loop, but not parade" ("20,000 Strikers" 3).

When permits for labor marches are denied by the state, strikers may occupy the street under the guise of other actions that feature bodies on the move. A common revision to the march is to emphasize its celebratory function and turn it into a parade. Labor parades have been taking place since at least 1882, when working men called a one-day strike and parade in New York and risked losing their jobs because when parading they revealed their identities as strikers. Slowly, the labor parade became appropriated by the state. In 1894, President Grover Cleveland declared Labor Day a national holiday, and the parade became a state-sanctioned form of street movement. Another kind of street movement strikers may organize around is the funeral procession. The Haymarket rally was technically a funeral procession, organized in response to police killing a picketing striker. So, too, was the December 1910 garment strikers' march. The day before this march, several thousand workers had attended the funeral and procession for Charles Lazinskas, a garment worker who had been killed by a police officer. As a funeral procession, the December march appealed to the public for support against police brutality. Photos show strikers holding signs that both mourn Lazinskas and demand better working conditions.

Both Haymarket and the 1910 Garment Workers Strike started at industries in Pilsen, but found their public expression miles north on the streets of Chicago's west side. Taking place decades earlier, the Haymarket incident had begun as a march on the McCormick Reaper Works and ended in a rally in Haymarket square, eventually spiraling into a deadly riot. Unlike the Haymarket rally, the December 1910 garment march did not end in violence. When garment marchers paraded west rather than east toward downtown, they made the march less about challenging manufacturers and police, and more about calling for support from immigrant communities. From Jackson Street, marchers headed south and west toward the West Side Grounds National League Baseball Park, where the Chicago Cubs played. By moving west instead of east, the marchers moved through different neighborhood enclaves of the immigrant communities employed by the garment industries. In so doing, it was a march in which collective bodily movement challenged the claims to the street Starr had made based on her social status, whiteness, citizenship, and family history. Many strikers did not share these identities with Starr, yet claimed the street for themselves and their communities, nonetheless. In a comparative study of garment protests in London and Chicago, historian Ruth Percy makes the point that several of the Chicago garment strikers' marches in the fall and winter of 1910 started outside the garment shops and then wound through immigrant neighborhoods, becoming opportunities to build community (475). Her analysis focuses, for example, on a November march when five thousand Bohemian and Polish strikers walked through the streets of Pilsen, which had sizeable Bohemian and Polish communities at this time. While smaller marches like this one built support for particular ethnic communities, the December march was unique in its size and the diversity of participants. Marchers shed new light on the cosmopolitan character of the economy, revealing that the world market required the cooperation of nationally diverse people, but also that those same people understood the value of their labor and could stop production and consumption with a strike. The coming together of a cosmopolitan alliance of workers was also key to speaking back to the ways garment industry employers had used their linguistic differences against them. The power of the march to communicate alliance across national and linguistic difference was brought into relief at the end of the march during the rally at the baseball park. There, differences of language constrained communication once again as the crowd broke up into smaller groups by shop and language, and speakers addressed them in English, Polish, Italian, Bohemian, and Lithuanian. This atomizing of the marchers once again highlights the limits of oratory to bring workers together and the power of the nonverbal, bodily action of moving together to invite broader alliance.

When marching through the west side of the city, strikers not only built immigrant community support, but also challenged their neighbors' rote participation in using the street as a site of distribution and exchange. West side streets—conduits for people and goods moving from one place to another—were also spaces for buying and selling. In her oral history account of living on Chicago's west side, artist and teacher Sadie Garland Dreikurs offered insight into the street as a site of exchange. Recalling the early 1900s, Dreikurs recalled "hawkers all down the street. It wasn't a market but you lived a market life more or less because you bought everything from a truck . . . . It was colorful. The horses, the wagons and all the activities of the street" (12). Sellers brought milk, ice, peanuts, vegetables and more into the neighborhood on a truck bed. So significant was the buying and selling of items on the street that Dreikurs called west side living a "market life," a phrase that captures the centrality of exchange on the street to shaping the rituals, routines and rhythms that made life, in the words of the artist Dreikurs, "colorful" (12). Dreikurs's account of the street as the location of exchange for so many on the west side is crucial context for how a march offered neighborhood people a glimpse at a different way of using the street. Through marching, strikers temporarily halted their exchange activities that kept the industrial economy churning and offered their fellow Chicagoans evidence that alternatives were possible.

During the December 1910 march, strikers undertook complicated rhetorical work: They combined a funeral procession with a protest march, revisited the geographies of labor in the city that gave meaning to their action, replayed some but not all of the movements of Haymarket strikers, and traversed through immigrant enclaves to hail support from communities. Their garments, combined with their unified movement, signaled alliance across gendered differences. Meanwhile, their route through Chicago's west side acknowledged the diverse ethnic identities of the marchers. The march was different from a walkout or picket, actions through which it is possible to identify individual actors or leaders. The ballpark rally, too, centered individual speakers. Being an identifiable leader was risky. Starr had taken on that risk understanding her identities would likely protect her. Haymarket rally speakers August Spies and Albert Parsons had also taken this risk, but had been hanged for their roles as identifiable leaders. During the 1910 garment workers' march, risk was dispersed across thousands and individuality subsumed as the collective came together across differences of gender, class, and ethnicity.

Alliance and Enduring Solidarity

The Chicago Garment Strike lasted six months under difficult winter conditions. In February, strikers ran out of money. The strike fund was depleted. So, too, was the milk fund ("Union Calls" 1). Two days ahead of a blizzard that would have made continued street protest dangerous, Rickert negotiated an end of the strike that fell far short of workers' demands. Manufacturers did not agree to hire only union employees, and there were no processes put in place for addressing workers' future grievances. The UGW simply encouraged striking workers to return to their factories. This was a disappointing end to a deadly and costly strike. Yet, the effects of strikers' labor rhetorics cannot be evaluated on the basis of the final negotiation alone. That women initiated and led the strike was its own kind of accomplishment. They reimagined the street, a public space often hostile to women, as where women could appear and invite others to come together there across differences of identity. Whereas in Hull House, speakers had to work out rhetorical conventions and traditions for mutual understanding among those with different backgrounds and languages, strikers accomplished an expression of collective solidarity through embodied mobile action that did not require the specialized literacies of individuals who could engage in spoken or written negotiation, practices that excluded workers without the power, language, or literacy skills to engage effectively. By allying in the street, garment workers gained the attention not only of the manufacturers exploiting them, but also the attention of the unions. While unions and manufacturers could ignore for a time spoken and written complaints, neither could ignore the absence of workers in the shops and presence on the streets. In Chicago, where the garment industry was stratified by gender and ethnicity, it was crucial that strikers showed employers and the state they were unified as a workforce and had key support from communities and organizations. They did this by getting close on the street, taking routes through immigrant enclaves, and using signage and clothing to emphasize the visual message of their collective bodily movement.

Mobile labor rhetorics on the street were necessarily fleeting, as protest actions required resources to sustain them. Street alliances, though ephemeral, reveal a more enduring solidarity at the level of ritual. In distinguishing between solidarity and support, hooks argues that solidarity requires "a community of interests, shared beliefs, and goals around which to unite" (67). These requirements take time to put in place, and to this list I would add that seeking solidarity is aided by having shared space and shared rhetorical traditions. Walkouts, pickets and marches were by 1910 iconic protest actions in the labor movement that signaled collective protest against low wages, harassment from employers, and a ban on collective bargaining. Protest actions were how workers risked the safety of their bodies and thus demonstrated the urgency of their demands. Think of the collective knowledge required even for workers to reappropriate the sound of the whistle to signal a walkout. Everyone involved must understand its established meanings in a workplace setting to start and stop work, and then must also understand its reappropriated meaning to stop work when used to call for a walkout. This meaning making requires a collective of workers to share histories and traditions of protest.

Hull House was a complementary space to the street in building shared histories and traditions of protest. Strikers knew they could count on Hull House as a meeting space. During the strike, Hull House residents served as allies during the strike in visible and meaningful ways, as they had done during prior labor disputes. In September 1935, months after Addams's death, Sidney Hillman delivered a speech about Addams's role in the garment strike for the Women's International League of Peace and Freedom. In the speech, Hillman called Hull House the "nucleus around which there gravitated so many of us who were looking for light and leadership in a chaotic world," and noted Addams's attempts to negotiate between HSM and the strikers set important precedent for what garment workers achieved during the strike and afterward (1). Precedent mattered for both Hillman and his wife Bessie Abramowitz Hillman, who after witnessing the failures of the UGW to negotiate on behalf of garment workers in Chicago, served in leadership roles in other clothing workers unions over the next several decades. The difference between an ephemeral alliance and a more enduring kind of solidarity, though, also rests on participants' willingness to risk losing individual power in the service of creating collective power to redistribute property, wealth and resources, and dismantle social structures that allow inequality to persist. Between Hull House residents and women workers, a clear power imbalance was reified in their interactions. Addams had the power to stand up to the garment manufacturers on behalf of workers because her organization had its own power, wealth and connections.

Starr, too, was a public ally during the strike by serving as a picket and by circulating accounts of police brutality, but Starr's allyship in these instances was limited in that it relied on her reasserting that her whiteness and wealth were measures that granted her access to the street. In distinguishing between solidarity and support, hooks argues that white women's support will begin to look more like solidarity when they confront the racism and classism in society and actively unlearn racist socialization patterns that lead them to perpetuate these patterns in the feminist movement. For white women, solidarity can look like listening to and collaborating with women of color, and working-class and poor women, rather than assuming leadership roles (56–57). Across twenty years, Hull House residents' allyship with women workers was uneven, imperfect, and sometimes harmful. Throughout their efforts as allies, the Hull House founders claimed leadership roles in labor negotiations on behalf of working-class women and women of color without interrogating how their arguments sustained inequality along axes beyond gender.

The street leveled any individual's ability to assume a leadership role. On the street, garment workers claimed the right to appear, and women garment workers, who were the most inexperienced and unorganized, collectively led the strike and challenged the exclusionary practices of the very unions that had innovated the forms of labor walkouts and marches in the first place. By adding gendered variation to these traditional forms, women workers called for the support of those with access to different kinds of power, such as unionized men garment workers and the well-connected reformers who supported them. The 1910 strike is significant, ultimately, because it was part of a moment when women workers asserted their place in these labor traditions in significant numbers and began initiating use of established labor rhetorics.

Chicago women workers were linked in a network of garment strikes that included ones that had taken place the year before in New York, Cleveland, and Philadelphia, and a year later in Lawrence, Massachusetts and London. The women who led these strikes occupied streets previously occupied by men protestors and challenged broader societal beliefs about gendered labor. When women took to the street, a literal route away from the home, they were communicating that traditional gendered divisions of labor were no longer sufficient. Across time, and on the street, women shared this message in new ways and connected it to other social causes. In May 1911, for example, women in New York City merged the causes of labor reform and suffrage by marching down Fifth Avenue with a sign that read, "Women Need Votes to End Sweatshops," a message made all the more urgent because it responded to the deadly Triangle Shirtwaist factory fire that took place three months earlier in which 146 employees, most of whom were women, perished in a fire ("Great Parade" 146). This combined labor and suffrage march was also fused with a funeral procession. Their signs were painted in red for revolution, draped in black for mourning.

As I stood on Halsted Street in Pilsen with my daughter to see where the 1910 garment walkout had taken place, I wondered what enduring solidarity meant from my vantage point, next to where the public commemorative plaque to the walkout was graffitied over. Halsted Street, formerly the great north-south thoroughfare through the city, was overshadowed by the massive interstate highway that now looms over it. This spot in Pilsen no longer seemed to me to be a place of making and instead the converted factories seemed more like storehouses for capital in the form of the art displayed inside the loft buildings. Perhaps what I saw on Halsted Street was not a space ripe for protest, but symptomatic of the larger, interstate economic geography of inequality. People still appear in mobile street alliances at moments when the interests of labor and capital are furthest apart and the organizations that are supposed to represent their interests fail to secure fair and safe working conditions. For example, teachers in West Virginia participated in largely successful walkouts and marches in 2018, securing a significant pay raise and inspiring teachers in other states to follow with their own strikes. In West Virginia, a state with powerful anti-union laws, teachers reimagined local and masculine traditions of organized labor developed in industries like mining to protest ever expanding job responsibilities, decreased pay, and more, simultaneously merging the traditionally unpaid gendered labor of mothering and caring for community with their paid role as teachers (Hanrahan and Amsler 159). By networking specific moments of protest together, a more enduring kind of solidarity emerges among women and workers who build on each other's labor rhetorics. Across time, the intergenerational dimension of labor solidarity is the link through which the rituals of alliance that seem dormant are passed down for use when they are needed.

Conclusion: Networking Labor Rhetorics

> Do you think you will help the people more by adding yourself to the crowded city than you would by tilling your own soil?
>
> —Leo Tolstoy, quoted in Jane Addams's
> *Twenty Years at Hull House*

Throughout *City Housekeeping*, the metaphor of the network, evoking a product of and process from the historical context of garment making, has helped me to notice how rhetorical events occurring within the context of social movements are linked, though not necessarily through direct or chronological relationships. As I wrote about women who were participating in a growing labor movement, the idea of the network helped me to emphasize links between instances of their labor rhetorics, a term offered by this book to name a distinct area of inquiry into how rhetors communicate the meaning of activities that make life possible and the value of those activities on a variety of scales of space and time. Simultaneous to their negotiation of economic value, labor rhetorics participate in investing identities of gender, race, ethnicity, and nationality with meaning. Through tracing labor rhetorics across space and time, we might better notice recurrent uses of arguments, conventions, and practices that have developed in labor discourse, persisted into the contemporary moment, and shape the resources labor rhetors draw on today. To conclude this book, I revisit the arguments about labor that women deployed across space and time that I discussed in the chapters. I also expand my use of the metaphor of the network and apply it to the concerns of feminist rhetorics more broadly to suggest possible future research paths through which feminist rhetoricians might build out the network of labor rhetorics. In doing so, I hope others might find entry into the larger feminist project of demonstrating how gender and womanhood are constantly redefined in relation to labor. Last, I suggest feminist rhetoricians explore their own spaces of writing and research, and situate themselves more explicitly in solidarity networks with the subjects they recover in their scholarship and with other researchers. To model this process, I end by offering brief scenes from my own spaces of writing and research where I noticed threads of connections to others and to the concerns of this book. But first, allow me to rearticulate the concerns of this book across the chapters and to synthesize the contributions this book makes as a whole.

Labor Rhetorics from Hull House and Beyond

Among the variety of spaces explored in this book, I considered Hull House a hub for women's labor rhetorical activity with local and national impact. Hull House was especially successful because it had an innovative leader in Addams, who reimagined the British idea of a settlement house for the US context. Through leading Hull House, Addams brought people together not only across class backgrounds, but across gender, ethnic, and national backgrounds as well. She and Starr crafted the settlement as a cosmopolitan space, one where diverse people recognized mutual interests and found entry into discussions about labor. Hull House was an imperfect but reliable space where unorganized women and men could meet to discuss labor and seek solidarity. The space of Hull House was used by thousands of west siders each year, though throughout I have emphasized that it was also a space that consolidated power for middle-class and wealthy white women who at times used the space to protect whiteness through constructing American domesticity as white-coded in relation to the foreign. One of the takeaways of this book is that we might think of today's ethical consumption campaigns as successors to a cosmopolitan labor rhetoric originating in spaces like Hull House, where well-to-do women imagined they could avoid identifying as producers or capitalists and instead intervene in labor politics through savvy purchasing of artisan wares. Through idealizing foreign artisanship, Hull House's approach to labor politics created rather than narrowed the distance between those occupying the identity categories of domestic and foreign, and of white and Black, and ultimately protected white women's authority over the home and expanded this authority to include the wider city and even the world.

While Hull House was a unique space that offered women entry into conversations about labor, the metaphor of the network guided me to understand it as rhetorically interesting because it was a node within a broader net in which city dwellers were responding to industrial upheaval. Shifting modes of production, an influx of immigrants and migrants, and rapidly multiplying houses and factories created new conditions of modernity that left Chicago's citizens in need of shared conventions and traditions for responding to change. One way to think of Hull House is as a space that welcomed the culture of labor organizing that was already developing on the west side when Addams and Starr settled there. Addams was challenged in her thinking about labor not only from the Russian novelist and philosopher Leo Tolstoy as quoted in the epigraph to this chapter, but also from recently immigrated Russian-Jewish tailors in her neighborhood who were already organizing their collective power through unions. Their spaces for organizing, however, and their rhetorical traditions, as I explored in chapter one, were segregated by ethnicity, gender, language, and skill in the garment trade. Hull House became a place where women excluded from existing unions could attempt to create integrated unions, and also to gather resources, invent arguments, and reimagine labor rhetorics and solidarity.

After locating this study first at Hull House, I committed to identifying other spaces women who connected through the settlement were rhetorically and materially remaking for the purpose of inviting solidarity. I followed women and their labor rhetorics from the hub of the settlement to the tenement, exhibition, and street to find out how their arguments shaped—and were shaped by—these spaces. I did this to model how the spaces important to the study of labor rhetorics go beyond traditional homes and workplaces. The settlement, tenement, exhibition, and street had porous boundaries, were all defined as alternative to traditional versions of home and work in their own ways, and were where diverse rhetors could collectively reimagine what home and work might look like. Then, I explored how labor rhetorics emerged through interactions within these spaces. In each chapter, I featured scenes of stakeholders—such as settlement residents, garment workers, manufacturers, and the public—expressing disparate motives and beliefs surrounding the topic of labor and negotiating how they might come together to reach common goals.

While space itself was often physically shared, rhetors were unequal in space. Power was distributed differently within the settlement, tenement, exhibition, and street. Because of unequal power dynamics, efforts to create solidarity were at times fleeting or ended in confusion or further stratification. For example, in chapter three I explored how exhibition organizers cast immigrant women artisans and sweatshop workers as representative of labor's past in their industrial progress narratives that idealized the factory. Garment workers disrupted these organizers' efforts to convey this kind of progress narrative through striking, and in so doing briefly enlisted solidarity for their working conditions within and beyond the exhibition from exhibit makers, other workers, and the public.

As I followed labor rhetors across spaces and times, I explored the affordances of spoken, written, visual, aural, and mobile labor rhetorics for the way these modes created mutual understanding and circulated messages beyond originating rhetorical situations. At times, Hull House residents and garment workers aligned their interests across modes of rhetoric. I explored these multimodal rhetorics in chapter four's discussion of the 1910 Chicago

Garment Workers Strike when garment workers allied across differences through visual, aural, and mobile modes to enlist solidarity across differences. Simultaneously, Hull House residents used spoken and written labor rhetorics to circulate arguments beyond the street and to negotiate the value of garment workers' labor with manufacturers. At other times, residents' and women workers' modes served cross purposes, such as in chapter two when Florence Kelley sought to protect women through visual and verbal representations of their labor conditions to the public who might then purchase more ethically or support labor laws specifically targeting women. Garment workers, meanwhile, resisted Kelley's efforts to document them in writing and visuals to make their labor visible. Throughout, I have shown labor rhetors not only chose the most fitting modes for their messages, but also chose the modes that were available to them based on their ability to access the material resources required to produce messages and leverage their literacy and language resources for negotiating purposes.

More broadly, Chicagoans in the late nineteenth and early twentieth centuries were seeking new modes and arguments to describe the city and its impact on shaping the conditions of modern labor. I frame this conclusion with an epigraph from Tolstoy because he questioned Addams's labor ethics as connected to her relocation from country to city. Addams had made a pilgrimage with her partner Smith in 1895 to visit Tolstoy in Russia. She wrote about this visit later in her 1910 book as part of reflecting on life at Hull House over twenty years. Prior to her visit to Russia, in 1894, Chicagoans had been hit hard by economic recession, and Addams recalled feeling a sense of shame in not sharing in her neighbors' misery. Addams and countless others visited Tolstoy for advice because they admired how he was attempting to merge his Christian beliefs with a practice of everyday living. In Russia, Addams found Tolstoy living and working among peasants, joining them in "bread labor," or farm labor, for the purpose of feeding others (272). When Tolstoy asked Addams how she obtained food and shelter, she told him she was a miller's daughter and was supported by the inheritance of her father's homestead in the northwest corner of Illinois. When Tolstoy asked, "do you think you will help the people more by adding yourself to the crowded city than you would by tilling your own soil," Addams declined to answer directly in the moment, but responded in the form of her reflection fifteen years later (269).

Addams's response reveals some of the ways the American city enabled and constrained women's means for reimagining labor. After her visit, Addams tried to live more like Tolstoy. A miller's daughter, Addams decided to spend a portion of her day performing labor more aligned with her early familial role by baking bread. This plan was soon halted by "the half dozen people invariably waiting to see [her] after breakfast, the piles of letters to be opened and answered, the demand of actual and pressing wants" (277–78). Addams ultimately decided that living like Tolstoy by doing the same labor, eating the same foods, and wearing the same clothes as her neighbors was not how she could be most helpful to people. It was also impossible for her to participate in all the steps of production. Tolstoy's theory of labor as ideally shared among peasants and landowners in rural Russia did not translate into a way of life for Americans occupying diverse economic roles in an ever-expanding geography of labor. Baking bread didn't make sense for Addams: industrialization had created new geographies of labor in which the harvesting of raw materials took place hundreds of miles away on places like her former homestead; then, those materials were brought into the city. Under the conditions of industrial mass production, when wheat was harvested and milled in places like Cedarville, Illinois, it was turned into bread by bakers in the city, sometimes in basement sweatshops, sometimes in unionized and modernized factories. The American city was a node in a recently and profoundly changed production landscape.

In this book I focused on women in the service of including their contributions to labor rhetorical traditions and to reveal them as navigating and intervening in gendered discourses. As historian Alice Kessler-Harris has argued, we still need women's history despite the pressing importance of conducting gender analysis of social systems because studying women reveals "the power of the individual to shed a different light — sometimes a liminal light — on historical processes." Women's labor rhetorics are an important site to research in hopes of better understanding how women articulated the shifting meanings of gender and womanhood for themselves. In response to Tolstoy, Addams articulated these meanings as they had been reshaped by her location in the industrial city. Addams found Tolstoy and his daughter Maria committed to doing the same kind of labor as their peasant neighbors, and though Addams could have followed their model, she also faced gendered obstacles to doing so that were specific in the American context and to the ideals embedded within American domestic discourse. For white women like Addams, claiming the role of producer was a masculinized way to identify. In chapter one, I explored how the organizer Mary Kenney had confronted this obstacle as the very reason women garment workers seeking middle-class and white identities did not want to join unions. Not only would unionizing have cemented their status as working-class and nonwhite; it would also have located them further away from embodying ideal womanhood.

Tolstoy further pressed Addams about her gendered presentation by asking why she did not dress like the peasants in Chicago, objecting to the size of her sleeves, which seemed to have been made with excessive amounts of material (268). Addams, familiar with the power of garments to reflect a wearer's gender and labor politics, reflected later that she could not wear the same style of clothes as her neighbors; there were too many different styles to choose from. Immigrants in Chicago had brought diverse styles of peasant dress with them, and working-class women were wearing puffy sleeves as a revival of what had been a particularly impractical and cumbersome Victorian trend and had reimagined it to make their silhouettes bigger. Working girls literally took up more space with those sleeves, and their presence signaled the new power they enjoyed in the city. Addams replied to Tolstoy that contrary to his logic that wealthier people would use more fabric, her sleeves did not "compare in size with those of the working girls in Chicago (269)." In the moment, it was difficult for Addams to explain the nuances of how garments reflected gendered style, national identity, and the labor politics of the wearer.

Overall, in Tolstoy's presence, Addams struggled to respond to his question about whether she was helping more people in the city than she might if she had stayed in the country, but in her reflections, and, in the record of her life after twenty years at Hull House, she answered with a resounding yes. At the time of her writing in 1910, she was supporting women garment workers through leading an industry-wide strike that revealed women's growing power to organize their labor. Throughout the previous two decades, her settlement had served countless Progressive reformers in launching careers into newly emerging professions that they had helped to invent. In addition, Addams's own life looked something like a model for gendered progress. Addams was no longer relegated to baking bread on her father's farm, and was by 1910 a settlement leader, writer, speaker, fundraiser, diplomat, political consultant, and more. She was also living a life beyond the bounds of traditional domesticity and had expanded her family to include Smith and the larger group of Hull House residents.

I recount Addams's reflection on her visit to Tolstoy because she explores how the American city was a geography that reshaped possibilities for women's lives and labor. Also, her visit highlights that she and Tolstoy shared an overarching interest in asking "what to do" to help the people (261). Their very question set limits on possibilities for how they would imagine possibilities for solidarity. Helping the people as an individual acting and seeking relations of solidarity with people are not the same. Solidarity is not about doing the same kind of labor as others, nor is it about using one's privileges to help without reassessing the origins of a system that confers privilege to some and withholds it from others. Solidarity often begins with recognizing differences, and it manifests because of, rather than despite differences, as various actors find common ground. As I have discussed throughout this book, the Progressive impulse to center the individual as the driver of change often became a constraint to efforts to achieve solidarity.

It is possible to ask different questions. Rather than ask what can be done to help, someone seeking solidarity with others might begin with reflection, as Addams did twenty years after her visit to Tolstoy. In reflecting on her encounter with Tolstoy, Addams finally began the work of claiming the origins of her privilege as the inheritor of the profits from a successful mill. Addams also understood the impracticality of reclaiming the identity of miller's daughter; she had worked her whole adult life to expand economic and social roles for herself and other women. Unfortunately, Addams did not use the opportunity offered by the encounter to reflect on her earlier idealizing of cosmopolitan artisan wares to help producers. She did not explicitly connect the impracticality of her returning to the labor of baking bread to her imagining neighbors' lives might be righted if they returned to the conditions of a peasant past and rejected industrialization, along with the incredible changes it brought to culture. By making comparisons between her own labor history and those of her neighbors, Addams might have decentered herself and joined others in a process of considering why industrial capitalism benefited some but not all, and of reimagining a world that did not repeat current economic logics.

In the remainder of this chapter, I move beyond reviewing the topics and arguments covered throughout this book to think broadly about why labor matters more generally to feminist rhetorics and how the topic can propel new scholarship. I invite feminist rhetoricians to pursue projects in labor rhetorics at new sites and times to continue recovering and retheorizing rhetoric. Finally, I discuss how rhetoricians can write about their own spaces of research and writing as part of a feminist method of centering labor and spaces for solidarity. Below, I return to an overarching theme of this book— building a network— to suggest new pathways for research.

NETWORKING FEMINIST STUDIES OF LABOR RHETORICS

As I mentioned previously, I took up the topic of labor rhetorics in part to join other feminist rhetoricians in engaging in the complementary projects of recovering women's rhetorics and conducting gender analysis to help expand what counts as rhetoric. Within the broader projects of recovery and retheorizing, I was also interested in diversifying rhetorical history by writing a relational history in which gendered labor rhetorics emerged not from singular figures, but in negotiation when stakeholders interacted. My recovery project was a feminist one of networking people, spaces, and arguments together. According to feminist rhetorician Rebecca Dingo, networking draws "attention to the links between women's diverse experiences, aspirations, and identities" (11). In focusing attention on these experiential, aspirational, and identity links, I hope to have shed light on the possibilities and missed opportunities for solidarity among women. Networking arguments, as Dingo's work illustrates, also guides researchers beyond the study of discrete rhetorical events and toward glimpsing the circulation of claims about women and gender in a broader ecosystems. I hope to have added to this process by following women across city spaces where they reimagined labor rhetorical conventions and traditions and developed collective strategies for negotiating the value of their labor power.

Here, I also want to cast the projects of recovery and expansion of what counts as rhetoric as central to allying across differences within the discipline. In chapter four I described alliance in the context of the labor movement as the coming together of groups facing discrimination or crisis, a mutually beneficial process that highlights their differences of identity and power rather than erases them. The concept of alliance is also grounded in other historical conversations. For example, Malea D. Powell applied the idea of alliance used to describe Native communities recognizing each other's sovereignty while simultaneously working toward mutual understanding to develop the concept of a "Rhetoric and Composition alliance" and call attention to how the discipline could change through multiple histories of rhetoric informing one another (rather than continuing to center Greek, Roman, and Euro-centric histories) (39–40). Such a rhet/comp alliance, Powell argues, might help decenter any one historical tradition and move the discipline beyond mere inclusion and toward developing histories and theories that are more interconnected and reciprocal, ultimately leading those working in the field to use the resource of history to narrate possibilities in the contemporary moment for growth and change. In the service of furthering the project of building a rhetoric and composition alliance, I invite feminist rhetoricians to diversify the study of labor rhetorics and build out a network of connections. There is still much to explore. I offer some possibilities for future lines of inquiry into labor rhetorics that are linked to this book's concerns of women, labor, and space. I suggest these topics toward the goal of creating a centerless network that includes multiple histories, while acknowledging there are countless other entry points into labor rhetorics beyond the ones I mention here.

Throughout this book I have focused on a group of women connected to one organization in Progressive Era Chicago. Clearly, the task of making spaces for labor rhetorics was not solved in this place at the close of this era. One way to build out a network would be to update research on women's labor rhetorics in the American city, especially surrounding questions regarding how women have negotiated domestic discourse and gendered divisions of labor. To update this history, one might explore debates in the mid- to late- twentieth century city over where to build public housing complexes and who should live in them. Like "city housekeeping," the phrase "public housing" juxtaposes public and private space, civic and home space, and suggests tensions between these terms. The public housing crisis is an area of inquiry for feminist study because it is also the successor to the tenement housing crisis. In Chicago, for example, one of the first public housing projects was called the Jane Addams Homes because Addams had continued to seek remedies to the tenement problem in Chicago throughout her life and had suggested the site for the project prior to her death in 1935 ("U.S. Government" 12). In *City Housekeeping*, I explored how the tenement was a kind of housing that emerged in cities in response to the need for the newly immigrated to live near industry. The tenement was where home was also a workshop, and people lived outside of normative family relations there. For these reasons, it was considered a foreign geography in contrast to a more traditionally domestic one. From Florence Kelley's efforts to create knowledge about and regulate tenement homes emerged a longer legacy of government oversight over this kind of housing. In the twentieth century, public housing in Chicago became racialized in ways different from the tenement, as Black residents moved into public housing during and after the Great Migration. The city itself also used public housing to further segregation. In his rhetorical history of a Chicago public housing project, David Fleming argues the Chicago Housing Authority participated in further separating the city's Black residents into public housing through racist policies that built this kind of housing in already segregated areas. To update research on how women used rhetoric to imagine public housing as a space of gendered and racialized labor in a more contemporary moment, we might look to Candice Rai's rhetorical and ethnographic study of a Chicago housing development as a model for understanding it as contested space. In her book, Rai explores the debate over whether fair housing is a right of citizens, or whether it is subject to market forces and those who can own property. Within this debate, women's authority over the private and domestic is subordinated to the realm of public and economic concern. Perhaps especially when housing is left subject to market forces, women are disadvantaged. As the feminist writer and former Chicago public housing resident Mikki Kendall explains, affordable housing remains a pressing feminist issue because the persistent wage gaps along gender and racial lines means that "households supported by women are paying larger-than-average proportions of income toward rent," which over time affects women's ability to secure quality and safe housing for themselves and their families (206). Today the former Jane Addams Homes at 1306 West Taylor Street is the site of the National Public Housing Museum, which as of the time of this writing is scheduled to open in 2025. When it opens, it will be a space potentially ripe for making feminist rhetorical inquiries into how women navigated the boundaries of domestic and public space, and Black and white racialized geographies, in public housing developments.

Another link to feminist studies of labor rhetorics are projects that move beyond the domestic as the word applies to the concept of home and housing and toward exploring its meanings at the level of nation. Specifically, feminist rhetoricians might explore women's labor rhetorics as they move across transnational contexts. The economies of nations have been interconnected for centuries, and I have highlighted a group of women who thought of the cosmopolitan character of the market as an entry point for white American women seeking authority in conversations about industry. In chapter one, for example, I explored Addams's and Starr's anti-industrial stance and efforts to create a cosmopolitan space by decorating Hull House with imported art and furnishings that reflected diverse foreign locales. I also suggested that instead of imported artisan wares, it was the cloaks the garment workers were making and manufacturers selling that might have been a better analytic key to building a labor network of solidarity across a chain of production and consumption. Today, Chicago is no longer a city where clothing is mass manufactured, so if feminist rhetoricians were to update the practice of "looking for the union label" started by the International Ladies Union to trace how garments travel through production and distribution networks, they would find that many garment manufacturers have moved their production facilities overseas, where 85 percent of garment workers are women of color (Pham 133). Media studies scholar Minh-Ha T. Pham has framed the global production of garments as a pressing feminist issue, especially in response to a supposedly feminist stance in which some argue the garment industry offers women in the Global South new opportunity to earn money and modernize their labor. Furthermore, Pham has found young women in the Global North attempting to shore up the problem of underpaid labor through ethical consumption campaigns (144). Feminist rhetoricians who follow Pham's research path into the contemporary garment industry might network contemporary arguments about the benefits of hiring women garment workers overseas and the historical arguments about women's entrance into the factory as a sign of industrial progress that I discussed as prevalent in labor discourse in early 1900s Chicago.

Contemporary research on gendered labor need not be confined to industrializing cities and can certainly expand beyond a focus on the garment industry. The study of women's labor rhetorics would be made more robust by truly transnational labor studies that followed people and rhetoric across borders. Literacy scholar Eileen Lagman provides a model for what this kind of scholarship might look like. In "Moving Labor: Transnational Migrant Workers and Affective Literacies of Care," Lagman shares insights from her ethnography that included sites in the Philippines and the US to explore how state-sponsored literacy education facilitated the movement of Filipina labor migrants. Her study reveals literacies performed through the body move across borders via a series of emotional and legal attachments between state and worker-citizen. When scholars like Lagman network labor rhetorics across transnational boundaries, they participate in creating a better understanding of what it takes to enact what Mohanty identified as the first step in creating solidarity, which is to recognize women as workers across global divisions and borders.

Considering labor rhetorics in global context might further illuminate the economics of domestic labor. In fact, a global perspective can be helpful for re-evaluating the labor rhetorics surrounding the most feminized and domestic kinds of social reproduction. In chapter three, I discussed a pervasive, Progressive home-to-work narrative in which women's unpaid domestic labor was understood to easily convert into paid labor in the factory setting. Other feminist rhetoricians might pursue inquiry into how contemporary domestic labor is revalued as workplace labor. For example, writer Angela Garbes models this kind of inquiry in her exploration of mothering as necessary for the global economy to function and therefore a site where women hold power and might collectively use it to create social change. Through personal and social history, Garbes investigates how the reproductive labor of pregnancy and childcare has come to be devalued and simultaneously highly regulated by the state because reproductive labor propels the functioning of the global economy. Furthermore, Garbes explains her own thinking about labor as shaped by her family's history of Philipina-US labor migration in which her family members' domestic labor of caring was revalued as paid work and facilitated their migration to the US. Garbes finds in mothering possibilities for revaluing labor as a form of connection to one's own body and to others. Rhetorical inquiry can help us better understand the arguments that devalue reproductive labor and caregiving as shaped in transnational economies, but also how women find value in it that is beyond monetary.

Creating links across studies of women's labor rhetorics may also mean looking closer to where feminist rhetoricians work. Melissa Nivens interrogates the history of her own workplace through her research on the home management house opened in the 1930s at East Texas State, now East Texas

A&M University. Then and there, white rural women were able to leave their farms to occupy a combined home/classroom/laboratory space, one that helped them to learn how to run households and join the middle class. Studying 1930s Texas, Nivens found progress narratives similar to the ones that were circulating in the 1900s industrial city; that is, she found that white women's movement from farm to middle-class household was mediated by the argument that traditional gender roles were helpful for moving into the new modern role of savvy consumer. White women who attended the home management house were trained in occupying the role of manager, one that Nivens rightly points to needing further exploration. The home management house was where white farm girls at a segregated school learned to be managers over servants at a time when many domestic servants in East Texas were Black women (297). Further study could explore the racist labor dynamics of the Southern US and connect what at first appears to be a local and rural study about white women's labor in the twentieth century not only to histories of Black women's labor of the same period, but also to white and Black women's labor and their relations to one another as shaped by the legacy of the global slave trade of the seventeenth and eighteenth centuries.

These are a few possibilities feminist rhetoricians could pursue among many others. Powell's interest in alliance for the discipline is as a decentering practice, and feminist rhetoricians are key participants in creating new nodes in a centerless network of rhetorical studies. As feminist rhetoricians multiply studies of labor rhetorics, we can better notice how arguments appear and reappear in different formats, often in nonlinear relationships, and across time. We can also notice how gender and class are constructed in relation to the identities of race, ethnicity, and nationality. Finally, a network of rhetorical scholarship offers opportunities to consider geographic scale. We might better notice that what appear to be local labor rhetorical practices are in fact shaped by the global economy.

Writing Spaces of Labor into Feminist Rhetorical Methods

I use this final section of the conclusion to reflect on possibilities available to those who take up feminist research to write their own spaces of labor into their scholarship as an act of solidarity across space and time. I do this primarily by writing about some of the spaces of labor I occupied while collecting research from an archival collection in Chicago, analyzing my sources back in my office at a public research university in North Texas, and writing this book from home in 2020 during the first year of the COVID-19 pandemic. I saw in all of these spaces of archive, office, and home parallels to the spaces I discuss in this book in the sense that their meanings for gender and labor shift during times of economic and social upheaval. The space of the archive, for example, can serve as a space of selective memory preservation about gender and labor, much like the labor exhibitions created by Hull House residents and Chicago philanthropists in the early twentieth century. In addition to drawing out similarities between my own workspaces and those in this rhetorical history, I write about my workspaces here primarily to gesture toward how feminist rhetoricians might invite solidarity with colleagues engaging in the shared labor of writing and research.

First, an aside: One space I have not explicitly discussed in this history is the classroom; however, my own teaching of writing was always on my mind while I researched labor. While it is beyond the scope of this study to draw direct pedagogical inferences, I offer a connection. In rhetoric and composition studies, there is already a strong tradition of accounting for the classroom as a space of labor where students write and produce texts. Compositionists such as Bruce Horner and John Trimbur are examples of scholars who have focused on making visible the labor of writing in contemporary classrooms, a project that matters for students who deserve equitable conditions and to maintain ownership of their writing and a say over how their writing circulates. Feminist rhetoricians might continue to explore the labor dynamics of student writing in the classroom while also including analysis of their own labor toward the goal of noticing what equitable conditions might look like across the experiences of teaching and learning. The classroom is one possible space to notice where this kind of work happens.

In addition, feminist rhetoricians might begin with what Adrienne Rich has called "the geography closest in —the body" and notice where else they research and write (212). Such a practice of locating, as Rich theorizes it, is a feminist one that guards against abstractions and absolutes in favor of the specificity of asking "where, when, and under what conditions" one acts as is acted upon (214). Many already articulate their processes of research and writing as part of what accounts for the methods of how they conduct scholarship and report results. By broadening an account of methods to include where and when writing and research labor occurs, it becomes more possible to trouble progress narratives about labor that persist today and to notice the shared values, practices, and conditions that make writing and research possible.

Writing about spaces of labor also has the potential to trouble persistent home-to-work progress narratives about women gaining equality in the workplace with men, which continue to be tempting to write. This kind of progress narrative seeps through, for example, in the 2008 *Women's Ways of Making It in Rhetoric and Composition*. Authors Michelle Ballif, Diane Davis, and Roxanne Mountford synthesize insights from women in the discipline who share their stories and strategies, but the book's focus on "making it" and success is ultimately narrow. Though survey respondents troubled narrow versions of success and shared stories of discrimination and harassment, the women profiled were ones that "hold a PhD; are full professors at an academic institution; are tenured; are well published; are cited regularly; have contributed a consummate piece in the field; are frequently keynote speakers at national conferences; are actively mentoring other women in the field; are able to have a 'real' life, in addition to their scholarly activities" (7). As the last item about having a "real' life" makes clear, there remains a connection between making it and having it all, or overcoming a gendered separation of home and work. I argue that providing snapshots of spaces where one labors helps to trouble this idealized separation and gives needed dimension to narratives about where, how, and under what conditions women labor. Such questions are important ultimately for critiquing structures of, for example, a sexist academy that supports some in making it and not others.

Troubling Progress Narratives

At this point I want to offer examples by describing my own spaces of labor while writing this book, spaces that entwined me in a web of relations with the historical subjects I recovered and other scholars working in rhetoric and composition. By writing about the spaces where I labored, I hope to be better able to trouble idealized progress narratives about my own labor that were tempting for me to participate in because they are easier to write about than the messy lived reality. Much of my own embodied process of collecting archival materials was spent in the Richard J. Daley Library at the University of Illinois Chicago. There, during visits across many years, I looked at items in the Jane Addams Memorial Collection, which served as the primary repository for the records, photographs, manuscripts, clippings, and yearbooks that made this study possible. When first there, I appreciated the abundance of records that spoke to diverse women's lives and labor in the late nineteenth and early twentieth centuries. I thought of this abundance in connection to the largely absent records that spoke to my own family's history in the garment trade. After several visits, though, I began to see the absence of family records as a potential choice that my ancestors had made, one that opened up opportunity to reimagine and rewrite their own identities without the constraints of records. I began to wonder also if a desire to recover records that spoke to my own family history was a little bit too close to Addams's and Starr's idealizing of an immigrant peasant culture that was irrevocably lost in the American city and needed preserving in the first place.

At UIC, among endless boxes and files from Hull House, I thought about the privilege required to invent identity through writing and then to preserve it. As I had learned by studying the multimodal rhetorics of garment workers, writing was one possible mode among several, and usually labor intensive to learn, produce and circulate. While in the UIC reading room, looking through box after box of records, I appreciated the labor of so many who had not only produced these records, but subsequently organized, preserved, and protected these records. These records, unmoved from their location over time, were a sign of the tremendous privilege the women who created them enjoyed.

Or were they? What did the abundance of preserved texts in the Richard J. Daley Library really communicate about the privilege of Hull House residents, about the status of Hull House as a valued place? In the larger landscape of my surroundings, the Daley Library sits on the site that was formerly Hull House. In the Special Collections and University Archives, I was physically on the plant of what used to be the Hull House settlement, most of which was demolished in the 1960s to make room for the University of Illinois Chicago. Today, only two buildings from the original settlement remain as part of the Jane Addams Hull House Museum. By occupying this archival space, I was also undertaking my process of occupying contemporary places related to the historical ones I wrote about to critically imagine in support of my reading of texts. Earlier I discussed how I used contemporary place as a source, not as evidence of what existed in the past, but as part of understanding the present as inextricably networked to past historical events in which rhetoric was central to the action. In chapter four, for example, I described being at the site of Hannah Shapiro's garment factory walkout, which helped me understand how spontaneous and embodied labor rhetorics afforded strikers the ability to create sights and sounds for other workers to follow out of the factory and into the street. Moments like this one helped me to better appreciate women's innovative responses to common labor exigencies and the diversity of modes of expression that they used to respond. While in the reading room, I questioned what occupying this contemporary version of place where Hull House once stood told me about its meaning in relation to the past. One way to interpret its meaning, for example, would be through Addams's lens. The demolition of Hull House and the building of UIC in the 1960s was further evidence justifying Addams's fear the city was overtaking any service or role that Hull House, and by extension women, had claimed as part of their authority over the private and domestic realm of life and turning it into a public good. While it was remarkable that Hull House records remained preserved in UIC's library reading room and physically in the same space where Hull House once stood, the actual women-led institution that was Hull House had been mostly erased from the landscape. I thought about how it was easier to save boxes of papers than it was the buildings where a group of women had lived and worked to reimagine gendered labor.

What would it have meant to view the Hull House archive in the space of Hull House, had it survived as a living institution into the twenty-first century? I caught a glimpse of an answer to this question as I brought back the records I collected from Hull House to analyze them at the library close to where I was living in western Massachusetts, Smith College's Neilson Library. Smith College is not a perfect parallel to Hull House. Its bucolic Northeastern setting, for example, means it was never subject to the pressures of industrialization like Hull House's city campus. Still, it is a women's institution that has persisted into the present. It remains an institution for women, premised on societal gender inequality, and is still a place where conversations about gender and womanhood are at the forefront of discourse, and where women are innovating traditions and inventing their own. The Sophia Smith Collection of Women's History is a place where Smith College not only preserves its own history, but preserves a wider expanse of women's history. It is a place to ponder who has been included in the category woman and how that category has been constructed in relation to labor at different times and places.

In this archival space I had time to contemplate why the Hull House records remained preserved at all and the ethics of my participation in using them. I was making use of, even sponsored by, the institution that erased the physical structures of the most prominent women-led institution of the Midwest. For a short time, my research was funded by a small grant from the UIC Special Collections and University Archives. When I asked a librarian where the money originated, she told me it was "Daley money," meaning connected to the family of the long serving mayor Richard J. Daley for whom the library was named and who authorized the demolition of Hull House to build it, a small part of his greater legacy of "slum clearance" and creating Chicago as a segregated city. I thought about how Daley's legacy benefited from funding research into UIC's past when researchers understood his demolition of Hull House and the west side tenement district and building of a large public research university as part of a progress narrative about Chicago becoming a modern city. It was easy for me to see how I might participate in furthering such a progress narrative. I have worked in large public research universities and think of public universities as sustaining some of the best functions of Hull House, including educating citizens and serving local people from diverse educational backgrounds. I am also a product of the public university educational system and can see my own labor of writing and research as motivated by my interest in participating in what Harvey Graff has called the literacy myth. In my own experience, acquiring literacy has led to class mobility. I am not a garment worker like my great-great-grandmother, but a white, middle-class academic who has acquired some specialized literacies needed for making meaning of the texts Hull House residents produced in the early twentieth century. I realized that I had assumed that historical subjects, some of whom were my ancestors, would be just as invested in writing as a mode because of my own internalized belief that writing is a tool of transformation. Being in the UIC Special Collections and University Archives Reading Room helped to further underscore that progress narratives too easily cover over what gets lost. What was lost in demolition was Hull House as a space of gendered power and community building for women and immigrants in a city. In the larger demolition of the west side tenement district completed in the name of progress, locals lost their homes, streets, connections to culture, and other spaces for solidarity. Given this, I hope to have pushed back against the building of a public university as part of a literacy myth and instead recovered a multimodal rhetorical history of Hull House and its neighborhood that offered a glimpse into places that have not physically endured, all without idealizing or sentimentalizing a version of the past.

RECOGNIZING SHARED CONDITIONS

Writing and research are acts of gendered labor, and as such locating the self in relation to this labor can involve risk and reward. In the book, I gestured toward some of those risks and rewards in chapter two through my analysis of the production history of the labor treatise *Hull-House Maps and Papers*. For example, I discussed how *Hull-House Maps and Papers* contains several photographs of Hull House interiors, but there are no women doing or making in those photos. For Hull House residents, making their own labor visible would have been risky and invited others to question their radical rearrangement of domestic labor, their eschewing of heteronormative family structures in favor of group living, and ultimately their womanhood. Yet, residents could have taken a risk and modeled possibilities for reimagining gendered labor for others, especially for those who did not have similar privilege. For those who have the privilege to make visible their labor from relative safety, such an act can be a first step in allying in a network of solidarity among others who may not be able to decide whether to make their spaces of labor visible or withhold them from view.

Addams shared in reflecting on her visit with Tolstoy a story about where and how she labored. Simultaneously, Addams shared a story about how she stopped looking to great men for advice about where and how to labor. Back in Chicago, Addams rejected Tolstoy's advice about how to labor because of "the piles of letters to be opened and answered," offering finally a scene of the kind of labor she shared with Tolstoy: writing. Addams modeled that a writer is not someone who is isolated and "irrevocably male," as Linda Brodkey characterized the modernist ideal (70). By locating in the scene of writing, we might join Addams in multiplying who occupies that scene to include women and others with minoritized identities. In so doing, we might contribute alongside Brodkey to reimagining who a writer can be and strengthen a theory of writing as a social and historical act connected to the material world rather than imagine it as the product of an individual's mental process. Writing spaces of labor into feminist rhetorical methods recognizes that research and writing processes are labor, and as such, they are processes that are social, shared, and require space and time. By writing spaces of labor into feminist rhetorical scholarship, we might also push back on the modernist ideal of the (white) male writing alone in a room.

At this point I want to explore the meanings of the office and the home in my own writing and research process. In 2019, I spent much of my time in my university office and took for granted this office as a space necessary to write up my findings, store books and materials, create lessons, hold conferences and meetings, and offer feedback on my students' writing. While this list of activities is specific to the role of university professor, the use of offices for writing and research is widespread. As Deborah Brandt has explained in her study of the rise of mass writing in the workplace, "millions of Americans now engage in creating, processing, and managing written communications as a major aspect of their work. It is not unusual for many American adults to spend 50 percent or more of the workday with their hands on keyboards and their minds on audiences" (3). In occupying an office for writing, I shared working conditions with many other white-collar workers across sectors.

In 2020, I also joined many of these workers in experiencing the loss of a dedicated office space and the collapse of home and work into one because of the COVID-19 pandemic. My office was now also a bedroom in a detached single-family home. It was also a classroom where I taught university students who met with me through a synchronous learning management system. My home itself served multiple functions for my other family members. It was now the workplace for my spouse who was also employed as a faculty member at the university. For my school-aged daughter, it was her elementary school classroom. For my newborn daughter, home now served the functions previously provided by a childcare center. When the spaces of home, office, classroom, and childcare center became one, I thought newly about how the constraints on and opportunities for making space and organizing were experienced by those who lived in Progressive-era settlements and tenements. In exploring parallels, I do not wish to overstate the comparison between my contemporary work of writing and research and historical garment making. They are obviously not the same. Garment making, especially as sweatshop labor, was and is physically brutal and relentlessly punishing. I remain curious, though, about the pandemic's effect of suddenly and surprisingly revealing links among people across space and time. As it had the effect, for example, of collapsing the spaces of home and work into one for many including myself, the pandemic changed what Addams had called the "hours and immediate conditions" of work (*Modern City* 9). When she said this, Addams was specifically worried women who entered the factory were ceding their authority over previously domestic labor to employers. The pandemic, though, did not restore women's authority over the home and re-privatize certain kinds of labor. Instead, the pandemic isolated workers and made it more difficult to meet together to organize, and it allowed employers to benefit when workers used their own resources and spaces.

Feeling isolated during this time, I joined a writing group made up of colleagues working in the discipline of rhetoric and composition from across the US. We were not sponsored by a university or organization, and we met online weekly. For a time, one of our informal practices as a group was to keep track of the hours spent on writing to better recognize when we were prioritizing writing scholarship over other kinds of work. In *Labor-Based Grading Contracts*, Asao B. Inoue suggests students keep track of their hours working on writing as part of a larger anti-racist process of valuing the time spent laboring on writing rather than the product of writing. I found a model for documenting my own labor time in Inoue's work and noticed that in my home during the pandemic I was writing an average of two to four hours per week. The meaning I eventually made from this average was not so much based on the length of time, but the texture of the experience across two to four hours of weekly writing. Those hours were not consecutive, instead split across the minutes I had available while trading off childcare duties with my spouse so we could both carry on a version of teaching from home. I expanded the practice of the labor log to keep track of *where* and *how* I was writing as well. In my home, I was writing in my makeshift office, at the kitchen table, in the backyard, in my bed, and on a personal laptop or on my phone while nursing a baby. In 2021, once I returned to working in an office, I was able to log an average of fifteen hours of writing time per week, completed in more regular time blocks at both home and work, and made possible only because I had an office, a university-issued computer, access to library books, and access to school and childcare centers for my children.

The value in keeping a writing labor log is not just for personal growth or understanding, but to be able to make comparisons. A labor log allows one to notice patterns across how time use is impacted by gendered, raced, and classed differences. For example, researchers who conduct time use surveys of household labor notice that the gendered division of labor in the home remains unequal. Women take on twice as much housework as men. This is a finding that has held steady over the last three decades, even as more women have entered the paid workforce outside the home (Lachance-Grzela & Bouchard 768). By keeping a labor log and documenting my space, time, and technologies, I was able to informally compare writing as labor with other members of my writing group, and through this process to find that the conditions of our writing were similarly impacted by the lack of division between home and work, and paid and unpaid labor. It may be unsurprising that these conditions were shared in retrospect, but my fellow colleagues and I were isolated at the time. Keeping and comparing a labor log during the pandemic helped me to appreciate that the product of writing valued by so many employers requires material resources beyond pay. It has always required the labor of others, such as childcare workers and family members who care for children. It has required the resources of literacy sponsors like employers who offer space, equipment, and technologies. University employers, for example, had previously offered offices to support the process of writing. During the pandemic, such support for process vanished, but the product of writing was still valued and expected.

What emerged unexpectedly from this experience of rebuilding my networks of support from my home/office with an online community of writers was that I began to see possibilities for solidarity open that had been foreclosed by the office. In chapter two, I discuss Kelley's belief that isolation in tenement homes kept garment workers from discussing their labor and organizing. While Kelley took this belief to the extreme conclusion that she could ignore workers who could never organize and instead seek public and legal remedies to protect them, she understood that labor rhetorics for organizing and solidarity were difficult to communicate without shared space and channels of communication. I learned firsthand that an office is certainly a space where one can speak to colleagues and discuss shared problems, but it is also owned and controlled by an employer and can be monitored and taken away. As I discussed in chapter four, workers who seek to organize are often thwarted in their efforts when the most direct channels for communicating with other workers are through using the spaces and technologies provided by the employer who can monitor them and withhold them. Through online spaces and digital networks I was able to find ways to connect with other colleagues beyond the gaze of an employer and thereby begin to articulate new labor rhetorics about the value of writing and research. Part of the writing group's motivation for keeping track of hours for writing in the first place was to reimagine the value of writing. Universities value the product of research and writing far more than the process, with that value granted in the form of continued employment, and for some, the protections of tenure. The members of the writing group and I joined with many academics who have sought to articulate the value of the process of writing for ourselves, as interrelated to and apart from the product of writing valued by universities. I took away a renewed appreciation for writing as a process that has value beyond criteria defined by the workplace. Members of my writing group, for example, reminded me that writing has value not simply because it is a workplace product, but because it is a shared process through which to build community, share and compare information, and support others in inquiry.

One of the goals of this book is to shed light on how today's labor rhetorics are connected to a too-easy Progressive Era narrative in which unpaid labor moved beyond the home and became paid labor in the factory. This shift in where and when women worked also reshaped how gendered labor was valued. Yet, the meaning of this movement for many in the past was not necessarily progress, nor was there ever a clean division between unpaid and paid labor, or the spaces of home and work, for most individuals. There is certainly not a clean division between kinds of space and labor for many today. As feminist rhetoricians, we might locate ourselves in the contested spaces in between home and work and see ourselves more clearly in our own homes or workplaces to explore how our conditions of space and time impact labor, including the labor of writing and research. To do so connects us with the subjects we recover and to fellow feminists, writers, and workers. The women's labor rhetorics I recovered in archives and elsewhere are important, but my hope is that historical study of rhetorics that mediated the meanings of gender and labor in the past are understood as networked to the meanings of gendered labor today. Gender remains a pressing axis across which to find common ground, but it is not the only difference that matters. Solidarity requires noticing everyone's labor is reciprocal, and feminists can and should learn from past efforts to establish it.

Works Cited

"5,000 Babies Starve; Big Strike is Cause." *Chicago Record-Herald*, 26 November 1910, p. 2.

"20,000 Strikers in West Side Parade." *Chicago Inter Ocean*, 8 December 1910, p. 3.

Addams, Jane. "Appendix: Outline Sketch Descriptive of Hull House." *Hull-House Maps and Papers*, 1895, U of Illinois P, 2007, pp. 151–70.

—. "The Art-Work Done by Hull House, Chicago." *The Forum*, Vol. 19, 1895, pp. 614–17.

—. "The College Woman and the Family Claim." *Commons*, No. 29, Sept. 1898, pp. 1–7.

—. "Domestic Service and the Family Claim." *The World's Congress of Representative Women: A Historical Resume for Popular Circulation*, Vol. 2, edited by May Wright Sewall, Rand McNally & Co., 1894, pp. 626–31.

—. "First Report of the Labor Museum at Hull House, Chicago." 1902, pp. 1–16, Hull House Collection, Special Collections and University Archives, University of Illinois-Chicago, Chicago, IL, Box 52, Folder 586, Accessed 03 January 2020.

—. Letter to D.C. Davies. 14 March 1924, Accession Files A1507, Department of Anthropology, Field Museum of Natural History Archives, Accessed 20 June 2018.

—. Letter to Mary Rozet Smith. 3 February 1895, *The Jane Addams Papers, 1860–1960 (Microfilm)*, 1984, Reel 2.

—. Letter to Mary Rozet Smith. 22 November 1910. *Jane Addams Digital Edition*, https://digital.janeaddams.ramapo.edu/items/show/3242. Accessed 9 December 2022.

—. Letter to Richard T. Ely. 31 October 1894, Richard T. Ely Papers, *The Jane Addams Papers, 1860-1960 (Microfilm)*, 1984, Reel 6.

—. Letter to Richard T. Ely. 3 January 1911, *The Jane Addams Papers, 1860–1960 (Microfilm)*, 1984, Reel 6.

—. *The Modern City and the Municipal Franchise for Women*. National American Woman Suffrage Association, 1906.

—. "The Objective Value of a Social Settlement." *Philanthropy and Social Progress*, Thomas Y. Crowell, 1893, pp. 27–56.

—. "Respect for Law," *The Independent*, Vol. 53, No. 2718, 1901, pp. 18–20.

—. "The Settlement as a Factor in the Labor Movement." *Hull-House Maps and Papers*, 1895, U of Illinois P, 2007, pp. 138–50.

—. *The Spirit of Youth in the City Streets*. Macmillan, 1909.

—. *Twenty Years at Hull House*. Macmillan, 1912.

"All Cloakmakers Musical Entertainment." Hull House Collection, Special Collections and University Archives, University of Illinois at Chicago, Chicago, IL, Scrapbook II, p. 17, Accessed 3 January 2020.

"A Local Toynbee Hall." *Chicago Inter-Ocean*, 24 April 1892, p. 4.

Anzaldúa, Gloria. "Bridge, Drawbridge, Sandbar or Island: Lesbians-of-Color *Hacienda Alianzas*." *Bridges of Power: Women's Multicultural Alliances*, Edited by Lisa Albrecht & Rose M. Brewer, New Society Publishers, 1990, pp. 216–31.

Appiah, Kwame Anthony. *Cosmopolitanism: Ethics in a World of Strangers*. Norton, 2006.

Applegarth, Risa. *Rhetoric in American Anthropology: Gender, Genre, and Science*. U of Pittsburgh P, 2014.

Arendt, Hannah. *The Human Condition*. U of Chicago P, 1958.

Aristotle. *On Rhetoric*. Translated by George A. Kennedy. Oxford UP, 2007.

Bae, Youngsoo. *Labor in Retreat: Class and Community among Men's Clothing Workers of Chicago, 1871–1929*. SUNY P, 2001.

Baker, George M. *The Handy Speaker*. Lee and Shepard Publishers, 1876.

Ballif, Michelle, Diane Davis, and Roxanne Mountford. *Women's Ways of Making It in Rhetoric and Composition*. Routledge, 2008.

Balser, Diane. *Sisterhood and Solidarity: Feminism and Labor in Modern Times*. South End P, 1987.

Benjamin, Walter. "The Work of Art in the Age of Mechanical Reproduction." *Illuminations: Essays and Reflections*, translated by Harry Zohn, edited by Hannah Arendt, Schocken Books, 1969.

Benton, Megan. "Unruly Servants: Machines, Modernity, and the Printed Page." *A History of the Book in America*, Vol. 4, edited by Carl F. Kaestle and Janice A. Radway, U of North Carolina P, 2009.

Bisno, Abraham. *Abraham Bisno, Union Pioneer*. U of Wisconsin P, 1967.

Bodnar, John. *The Transplanted: A History of Immigrants in Urban America*. Indiana UP, 1987.

Booth, Charles. *Life and Labour of the People in London*. Williams and Norgate, 1891.

Brandt, Deborah. *The Rise of Writing: Redefining Mass Literacy*. Cambridge UP, 2014.

Breckinridge, Sophonisba P. "Chicago Exhibit." *Women's Industrial News*, Vol. 40, 1907, pp. 656–58.

Breckinridge, Sophonisba P., and Edith Abbott. "Chicago Housing Conditions, IV: The West Side Revisited." *American Journal of Sociology*, Vol. 17, No. 1, U of Chicago P, 1911, pp. 1–34.

Breckinridge, Sophonisba P., and George H. Meade. "Concerning the Garment Workers' Strike: Report of the Sub-Committee to the Citizens' Committee." 5 November 1910. *Nineteenth Century Collections Online*, Accessed 8 July 2022.

Brodkey, Linda. *Writing Permitted in Designated Areas Only*. U of Minnesota P, 1996.

Brown, Charles Walter. *The American Star Speaker and Model Elocutionist*. M.A. Donohue & Co., 1902.

Brown, Helen Gurley. *Having it All: Love, Success, Sex, Money, Even If You're Starting with Nothing.* Simon & Schuster, 1982.
Buchanan, Lindal. *Regendering Delivery: The Fifth Canon and Antebellum Women Rhetors.* Southern Illinois UP, 2005.
Buechler, Steven M. *Women's Movements in the United States: Woman Suffrage, Equal Rights, and Beyond.* Rutgers UP, 1990.
Burke, Kenneth. *A Rhetoric of Motives.* 1950, U of California P, 1969.
Butler, Judith. *Notes Toward a Performative Theory of Assembly.* Harvard UP, 2018.
Campbell, Karlyn Kohrs. *Man Cannot Speak for Her: A Critical Study of Early Feminist Rhetoric.* Greenwood P, 1989.
Carsel, Wilfred. *A History of the Chicago Ladies' Garment Workers' Union.* Normandie House, 1940.
Chaplin, Ralph. *Wobbly: The Rough-and-Tumble Story of an American Radical.* U of Chicago P, 1948.
Chávez, Karma. *Queer Migration Politics: Activist Rhetoric and Coalitional Possibilities.* U of Illinois P, 2013.
Chicago Commission on Race Relations. *The Negro in Chicago: A Study of Race Relations and A Race Riot.* U of Chicago P, 1922.
Civic Federation of Chicago. "Laws of Various Cities Relating to the Construction of Tenement Houses." 1911, Newberry Library General Collections, Chicago, IL, Accessed 19 July 2019.
Cloakmakers' Entertainment Invitation. *The Jane Addams Papers, 1860–1960 (Microfilm),* 1984, Reel 52.
"Club Women in New Role." *Chicago Tribune,* 8 March 1907, p. 7.
Cohen, Lizabeth. *Making a New Deal: Industrial Workers in Chicago, 1919–1939.* Cambridge UP, 1990.
Coman, Katherine. "Bricks Without Straw: The Story of an Italian Girl Among the Striking Garment Workers in Chicago, Taken Down Verbatim by Prof. Katharine Coman of Wellesley College." *Survey,* Vol. 5, No. 25, 1910, pp. 424–28.
Commonwealth of Massachusetts Bureau of Statistics of Labor. "Exhibits of Industrial Conditions." *Labor Bulletin of the Commonwealth of Massachusetts,* Wright & Potter Printing Co., 1907, p. 357.
Cott, Nancy. *The Bonds of Womanhood: "Woman's Sphere" in New England, 1780–1835.* Yale UP, 1997.
Crenshaw, Kimberlé. "Mapping the Margins: Intersectionality, Identity Politics, and Violence against Women of Color." *Critical Race Theory: The Key Writings that Formed the Movement,* edited by Crenshaw, Neil Gotanda, Gary Peller, & Kendall Thomas, The New Press, 1995, pp. 384–425.
Crick, Nathan. "From Cosmopolis to Cosmopolitics: The Rhetorical Study of Social Movements." *The Rhetoric of Social Movements: Networks, Power, and New Media,* edited by Nathan Crick, Routledge, 2020, pp. 3–30.
Crozier, Mamie. "Diary and Ornament from 1893 World's Fair." Exhibited at Frisco Heritage Museum, 4 September 2021, Frisco, Texas.
Davis, Diane. *Inessential Solidarity: Rhetoric and Foreigner Relations.* U of Pittsburgh P, 2010.

Deutsch, Sarah. *Women and the City: Gender, Space and Power in Boston, 1870–1940*. Oxford UP, 2000.

Dingo, Rebecca. *Networking Arguments: Rhetoric, Transnational Feminism, and Public Policy Writing*. U of Pittsburgh P, 2012.

Donawerth, Jane. *Conversational Rhetoric: The Rise and Fall of a Woman's Tradition, 1600–1900*. Southern Illinois UP, 2011.

Dreikurs, Sadie Garland. Interview by Mary Ann Johnson. Hull-House Oral History Collection, 1980, Special Collections and University Archives, University of Illinois at Chicago, Chicago, IL, Box 2, Folder 26, Accessed 25 March 2016.

Dreiser, Theodore. *Sister Carrie*. 3rd edition, Norton, 2005.

Du Bois, W.E.B. *The Philadelphia Negro: A Social Study, Together with a Special Report on Domestic Service by Isabel Eaton*. Schocken Books, 1899.

Duffy, William. "Remembering is the Remedy: Jane Addams's Response to Conflicted Discourse." *Rhetoric Review*, Vol. 30, No. 2, 2011, pp. 135–52.

Durkheim, Émile. *The Division of Labor in Society*. Translated by George Simpson, Free Press, 1965.

"Electrical Workers Defiant." *Chicago Inter Ocean*, 12 Mar. 1907, p. 3.

Ellis, S.F. "The Life-Work of William Morris." *Journal of the Society of Arts*, Vol. 46, May 1898, pp. 618–30.

Ely, Richard T. Letter to Jane Addams. 31 December 1910, *The Jane Addams Papers, 1860–1960 (Microfilm)*, 1984, Reel 6.

"End of Strike Near; Victory Is Workers'." *Chicago Inter Ocean*, 4 December 1910, p. 2.

Engels, Frederick. "To the Working Classes of Great Britain." *The Condition of the Working Class in England in 1844*, Otto Wigand, 1845.

—. "To Florence Kelley." 25 February 1886, *Letters to Americans, 1848–1895*, Translated by Leonard E. Mins, International Publishers, 1953, pp. 151–52.

—. "To Florence Kelley." 28 December 1886, *Letters to Americans, 1848-1895*, Translated by Leonard E. Mins, International Publishers, 1953, pp. 165–67.

Enoch, Jessica. *Domestic Occupations: Spatial Rhetorics and Women's Work*. Southern Illinois UP, 2019.

—. *Refiguring Rhetorical Education: Women Teaching African American, Native American, and Chicano/a Students, 1865–1911*. Southern Illinois UP, 2008.

Enoch, Jessica, Danielle Griffin, and Karen Nelson, editors. *Feminist Circulations: Rhetorical Explorations Across Space and Time*. Parlor P, 2021.

Enstad, Nan. *Ladies of Labor, Girls of Adventure: Working Women, Popular Culture, and Labor Politics at the Turn of the Twentieth Century*. Columbia UP, 1999.

Etsy, Inc. "About Page," Etsy, 2022, https://www.etsy.com/about?ref=ftr. Accessed 31 August 2022.

"Exhibits Go on Strike." *Chicago Record Herald*, 12 Mar. 1907, p. 3.

Fabian, Johannes. *Time and the Other: How Anthropology Makes its Object*. New York: Columbia UP, 2002.

"Factories and Workshops." Laws of the State of Illinois, Passed by the Thirty-Eighth General Assembly, H.W. Rokker, 1893, pp. 99–102.

Field Museum. "FMNH Textile Collections Sent to Hull House in 1902." Prepared by Jackie Pozza, 18 May 2018, Microsoft Excel File, Accessed 20 June 2018.

Finnegan, Cara A. "Studying Visual Modes of Public Address: Lewis Hine's Progressive-Era Child Labor Rhetoric." *The Handbook of Rhetoric and Public Address,* edited by Shawn J. Parry-Giles and J. Michael Hogan, Blackwell, 2010, pp. 250–70.

Fleming, David. *City of Rhetoric: Revitalizing the Public Sphere in Metropolitan America.* SUNY P, 2009.

Foner, Philip S. *History of the Labor Movement in the United States.* Vol. III, International Publishers, 1964.

—. *Organized Labor and the Black Worker, 1619-1981.* Haymarket Books, 2017.

—. *Women and the American Labor Movement: From Colonial Times to the Eve of World War I.* The Free Press, 1979.

Frank, Dana. *Purchasing Power: Consumer Organizing, Gender, and the Seattle Labor Movement, 1919–1929.* Cambridge UP, 1994.

"From the Industrial Exhibition in Brooke's Casino." *Polish Daily News,* 12 March 1907, p. 1.

Ganz, Cheryl R. and Margaret Strobel, editors. *Pots of Promise: Mexicans and Pottery at Hull House, 1920-1940.* U of Illinois P, 2004.

Garbes, Angela. *Essential Labor: Mothering as Social Change.* Harper Collins, 2022.

"Garment Workers and Clothing Firm Agree to Arbitrate." *Chicago Evening Post,* 5 November 1910, *The Jane Addams Papers, 1860-1960 (Microfilm),* 1984, Reel 53.

Gere, Anne Ruggles. *Intimate Practices: Literacy and Cultural Work in U.S. Women's Clubs, 1880-1920.* U of Illinois P, 1997.

—. "Kitchen Tables and Rented Rooms: The Extracurriculum of Composition." *College Composition and Communication,* Vol. 45, No. 1, 1994, pp. 75–92.

"Ghetto Tires of Invasion: Resents Intrusion of Sociologists into Humble Homes." *Chicago Daily Tribune,* 18 June 1906.

Gilbert, James. *Perfect Cities: Chicago's Utopias of 1893.* U of Chicago P, 1991.

Gold, David and Jessica Enoch, editors. *Women at Work: Rhetorics of Gender and Labor.* U of Pittsburgh P, 2019.

Goldman, Emma. "From 'Marriage and Love.'" *Available Means: An Anthology of Women's Rhetoric(s).* Edited by Joy Ritchie and Kate Ronald, U of Pittsburgh P, 2001, pp. 227–32.

Graff, Harvey J. *The Legacies of Literacy.* Indiana UP, 1987.

"Great Parade." *The Woman's Journal,* 13 May 1911, Vol. 42, No. 18, pp. 145–47.

Gries, Laurie E. "Circulation as an Emerging Threshold Concept." *Circulation, Writing and Rhetoric,* edited by Gries and Collin Gifford Brooke, Utah State UP, 2018, pp. 3–26.

Guglielmo, Thomas A. *White on Arrival: Italians, Race, Color, and Power in Chicago, 1890–1945.* Oxford UP, 2003.

Hallenbeck, Sarah, and Michelle Smith. "Mapping Topoi in the Rhetorical Gendering of Work." *Peitho,* Vol. 17, No. 2, 2015, pp. 200–25.

Hamilton, Alice. *Exploring the Dangerous Trades*. Northeastern UP, 1985.

Handbook of the Chicago Industrial Exhibit. Kirchner, Mecket & Co., 1907.

Haney López, Ian F. *White by Law: The Legal Construction of Race*. New York UP, 1996.

Hanrahan, Nancy Weiss and Sarah Amsler. "'Who Else is Gonna Do it if We Don't': Gender, Education, and the Crisis of Care in the 2018 West Virginia Teachers' Strike." *Gender, Work, & Organization*, Vol. 29, No. 1, 2021, pp. 151–66.

Hapke, Laura. *Sweatshop: The History of an American Idea*. Rutgers UP, 2004.

Harris, Barbara J. *Beyond Her Sphere: Women and the Professions in American History*. Greenwood Press, 1978.

Harris, Cheryl. "Whiteness as Property." *Critical Race Theory: The Key Writings that Formed the Movement*, edited by Kimberlé Crenshaw, Neil Gotanda, Gary Peller, & Kendall Thomas, New Press, 1995, pp. 276–91.

Harris, Leslie J. "Rhetorical Mobilities and the City: The White Slavery Controversy and Racialized Protection of Women in the U.S." *Quarterly Journal of Speech*, Vol. 104, No. 1, 2018, pp. 22–46.

Hart, Sara. *The Pleasure Is Mine: An Autobiography*. Valentine-Newman, 1947.

Heinze, Hermann. "Souvenir Map of the World's Columbian Exposition at Jackson Park and Midway Plaisance." A. Zeese & Co., 1893.

Henrotin, Ellen M. "An Outsider's View of the Woman's Exhibit." *Cosmopolitan Magazine,* September 1893. pp. 560–66.

Hillman, Sidney. Address in Honor of Jane Addams. 6 September 1935, pp. 1–2, Amalgamated Clothing Workers of America Records, 1914–1980, Kheel Center for Labor-Management Documentation & Archives, Cornell University, Box 88, Folder 25, Accessed 12 December 2022.

Hoganson, Kristin L. *Consumers' Imperium: The Global Production of American Domesticity, 1865–1920*. U of North Carolina P, 2007.

hooks, bell. *Feminist Theory: From Margin to Center*. Routledge, 2015.

Horner, Bruce. *Terms of Work for Composition: A Materialist Critique*. SUNY P, 2000.

"Hull-House Bulletin." Vol. 5, No. 2, Hull House, 1902, *Bulletin: Vols 5–7*, Google Books. https://play.google.com/books/reader?id=hJQgAQAAMAAJ&hl=en. Accessed 12 August 2017.

Hull-House Exhibition. 17-22 April 1895, *Jane Addams Papers, 1860–1960 (Microfilm)*, 1984, Reel 52.

Hull-House Minutes of Meetings, 1893–96. Hull House Collection, Special Collections and University Archives, University of Illinois at Chicago, Chicago, IL, Box 32, Folder 295, Accessed 16 August 2016.

Hull House Yearbook, 1910. Hull House Collection, Special Collections and University Archives, University of Illinois at Chicago, Chicago, IL, Box 44, Folder 435, Accessed 3 January 2020.

Hunt-Hendrix, Leah, and Astra Taylor. *Solidarity: The Past, Present, and Future of a World-Changing Idea*. Pantheon Books, 2024.

Ignatiev, Noel. *How the Irish Became White*. Routledge, 1995.

Indigenous Action. "Accomplices Not Allies: Abolishing the Ally Industrial Complex." 4 May 2014, http://www.indigenousaction.org/accomplices-not-allies-abolishing-the-ally-industrial-complex. Accessed 11 June 2024.

"Industrial Show to Be Permanent." *Chicago Daily Tribune*, 17 March 1907, p. 5.

"In the Butler Gallery: Venetian Architecture on South Halsted Street." *Chicago Tribune*, 31 May 1891, p. 38.

Inoue, Asao B. *Labor-Based Grading Contracts: Building Equity and Inclusion in the Compassionate Writing Classroom.* UP of Colorado, 2019.

Jacobson, Matthew Frye. *Whiteness of a Different Color: European Immigrants and the Alchemy of Race.* Harvard UP, 1999.

"Jane Addams Wears a Star: Appointed to the Force of Garbage Inspectors by Commissioner Kent." *Chicago Record*, 25 April 1895, p. 6.

Johnson, Nan. *Gender and Rhetorical Space in American Life, 1866–1910*. SIU P, 2002.

Kaplan, Amy. "Manifest Domesticity." *American Literature*, Vol. 70, No. 3, 1998, pp. 581–606.

Keiser, John H. "Black Strikebreakers and Racism in Illinois, 1865–1900." *Journal of the Illinois State Historical Society*, Vol. 65, No. 3, 1972, pp. 313–26.

Kelley, Florence. "Description and Work of Hull House." *The New England Magazine*, July 1898, pp. 550–56.

—. *First Special Report of the Factory Inspectors of Illinois, on Small-Pox in the Tenement House Sweatshops of Chicago.* State of Illinois, 1894.

—. *Notes of Sixty Years: The Autobiography of Florence Kelley.* Charles H. Kerr, 1986.

—. "To Frederick Engels." 9 June 1886, *The Selected Letters of Florence Kelley, 1869–1931*, edited by Kathryn Kish Sklar and Beverly Wilson Palmer. U of Illinois P., 2009, pp. 31–33.

—. "To Henry Demarest Lloyd." 10 October 1893, *The Selected Letters of Florence Kelley, 1869–1931*, edited by Kathryn Kish Sklar and Beverly Wilson Palmer, U of Illinois P, 2009, pp. 68–69.

—. "To Richard T. Ely." 14 November 1894, *The Selected Letters of Florence Kelley, 1869–1931*, edited by Kathryn Kish Sklar and Beverly Wilson Palmer, U of Illinois P, 2009, pp. 77–78.

—. "The Sweating-System." *Hull-House Maps and Papers*, 1895, U of Illinois P, 2007, pp. 63–72.

Kendall, Mikki. "#SolidarityIsForWhiteWomen: Women of Color's Issue with Digital Feminism." *The Guardian*, 14 August 2013, Accessed 15 April 2021.

—. *Hood Feminism: Notes from the Women that a Movement Forgot.* Penguin, 2021.

Kenney, Mary. "Organization of Working Women Address." *The World's Congress of Representative Women*, edited by May Wright Sewall, Rand McNally & Co., 1894, pp. 871–73.

Kenney O'Sullivan, Mary. Unpublished Autobiography. n.d, MS Women's Trade Union League and Its Leaders: Smaller Collections Reel, Arthur and Elizabeth Schlesinger Library on the History of Women in America, Harvard University, *Women's Studies Archive,* Accessed 20 November 2019.

Kessler-Harris Alice. "Do We Still Need Women's History?" *The Chronicle of Higher Education*, 7 December 2007, Accessed 27 February 2023.

—. *Women Have Always Worked: A Historical Overview.* The Feminist Press, 1981.

Kirkland, Joseph. *Among the Poor of Chicago.* Scribners, 1892.

Knight, Louise W. "Harriet Alleyne Rice." *Women Building Chicago, 1790–1990: A Biographical Dictionary*, Indiana UP, 2001, pp. 740–42.

Kynard, Carmen. "'All I Need Is One Mic': A Black Feminist Community Meditation on the Work, the Job, and the Hustle (& Why So Many of Yall Confuse This Stuff)." *Community Literacy Journal*, Vol. 14, No. 2, 2020, pp. 5–24.

"Labor Protests End of Strike." *Chicago Daily Tribune*, 6 February 1911, p. 4.

"Labor Troubles Mar Uplift Show." *Chicago Daily Tribune*, 12 March 1907, p. 3.

Laborers' International Union of North America. *Internal Organizing Guide for LIUNA Public Sector Local Unions.* 2017, https://www.liuna.org. Accessed 13 January 2023.

Lachance-Grzela, Mylène, and Geneviève Bouchard. "Why Do Women Do the Lion's Share of Housework? A Decade of Research." *Sex Roles*, 2010, Vol. 63, pp. 767–80.

Lagman, Eileen. "Moving Labor: Transnational Migrant Workers and Affective Literacies of Care." *Literacy in Composition Studies*, Vol. 3, No. 3, 2015, pp. 1–24.

LaGrand, James B. *Indian Metropolis: Native Americans in Chicago, 1945–75.* U of Illinois P, 2002.

LaPier, Rosalyn R., and David R.M. Beck. *City Indian: Native American Activism in Chicago, 1893–1934.* U of Nebraska P, 2015.

Lasch-Quinn, Elizabeth. *Black Neighbors: Race and the Limits of Reform in the American Settlement House Movement, 1890–1945.* U of North Carolina P, 1993.

Leonard, Thomas C. *Illiberal Reformers: Race, Eugenics, and American Economics in the Progressive Era.* Princeton UP, 2016.

Lissak, Rivka Shpak. *Pluralism and Progressives: Hull House and the New Immigrants, 1890–1919.* U of Chicago P, 1989.

Link, William A. *The Paradox of Southern Progressivism, 1880–1930.* University of North Carolina P, 1992.

Logan, Shirley Wilson. *Liberating Language: Sites of Rhetorical Education in Nineteenth-Century Black America.* Southern Illinois UP, 2008.

—. *'We Are Coming:' The Persuasive Discourse of Nineteenth-Century Black Women.* Southern Illinois UP, 1999.

Maddux, Kristy. *Practicing Citizenship: Women's Rhetoric at the 1893 Chicago World's Fair.* Penn State UP, 2019.

Marks, Nora. "Two Women's Work: The Misses Addams and Starr Astonish the West Siders." *Chicago Tribune*, 19 May 1890, pp. 1–2.

Marx, Karl. *Capital: A Critique of Political Economy, Volume 1.* Translated by Ben Fowkes, Penguin, 1990.

Marx, Karl, and Friedrich Engels. *The Communist Manifesto.* Edited and with an Introduction by Jeffrey C. Isaac, Yale UP, 2012.

Massey, Doreen. *Space, Place and Gender*. U of Minnesota P, 1994.
Matthews, Glenna. *'Just a Housewife': The Rise and Fall of Domesticity in America*. Oxford UP, 1987.
Mattingly, Carol. *Appropriate[Ing] Dress: Rhetorical Style in Nineteenth-Century America*. Southern Illinois UP, 2002.
—. *Well-Tempered Women. Nineteenth-Century Temperance Rhetoric*. Southern Illinois UP, 1998.
McCracken, Jill. *Street Sex Workers' Discourse: Realizing Material Change through Agential Choice*. Routledge, 2013.
McDowell, Mary. "Work for Normal Young Working Women." *Proceedings of the National Conference of Charities and Correction*, Ed. Alexander Johnson, Wm. B. Burford P, 1907, pp. 319–26.
McG, M. Letter to Jane Addams. 1911, *The Jane Addams Papers, 1860–1960 (Microfilm)*, 1984, Reel 6.
McLuhan, Marshall. *Understanding Media: The Extensions of Man*. McGraw-Hill, 1964.
McMillan, Gloria. "Keeping the Conversation Going: Jane Addams's Rhetorical Strategies in 'A Modern Lear.'" *Rhetoric Society Quarterly*, Vol. 32, No. 3, 2009, pp. 61–75.
"Men Fight Women Strikers." *Chicago Tribune*, 24 November 1910, p. 3.
Meyerowitz, Joanne J. *Women Adrift: Independent Wage Earners in Chicago, 1880–1930*. U of Chicago P, 1988.
Miller, Claire Cain. "Mississippi Asks: If Women Can Have It All, Is Roe Necessary?" *The New York Times*, 1 December 2021, https://www.nytimes.com/2021/12/01/upshot/mississippi-abortion-case-roe.html. Accessed 13 December 2021.
Mohanty, Chandra Talpade. *Feminism Without Borders: Decolonizing Theory, Practicing Solidarity*. Duke UP, 2003.
Mountford, Roxanne. *The Gendered Pulpit: Preaching in American Protestant Spaces*. Southern Illinois UP, 2003.
"Musical Entertainment with Addresses." Invitational Pamphlet, Hull House Collection, Special Collections and University Archives, University of Illinois at Chicago, Chicago, IL, Box 72, Folder 507, Accessed 3 January 2020.
Nestor, Agnes. *Woman's Labor Leader: The Autobiography of Agnes Nestor*. Bellevue Books, 1954.
Nivens, Melissa. "Farm to Table: The Home Management House as Rhetorical Space for Rural Women." *Peitho*, Vol. 19, No. 2, 2017, pp. 282–300.
Noon, Mark. "'It Ain't Your Color, It's Your Scabbing': Literary Depictions of African American Strikebreakers." *African American Review*, Vol. 38, No. 3, 2004, pp. 429–439.
N.W. Ayer & Son's American Newspaper Annual. N.W. Ayer & Son, 1907.
Orleck, Annelise. *Common Sense and a Little Fire: Women and Working-Class Politics in the United States, 1900-1965*. U of North Carolina P, 1995.
Painter, Nell Irvin. *Standing at Armageddon: A Grassroots History of the Progressive Era*. Norton, 1987.

Pastorello, Karen. *A Power among Them: Bessie Abramowitz Hillman and the Making of the Amalgamated Clothing Workers of America.* U of Illinois P, 2008.

Percy, Ruth. "Picket Lines and Parades: Labour and Urban Space in Early Twentieth-Century London and Chicago." *Urban History*, Vol. 41, No. 3, 2014, pp. 456–77.

Pham, Minh-Ha T. "A World Without Sweatshops: Abolition Not Reform." *Abolition Feminisms: Organizing, Survival, and Transformative Practice Vol.1*, edited by Alisa Bierria, Jakeya Caruthers, and Brooke Lober, Haymarket Books, 2022, pp. 133–52.

Philpott, Thomas Lee. *The Slum and the Ghetto: Immigrants, Blacks, and Reformers in Chicago, 1880–1930.* Wadsworth Publishing Co., 1991.

"picket, n.1." *OED Online*, Oxford UP, www.oed.com/view/Entry/143404. Accessed 9 December 2022.

"Plea to End Strike is Issued by Busse." *Chicago Inter Ocean*, 9 December 1910, p. 3.

Polachek, Hilda Satt. *I Came a Stranger: Story of a Hull-House Girl.* U of Illinois P, 1989.

"Police Told Not to Interfere with Peaceful Strikers." *Chicago Daily Socialist*, 8 December 1910, pp. 1–2.

Pond, Allen B. "The Settlement House." *The Brickbuilder*, Vol. 11, No. 9, 1902, pp. 178–85.

Potofsky, Jacob. Interview by Elizabeth Balanoff. *Roosevelt University Oral History Project in Labor History*, 4 August 1970, pp. 1-33, https://libguides.roosevelt.edu/c.php?g=748860. Accessed 13 July 2022.

Powell, Malea D. "Down by the River, or How Susan La Flesche Picotte Can Teach Us about Alliance as a Practice of Survivance." *College English*, Vol. 67, No. 1, 2004, pp. 38–60.

"Program of Conferences." Anita McCormick Blaine Correspondence and Papers, Wisconsin Historical Society Archives, Box 139, Accessed 13 September 2018.

Rai, Candice. *Democracy's Lot: Rhetoric, Publics, and the Places of Invention.* U of Alabama P, 2016.

Ramírez, Cristina Devereaux. *Occupying Our Space: The Mestiza Rhetorics of Mexican Women Journalists and Activists, 1875–1942.* U of Arizona P, 2015.

Rand McNally & Co. *Handy Guide to Chicago and World's Columbian Exposition.* Rand McNally, 1892.

"Real Strike Causes Delay." *Chicago Tribune*, 13 March 1907, p. 7.

"Reception to Germans." Hull House Weekly Program of March 1892, p. 8. Hull House Collection, Special Collections and University Archives, University of Illinois at Chicago, Chicago, IL, Box 72, Folder 507, Accessed 16 August 2016.

Residents of Hull House. *Hull-House Maps and Papers.* Thomas Y. Crowell & Co., 1895, Newberry Library General Collections, Chicago, IL, Accessed 11 July 2019.

Residents of Hull House. *Hull-House Maps and Papers.* 1895, U of Illinois P, 2007.

Reynolds, Nedra. "Ethos as Location: New Sites for Understanding Discursive Authority." *Rhetoric Review*, Vol. 11, No. 2, 1993, pp. 325–38.

Rice, Harriet. Letter to Jane Addams. 7 December 1928. *The Jane Addams Papers, 1860–1960. (Microfilm)*, 1984, Reel 20.

Rice, Jenny. *Distant Publics: Development Rhetoric and the Subject of Crisis*. U of Pittsburgh P, 2012.

Rich, Adrienne. "Notes toward a Politics of Location." *Blood, Bread, and Poetry: Selected Prose 1979–1985*, Norton, 1986, pp. 210–32.

Riis, Jacob. *How the Other Half Lives: Studies Among the Tenements of New York*. Scribners, 1890.

Rosaldo, Renato. "Imperialist Nostalgia." *Representations*, No. 26, 1989, pp. 107–22.

Rosenfeld, Morris. *Songs of Labor and Other Poems*. Translated by Rose Pastor Stokes & Helena Frank, Gorham P, 1914.

Roskelly, Hephzibah. "Hope for Peace and Bread." *Women and Rhetoric Between the Wars*, edited by Ann George, M. Elizabeth Weiser, & Janet Zepernick, SIU P, 2013, pp. 32–47.

Royster, Jacqueline Jones. *Traces of a Stream: Literacy and Social Change Among African American Women*. U of Pittsburgh P, 2000.

Royster, Jacqueline Jones, and Gesa E Kirsch. *Feminist Rhetorical Practices: New Horizons for Rhetoric, Composition, and Literacy Studies*. SIU P, 2012.

Ryan, Mary P. *Cradle of the Middle Class: The Family in Oneida County, New York, 1790–1865*. Cambridge UP, 1981.

Rydell, Robert W. *All the World's a Fair: Visions of Empire at American International Expositions, 1876–1916*. University of Chicago P, 1985.

Sandburg, Carl. "Blue Island Intersection." *Smoke and Steel*, Harcourt, Brace, & Co., 1920.

—. "Chicago." *Poetry Magazine*, Vol. 3, No. 6, 1914, p. 191.

Sandberg, Sheryl. "'Introduction: Internalizing the Revolution': Excerpt from *Lean In*." *Persuasive Acts: Women's Rhetorics in the Twenty-First Century*, Edited by Shari J. Stenberg & Charlotte Hogg, U of Pittsburgh P, 2020.

Schick, Louis. *Chicago and its Environs: A Handbook for the Traveler*. F. P. Kenkel, 1893.

"Seeking the Truth: Meetings in Other Halls." *Chicago Herald*, 21 July 1893.

Sharer, Wendy B. *Vote and Voice: Women's Organizations and Political Literacy, 1915–1930*. Southern Illinois UP, 2007.

Shaver, Lisa J. *Reforming Women: The Rhetorical Tactics of the American Female Moral Reform Society, 1834–1854*. U of Pittsburgh P, 2019.

"Sheep on Strike at Labor Exhibit." *Chicago Daily Tribune*, 14 Mar. 1907, p. 6.

Sinclair, Upton. *The Jungle*. Doubleday, Page & Co., 1906.

Sive-Tomashefsky, Rebecca. "Identifying a Lost Leader: Hannah Shapiro and the 1910 Chicago Garment Workers' Strike." *Signs*, Vol. 3, No. 4, 1978, pp. 936–39.

Skinner, Carolyn. *Women Physicians and Professional Ethos in Nineteenth-Century America*. Southern Illinois UP, 2014.

Sklar, Kathryn Kish. "Florence Kelley." *Women Building Chicago 1790–1990: A Biographical Dictionary*, edited by Rima Lunin Schultz & Adele Hast, Indiana UP, 2001, pp. 460–68.

—. "Who Funded Hull House?" *Lady Bountiful Revisited: Women, Philanthropy, and Power*, Rutgers UP, 1990, pp. 94–115.

The Slums of Baltimore, Chicago, New York, and Philadelphia. Edited by Carroll D. Wright, Government Printing Office, 1894.

"solidarity, n.1.a." *OED Online*, Oxford UP., https://doi.org/10.1093/OED/90852 24053. Accessed 1 August 2024.

The Speaker's Garland and Literary Bouquet. P. Garrett & Co., 1872.

Spear, Allan H. *Black Chicago: The Making of a Negro Ghetto, 1890–1920*. U of Chicago P, 1967.

Stansell, Christine. *City of Women: Sex and Class in New York, 1789–1860*. U of Illinois P, 1987.

"Stared at; Strike." *Chicago Chronicle*, 12 March 1907, p. 6.

Starr, Ellen Gates. "Art and Labor." *Hull-House Maps and Papers*, U of Illinois P, 2007, pp. 130–37.

—. "What the Artist Was Made For." Outline of Illustrated Lecture at Hull-House, 30 September 1895, *Jane Addams Papers, 1860–1960. (Microfilm)*, 1984, Reel 50.

Steghagen, Emma, and Alice Henry. "Why Working Women Must Organize." *The Papers of the Women's Trade Union League and Its Principal Leaders*, Collection 9, Reel 9, Research Publications, 1985.

"Strikers Barred from Downtown." *Chicago Daily Tribune*, 1 November 1910, p. 1.

"Strikers Parade to Show Number." *Chicago Daily Tribune*, 8 December 1910, p. 3.

"Stylish Cloaks." *The Ladies' Home Journal*, November 1893, p. 33

Taylor, Graham Romeyn. "The Chicago Industrial Exhibit." *Charities and the Commons*, Vol. 18, 1907, pp. 39–45.

"Tenement, n." *OED Online*, Oxford UP, www.oed.com/view/Entry/199111. Accessed 17 April 2023.

"They Help the Poor: Jane Addams and Ellen Starr's Self-Sacrificing Work Among the Lowly." *Chicago Times*, 23 March 1890, p. 2, Hull House Collection, Special Collections and University Archives, University of Illinois at Chicago, Chicago, IL, Box 70, Folder 506, Accessed 3 January 2020.

Triece, Mary E. *On the Picket Line: Strategies of Working-Class Women during the Depression*, U of Illinois P, 2007.

Trimbur, John. "Composition and the Circulation of Writing." *College Composition and Communication*, Vol. 52, No. 2, 2000, pp. 188–219.

Tuttle, Jr., William M. "Labor Conflict and Racial Violence: The Black Worker in Chicago, 1894–1919." *Labor History*, Vol. 10, No. 3, 1969, pp. 408–32.

Twelfth Census of the United States. 1900 Population Schedule for Cook County, Illinois, Bureau of the US Census, 1900.

"Union Calls off Garment Strike; Yields Claims." *Chicago Tribune*, 4 February 1911, p. 1.

"Urge Need of Labor Laws." *Chicago Daily Tribune*, 13 Mar. 1907, p. 7.

"U.S. Government Will Spend $1,720,000 for Chicago Housing Sites." *Chicago Tribune*, 3 November 1935, p. 12.

VintageClothingDream. "1890's First Edition Hull House Book." 6 June 2022, https://www.etsy.com/listing/709630479/1890s-first-edition-hull-house-book. *Etsy*, Accessed 31 August 2022.

Washburne, Marion Foster. "A Labor Museum." *The Craftsman*, Vol. 6, No. 6, 1904, pp. 570–80.

Washington, Jamie, and Nancy J. Evans. "Becoming an Ally." *Beyond Tolerance: Gays, Lesbians, and Bisexuals on Campus*," edited by Nancy J. Evans & Vernon A. Wall, American College Personnel Association, 1991, pp. 195–204.

"Weekly Programme of Lectures, Clubs, Classes, Etc." January 1891, Hull House Collection, Special Collections and University Archives, University of Illinois at Chicago, Chicago, IL, Box 72, Folder 507, Accessed 3 January 2020.

Weiler, N. Sue. "Walkout: The Chicago Men's Garment Worker's Strike, 1910–1911." *Chicago History*, Vol. 8, No. 4, 1979, pp. 238–49.

Wells, Ida B. "Lynching and the Excuse for It." *The Independent*, Vol. 53, No. 2737, 1901, pp. 1133–36.

—. "Preface." *The Reason Why the Colored American Is Not in the World's Columbian Exposition*, 1893, p. 1.

Wells, Susan. *Out of the Dead House: Nineteenth-Century Women Physicians and the Writing of Medicine*. U of Wisconsin P, 2001.

Wilder, Ralph. "An Exhibit at an Industrial Show of the Future." *Chicago Record-Herald*, 16 Mar. 1907, p. 1.

Wollstonecraft, Mary. *A Vindication of the Rights of Woman, With Strictures on Political and Moral Subjects*. Humboldt Publishing Co., 1891.

Woolf, Virginia. "Professions for Women." *The Rhetorical Tradition: Readings from Classical Times to the Present*, edited by Patricia Bizzell and Bruce Herzberg, Bedford/St. Martin's, 2001, pp. 1253–56.

"Work of Two Women." *Chicago Times*, 1890, Clippings Scrapbook, Ellen Gates Starr Collection, Smith College, Northampton, MA, 20 May 2016.

"Workers Strike for Clean Sweatshops." *Chicago Inter Ocean*, 12 March 1907, p. 3.

Wright, Frank Lloyd. "The Art and Craft of the Machine." *Brush and Pencil*, Vol. 8, No. 2, 1901, pp. 77–90.

Wright, Gwendolyn. *Moralism and the Model Home: Domestic Architecture and Cultural Conflict in Chicago, 1873–1913*. U of Chicago P, 1980.

Yoshihari, Mari. *Embracing the East: White Women and American Orientalism*. Oxford UP, 2003.

You, Xiaoye. *Cosmopolitan English and Transliteracy*. SIU P, 2016.

Index

Abbott, Edith, 53
Abbott, Grace, 10
Abramowitz, Bessie, 10, 108–110, 112–113, 119, 125
Addams, Jane, x, xii, xiii, 5, 7–10, 15, 31–40, 46–48, 50–51, 60–63, 71–73, 80–85, 88–90, 105–106, 114–119, 125, 128–129, 131–134, 136–137, 141–142, 145–146
alliances, xii, 20, 48, 107–108, 115, 117, 119–121, 123, 125, 127, 135, 139
Amalgamated Clothing Workers of America, 108
American Federation of Labor (AFL), xii, 45
American Woman Suffrage Association, 105
Anzaldúa, Gloria, 119
Appiah, Kwame Anthony, 24
archives, 140, 143
Arendt, Hannah, 12
Aristotle, 36
Art Institute, 84
artisan labor, 38, 58, 72, 82, 86
arts and crafts movement, 62

Bae, Youngsoo, 94, 106
Battle of the Halsted Street Viaduct, 112
Benedict, Enella, 71–72
Benjamin, Walter, 78
Bisno, Abraham, 40
Black Americans, xii, 38, 64–66
Black Neighbors (Quinn), xii, 38
Black/white labor relations, xii, xiii, 88
Blue Island Intersection, 113
Board of Lady Managers, 80

Booth, Charles, 56–57, 61, 63
Bowen Hall, 115
Bowen, Louise deKoven, 50
Brandt, Deborah, 145
Breckinridge, Sophonisba, 98, 103, 116–117
Brodkey, Linda, 145
Brosnahan, Honora, 86–87, 103
Burke, Kenneth, 19
Burlington and Quincy Railroad, 39
Busse, Fred, 120–121
Butler Art Gallery, 71
Butler Building, 45–46
Butler, Judith, 107, 111, 117

Campbell, Karlyn Kohrs, 22, 71
capitalism, 15, 19, 33, 38, 79
Carsel, Wilfred, 45
Cassatt, Mary, 92
Chaplin, Ralph, 19
Chávez, Karma, 107
Chicago Arts and Crafts Society, 37
Chicago Federation of Labor, 114
Chicago Fire, 52
Chicago Housing Authority, 136
Chicago Industrial Exhibit, xxii, 80–82, 90–92, 94, 96–97, 103
Civic Federation of Chicago, 52
class, x, xii, xv, 16–18, 33, 36–37, 42, 47–48, 50, 66, 75, 92, 115–116, 126, 129, 139
cloakmakers, 40–42, 44–49
clubwomen, 99–101
coalitions, 10, 50, 107, 114
coevalness, 85, 95, 100
collective, xi, xii, xvii, xxii, 2, 18, 21, 23, 51, 60, 77, 83, 87, 104, 107, 114, 119, 121–122, 124–125, 130, 135

163

colonialist, 84, 92, 101
Communist Manifesto (Marx and Engels), 19
Condition of the Working Class in England in 1844, The (Engels), 52, 60
consubstantiality, 19
consumers, xi, xvii, xviii, 26, 36, 66–68, 75–76, 99, 139
consumption: ethical, 129, 137
cosmopolitan, xi, xvii, 24–27, 31–39, 41, 44–47, 49–51, 54–55, 63, 65, 67–68, 70, 83–89, 91, 102, 122–123, 129, 134, 137
Cott, Nancy, 22–23
craft labor, 82
craft unions, xii, 31, 39, 45
Culver, Helen, 50

Daley, Richard J., 142–143
Department of Labor, 54, 64
Department of Labor (US), 54, 64
division of labor, 21, 90, 147
Dobbs v. Jackson Women's Health Organization (Supreme Court decision), 24
domestic discourse, 21–24, 42, 132, 136
domestic labor, xviii, 13, 22, 53, 60, 67, 74, 80, 84, 96, 102, 138, 144, 146
domesticity, 57, 70, 73, 129, 133
Dreikurs, Sadie Garland, 123
Dreiser, Theodore, 36
Durkheim, Émile, 19

Eaton, Isabel, 10
Ely, Richard T, 61, 63
embodied rhetoric, xviii
Engels, Frederick, 9, 33, 52, 59–61, 75–76
Enoch, Jessica, xxiii, 11, 14
ethos, xvii, 18, 35–36, 39, 42, 46–47, 61
exhibitions, x, 14, 71–72, 79–81, 85, 91, 101, 104, 130

exploitation, 2, 17, 19–21, 56, 66, 75, 102–103, 110, 115

Fabian, Johannes, 85
factories, 3–4, 7, 9–10, 12, 36, 40, 51–54, 68–69, 90–99, 101–103, 105–113, 116–117, 121, 126–127, 129–130, 137–138; inspectors, 54, 69, 73–74, 78–79, 95
Factories and Workshops Bill, 74
fast fashion, 3, 41, 99
feminism, xxiii, 27
feminist rhetoricians, xiii, xviii, 11, 29, 128, 134–135, 137–140, 148
Field Museum of Natural History, 29, 84
Finnegan, Cara A, 55
First Report of the Labor Museum at Hull House, Chicago, 82
Foner, Philip S., xii, 27, 50, 96, 113
Foster, Rachel, 61, 83

Gardner, Isabella Stewart, 80
garment district, 2, 6–7, 34, 36
garment industry, ix, xv, 3, 28–29, 107–108, 110, 123–124, 137
garment making, xv, 12, 27, 52, 87, 90, 109, 112, 128, 146
garment workers, xi, xiv–xviii, 1–4, 10–11, 18, 20, 31, 33, 39–41, 44, 46–48, 51–52, 77, 79, 92, 97, 104, 106–110, 112–113, 115, 117, 119–120, 124–126, 130–133, 137, 142, 147
Garment Workers' Strike (1910–1911), xvii
gender, 2, 4–7, 9, 17–18, 21–23, 36, 40–41, 47–50, 68, 102–103, 105, 107, 114–115, 120–121, 126, 128–130, 132–136, 143, 148
gendered labor, ix–xi, xiv, xviii, 14, 22–23, 30, 38, 105, 126–127, 134, 137, 143–144, 148
Gere, Anne Ruggles, 4, 6
Goldman, Emma, 41

Goode, G. Brown, 64
Goodrich, Helen, 45, 71
Graff, Harvey, xxii, 144
Great Migration, xii, 136
Greeley and Carlsen (mapmakers), 57

Halsted Street, 34, 36, 57, 111–112, 127
Hamilton, Alice, 6
Handy Guide to Chicago and the World's Columbian Exposition (Rand McNally), 67
Hapke, Laura, 92–93
Harper, Frances Ellen Watkins, 60
Haymarket Strike, xvii, 112
Hazenplug, Frank, 91
Heinze, Hermann, 64
Henrotin, Ellen, 10, 90, 92, 96, 99, 115, 119
Hillman, Bessie Abramowitz, 108, 125
Hillman, Sidney, 108, 125
Hine, Lewis, 68
Hoganson, Kristin, 24–25, 32
Holbrook, Agnes Sinclair, 10, 45, 54, 56–57, 63–64, 67, 69, 71–73, 76
home, 11–12, 22, 24–25, 35, 52–53, 66–70, 72, 78, 80–82, 93–94, 96–97, 102, 105–106, 129–130, 136–141, 145–148
home-to-work narrative, 11, 81, 138
hooks, bell, 18, 91, 102, 115, 125–126
How the Other Half Lives (Riis), 56, 93
Hull House, ix–xii, 5–13, 29, 31–42, 44–54, 56–60, 62, 66–68, 70–72, 74–78, 80–85, 114–119, 124–126, 128–131, 142–144; Labor Museum, xviii, 29, 80–82, 84, 87, 90, 101, 103, 112; residents, xi, xii, xvii, xviii, 8, 13, 27, 32, 37, 42, 44, 46–47, 49, 51, 54, 56, 60, 67, 70–71, 74–77, 80–81, 83–85, 87, 90, 101–103, 107–108, 115, 125–126, 130–131, 133, 140, 142, 144
Hull House Yearbook, x
Hull-House Bulletin, The, 83, 85
Hull-House Maps and Papers, xvii, 10, 35, 54–76, 144

I Came a Stranger (Polachek), 52
identity, xiv–xvi, 6–7, 17, 20–21, 24, 33, 37, 40, 42, 46, 49, 66, 68, 77–78, 88, 95, 102, 107, 118, 124, 129, 133–135, 142
Illinois Factory and Workshops Bill, 69
immigrants, x, xi, xii, xviii, 4, 9, 26, 31–32, 36–38, 51, 53, 56, 58, 65–67, 73, 77–78, 81, 83–86, 88–89, 93, 95, 99, 102, 104, 108, 110, 118, 122–124, 129–130, 142, 144; women, xi, xviii, 4, 9, 26, 51, 67, 81, 84–85, 102, 104, 118, 130
industrial capitalism, ix, 72, 134
industrial labor, 15, 24, 38, 44, 58, 70, 72, 75, 82
industrial progress, xviii, 37, 80, 91, 130, 137
inequality, xviii, xix, 20, 27, 84, 87, 101, 125–127, 143
Inoue, Asao B., 146
insanitary conditions, 92, 94–95, 99, 101
International Workers of the World, 20
intersectionality, 49

Jane Addams Homes (housing project), 136–137
Jane Addams Hull House Museum, 142
Jane Club, 10
Johnson, Nan, 22, 44–45
Jungle, The, 96

Kelley, Florence, xvii, xviii, 5, 9–10, 46, 53–79, 95, 116, 131, 136, 147
Kendall, Mikki, 27, 136

Kenney, Mary, 10, 31, 33, 39–45, 48, 60, 112, 132
Kessler-Harris, Alice, 91, 132
Kirkland, Joseph, 65
Knight, Louise W., 88–89
Knights of Labor, xii
Kynard, Carmen, 13

labor, ix–xix, xxi–xxiii, 1–30, 31–43, 48–62, 66–91, 92–96, 98, 100–138, 139–148; history, 29, 82, 85, 91, 96, 102, 112, 134; movements, 17–18, 27–28, 50, 72, 125, 128, 135; politics, 6, 9, 32–33, 36–37, 51, 103, 111, 129, 133; power, 11, 16, 135; progress, 80–81, 93, 102; reform, xvii, 5–6, 9–10, 17, 51, 54–57, 68, 126; relations, xii, xiii, xviii, 16, 78, 89; rhetorics, ix–xi, xiii–xv, xvii–xix, xxii, 2–4, 7–11, 13–18, 20–21, 27, 30, 33, 39, 43, 50–51, 54–55, 69, 75–76, 79–80, 107, 109–110, 113, 117, 124–128, 130–132, 134–139, 147–148
labor rhetorics: embodied, 110, 113, 142; mobile, xviii, 109, 119, 130
Lasch-Quinn, Elisabeth, xii, 38
Lazinskas, Charles, 122
Life and Labour of the People in London, the (Booth), 56
Lissak, Rivka Shpak, xii
literacy, xiv, 4, 6, 19, 107, 110, 124, 131, 138, 144, 147
Lloyd, Henry Demarest, 54, 68
Lloyd, Jesse Bross, 54, 68
Luther, Jessie, 82

MacMonnies, Mary, 92
Maddux, Kristy, 25
maps, 54, 56–64, 66–70, 72–76
marches, 1–3, 16, 20, 108, 112, 120–124, 127
Marks, Nora, 34
Marx, Karl, 11, 19, 33, 61, 81, 108
Marxism, 15, 78

Masilotti, Clara, 110, 113
Mastro-Valerio, Allesandro, 37, 71
McDowell, Mary, 90, 99, 103
McLuhan, Marshall, 76
Meyerowitz, Joanne J., 23
middle-class, ix, x, xii, xiv–xvi, 16–17, 22–23, 31, 37, 42, 44, 47, 66, 77, 87, 100–101, 129, 132, 139, 144
Midway Plaisance, 26, 63–64, 73–74
Midwest, 3, 51, 89, 143
Milligan, Josephine, 88
Minh-Ha T. Pham, 137
Mohanty, Chandra Talpade, 17, 138
Morris, William, 35, 80
Mountford, Roxanne, x, xi, 22, 141
multimodal rhetorics, xiv–xviii, 2, 10–11, 16, 130, 142, 144

Nancrede, Edith de, 91
narratives, xv, 9, 15–16, 22, 64, 81–82, 86, 92–94, 96–97, 102, 143, 148
National American Woman Suffrage Association, 61
Nationalities Map, 55–56, 58, 63–66
Native Americans, 32, 92
Nestor, Agnes, 113
networks, 5–6, 9, 27–28, 34, 51, 126, 128–129, 134–135, 137–139, 144
Newberry Library, xxii, 55, 62, 97

organizing, x, xii, xiv, xvii, xxi, xxii, 1–2, 4–5, 13, 18, 21, 26–27, 31–33, 39–40, 44, 46, 48–51, 55, 58, 60–61, 69, 77, 79, 84, 90, 98, 100, 108–110, 129–130, 146–147

Palmer, Bertha, 80
parlor rhetorics, 44–45, 47
Parsons Stevens, Alzina, 10
Parsons, Albert, 124
Pastorello, Karen, 109
performance, xviii, 45, 47, 86, 100
picketing, 16–17, 108, 117–118, 123, 126

Polachek, Hilda Satt, 52–53
Pond, Allen B., 34
Potofsky, Jacob, 110, 115
Powell, Malea D., 135, 139
power, x–xii, 9, 11, 18, 20–21, 25–26, 74–79, 81, 123–126, 129–130
privilege, 13, 16, 27, 66, 85, 88, 100, 115, 117–119, 133–134, 142, 144
progress: narratives of, xiv, xv, xviii, 7, 12, 15–16, 21, 26, 29, 64, 66, 80–82, 92, 99–103, 130, 139–141, 143–144
Progressive Era, xii, 4–5, 15, 54–57, 80, 90, 133–135, 138, 146, 148
protests, xiv, xviii, 1–2, 4, 10, 28, 66, 97, 104–105, 107–108, 112–113, 119, 123–125, 127
public housing, 136–137
publishing, 54, 56, 59, 61–62, 68–69, 75–79, 91
Pullman Strike, 8, 116

race, xii, xiii, xix, 2, 5, 7, 9, 17, 19, 22, 27, 38, 41, 44, 49, 64–65, 78, 88, 103, 119, 128, 139
racial discrimination, 74, 88, 95–96
racial identity, 37
Rai, Candice, 136
Rand McNally & Co, 67
reformers, x, xii, 9, 16, 18, 20, 39, 52–53, 75, 78–81, 84, 90, 93, 99, 102–103, 107, 126, 133
reproductive labor, 24, 138
Reynolds, Nedra, 36
rhetoric, ix, xiv–xvi, 8–10, 13–21, 32–36, 43–44, 55–56, 109, 129–130, 134–136, 140–142
Rice, Harriet, 10, 87–89
Rich, Adrienne, xviii, 91, 140
Richard J. Daley Library, 43, 141–142
Rickert, Thomas (UGWA), 114, 116, 124
Riis, Jacob, 56, 68, 93
Rosaldo, Renato, 84

Rosenfeld, Morris, 112
Royster, Jacqueline Jones, 28–29
Ruskin, John, 35–36
Ryan, Mary P., xxii, 23

saloons, 39–40, 47
Sandburg, Carl, 4, 113
segregation, xii, 65, 96, 136
settlement house, x, 5–6, 31, 34, 90, 118, 129
settlements, ix, x, xii, xvi, xvii, 5–10, 12–14, 31–36, 38–39, 44, 48–51, 55–56, 60, 75–76, 78, 87–90, 118–119, 129–130, 133, 142
Shapiro, Hannah, 10, 108–113, 119, 142
Sinclair, Upton, 10, 45, 54, 96
Sister Carrie (Dreiser), 36
Sklar, Kathryn Kish, 5, 50
smallpox, 73–74, 79
Smith College, ix, 143
Smith, Mary Rozet, 50, 88–89, 117, 131, 133
social movements, 2–3, 8–9, 27–28, 107, 128
solidarity, xvi–xix, 3–4, 16–21, 27, 32–33, 36–37, 48–51, 75–81, 98–99, 102, 109–110, 115, 119, 124–131, 133–135, 137–140, 147
spatial rhetorics, 14
Spies, August, 5, 124
Stanton, Elizabeth Cady, 60
Starr, Ellen Gates, x, 5, 7–9, 12, 31–37, 44, 50, 54, 58, 60, 66–67, 114, 117–119, 122, 124, 126, 129, 137, 142
strikers, 5, 118, 121–122
strikes, xv, 2, 5, 10, 16–17, 20, 39, 82, 98–101, 103–108, 112–117, 119–121, 123–126, 133
sweatshops, 51, 55, 79, 90, 92–102, 109, 130, 146

Taylor, Graham, 61, 93, 99, 137

tenements, x, xv, xviii, xix, 12, 14, 29, 34, 38, 51–58, 64, 66, 68–71, 73–77, 79, 90, 93–95, 99–103, 109–111, 130, 136, 143–144, 146–147
Tolstoy, Leo, 128, 130–134, 145
Toynbee Hall, 5, 56
Triangle Shirtwaist factory fire, 12, 92, 126
Triece, Mary E., 16, 109
Twenty Years at Hull House (Addams), 115–116, 128
Tyler, Alice Kellogg, 71–72, 75

unions, x, xii, xv, xvii, 4, 10, 13, 17–18, 31, 33, 39, 41–42, 45, 48–51, 55, 81, 92, 96–99, 103, 107–108, 112, 114–116, 119, 124–127, 130, 132, 137
United Auto Workers (UAW), xxi
United Garment Workers (UGW), 108, 114, 116, 121, 124–125

visual labor rhetorics, 54–56, 72
visual rhetorics, 55–56, 77, 79

Wages Map, 55–56, 58–59, 66–67, 69
walkouts, 107–115, 117, 123, 125, 127, 142
Washburne, Marion Foster, 83, 86–87, 103
Wells, Ida B, xiii, 11, 66
west side (Chicago), 6–7, 9, 53, 56–57, 63, 66–67, 72–73, 81, 83, 103, 105, 120–123, 129, 143–144
White City (Chicago World's Fair), 26, 63–65
white slavery, 106

whiteness, x, xi, xvii, 26–27, 31, 38, 64, 81–82, 97, 101, 106–107, 119, 122, 126, 129
Wilder, Ralph, 100
Willard, Frances, 39
Wollstonecraft, Mary, 21–22
Women at Work: Rhetorics of Gender and Labor (Gold and Enoch), 11, 91
Women Building Chicago, 1790-1990: A Biographical Dictionary, 88
Women Have Always Worked: A Historical Overview (Kessler-Harris), 91
women have always worked (banner), 84, 90, 92, 102
women workers, xvii, xviii, 1–2, 10, 26, 31, 40–42, 47–49, 51, 72, 82, 85, 90, 95, 98, 102, 106–108, 111, 114, 121, 125–126, 131
Women's Trade Union League (WTUL), 90, 96, 104, 110, 113–114
Woolf, Virginia, 23
work, xii, xv, xvii, 1–2, 7–9, 11–17, 20–24, 40, 50–55, 58, 68–73, 86–94, 96–103, 105–107, 109–113, 130, 145–148
working-class, ix, x, xii, xv, 5, 7, 16–17, 23, 33, 51, 56, 66–67, 72, 81, 90, 92, 101, 103, 115, 126, 132–133
Wright, Frank Lloyd, 62
writing, xii, xiv–xix, xxi, xxii, 4, 13, 17–18, 21, 23, 30, 34–35, 55, 60, 73, 76, 79, 86, 91–92, 109–110, 114, 118–119, 128, 131, 133–134, 137, 139–142, 144–148

Zeublin, Charles, 60

About the Author

Liane Malinowski is an assistant professor of Writing Studies at the University of Minnesota Twin-Cities whose essays have been published in *Rhetoric Society Quarterly* and *Rhetoric Review*. Her research and teaching focus on feminist rhetorics, rhetorical history, archival methods, and public writing.

Photograph of the author by Eric Miller.
Used by permission.

www.ingramcontent.com/pod-product-compliance
Lightning Source LLC
Chambersburg PA
CBHW020907180526
45163CB00007B/2658